MW01613645

Icons, Idols & Personal Heroes

A Tribute to Greatness with Gratitude

By

Kingston DuCoeur

Publishing Information

Pacific Blue Publishing

501 W. Glenoaks Blvd. # 746

Glendale, CA 91202

Phone: (818) 241-4797   Fax (818) 242-6450

E mail: kducoeur@sbcglobal.net

Copyright © 2007 by Kingston DuCoeur

Copyright number: TXu 1-336-581

First published, August, 2007

Library of Congress Catalogue Number: (pending)

All Rights Reserved

ISBN: 978-1-59975-633-2

Cover Designed by Kingston DuCoeur

FOREWORD

I had the pleasure of working with Kingston on the movie, "Seabiscuit". We became friends. We spent many of the long hours between 'takes' playing music and getting to know each other. Kingston would play on his portable keyboard; I picked on my guitar. We worked our way through the Beatles and Motown songbooks. The Fab Four and Smokey Robinson would not have been the least bit threatened by our dressing room renditions, but we had a great time. There's nothing like music to bring you close.

This guy is very easy to be around. He has an open heart and a willingness to see the best in things. I was also impressed with his sense of feeling lucky-of appreciating the life he has lead and all those who helped him on his way.

Kingston is a gracious man –a grateful man. This book is a celebration of his gratitude. Gratitude is a key to enjoying life to its fullest and can be a wonderful cure for the blues. But to do the trick it must be acknowledged and expressed. We all want to be appreciated, affirmed and, in some way, acknowledged for the good we do, however small or seemingly insignificant.

I think you'll find this book to be entertaining, informative and thought provoking. It was written by a man who has had a close connection with some fascinating people, and according to his own words, feels fortunate enough to give them flowers while most of them are still around to smell them. I'm delighted and honored that he considers me to be one of them.

Enjoy !

Jeff Bridges

Kingston DuCoeur

Table of Content
A - Z

Introduction

My name is Kingston DuCoeur, and since I started writing this book, I have been asked by a number of people why I decided to write such a book. So many queries led me to believe that others might want to know the answer to that question. Well, here are the plain and simple facts. I got the idea to write this book one day while having lunch with a friend at the Grill-a restaurant on the back lot at Universal Studios- Hollywood. We were talking about the Academy Awards and the time I attended the awards ceremony in 1998. I went on to tell my friend how I felt that night, sitting there waiting and hoping that our film, "Colors Straight Up" would win. I remember telling the film's producers, Julia Schacter and Michele Ohayon, that if we won I wanted just five seconds or less to thank my ninety-seven year old high school music teacher, Mrs. Maurine F. Bailey. She was the first one to make me believe that I could become a successful singer. I wanted with all my heart to thank her on national and international television, from the stage of the 70th Academy Awards Ceremony.

There are a few people to whom I would like to express my thanks publicly for what they have contributed to my growth and maturity as an artist and as a man. As we finished our lunch, my friend suggested that I write a book, thanking them collectively, in writing. That way, my encounter with and my gratitude for these remarkable people will be recorded not only for my own children, but for future generations as well. During the following weeks, the thought stayed with me, and I hit upon the idea of thanking one person for each of the letters in the alphabet. I wondered if I would be able to honestly express my appreciation for twenty-six people. It was not difficult at all. In fact, in some chapters I thanked more than one whose name begins with that particular letter of the alphabet. From that idea, came the title, concept, and the name of the book...

"ICONS, IDOLS, *and* PERSONAL HEROES"
A Tribute to Greatness with Gratitude

Preface

"Icons, Idols and Personal Heroes (A Tribute to Greatness with Gratitude)," is a collection of autobiographical essays, photos, and vignettes of my personal experiences with some magnificent people. We present the underlying reasons for the gratitude I feel towards these particular Icons, Idols and Personal Heroes. This work reveals little known facts about their contributions to America, and to humanity.

At no time am I attempting to speak for these individuals. My comments are based upon those areas of interest that I share with the people I write about, although our opinions may differ on certain points.

The phrase "down to earth", applies to a number of these people and is frequently used because it is a quality that I admire in people of stature and/or success, as opposed to those who have an elitist or snobbish disposition. In the body of my text, I often refer to my own dear mother, as "Mudear." This is an endearing name that many Black Folks in Texas, and other parts of the south, call their mother.

I use the words African-American and Black-Americans interchangeably when referring to my own race of people. The reason being, I am aware of the pros and cons of the exclusive use of those descriptive phrases. For an example, I personally most often prefer the use of African-American because African represents my ancestry and American identifies my legitimate domicile. None the less, I fully understand those who prefer the use of Black-American and reject the term African-American. Their rational has validity, which is: A white person, who was born in Africa and moves to America, is an African-American and qualifies for financial aid, etc., but he or she will get the jobs/pay, and privileges afforded whites.

The overriding reason to consider this fact according to statistics complied by the "Black Think Tank" hosted by Tavis Smiley on CNN during Black History Month, is as follows. While we as upwardly-mobile blacks are pleased to have carpet in our office, a secretary, have our name on the door, and earn a six figure income, we own very little, if anything of real significance. For example, at the time of this writing, how many black owned companies are there on the Wall Street Stock Exchange where Blacks own the majority or controlling interest of the stock? I invite you to consider the debate and decide for yourself which of the two terms resonates stronger with you.

The stories in this book represent my very best assessment of the contributions made by these Icons, Idols and Personal Heroes. Some were on a grass roots level and others from the pinnacle of success, fame and stardom. The stories and information will confirm their greatness, and are based on my intimate knowledge, and my best recollections.

Dedication

To my three sons, Carl Anthony, Kevin, Django, and my grandson, Demetrius, as well as their mother, Sandra, who gives them much love.

Acknowledgements

My thanks to Evelyn Palfrey, Imani Harris, Elizabeth Murphy, Reaux Flagg, Dr. Robin Kelley, Rose Gonzalez, Everett R. Van Vlear, Allen Marsh, Jo Ann Kim, Alex Aleman, and Jesse Sue Coburn

I extend special thanks to Robin Bissell for giving me the idea to write this book. Occasionally, when I felt stuck, I would reflect on the conversation we had that day while having lunch at "The Grill" restaurant on the back lot at Universal Studios. It helped me find the determination I needed to complete one of my goals, which was to present Robin with a signed copy of this book in gratitude for his encouragement.

Most of all, I want to thank the gifted individuals about whom I write. My encounter with each of them, however brief, however extended, has influenced my life in some way that has added to my spirit and my well-being as we make our numbered journeys around the sun.

Icons, Idols, & Personal Heroes
A Tribute to Greatness with Gratitude

Chapter

A

Muhammad Ali
American Icon

Muhammad Ali: "Float like a butterfly, sting like a Bee." No one did it better than Muhammad Ali. That statement is perhaps what most people around the world remember and revere about the almost super human skills, and athletic prowess of this man. I also remember the overpowering thrill and excitement he caused in the ring since 1964, when he dethroned the man who we believed to be unstoppable, Sonny Liston. And who can forget the "Thriller in Manila" against Joe Frazier? And years later, his unforgettable conquest of a bigger, meaner, heavier puncher named George Foreman at the "Rumble in the Jungle" in Zaire?

From the beginning of his reign as Heavyweight Champion of the World, we watched in stunned silence and with uncontrollable screams at the incredible grace, poise, and movements that were as smooth as a perfect heartbeat. It was indeed these and the many other exploits in the ring that earned him the right to declare, "I am the Greatest of all time!" Yet these things pale in the glow of his enormous heart, which is the habitat that harbors his indomitable courage. In the face of the raw and despicable injustice that took away his livelihood in the 1970s and threatened to take away his freedom, he was an even greater warrior.

Muhammad Ali did more to end the war in Vietnam than the great Martin Luther King Jr., the defiant Jane Fonda, and the infamous Lieutenant William Calley combined. Facing down boos and jeers from a self righteous middle class, Muhammad Ali took to college campuses across America. He began to ask a question whose answer most young people understood (many of whom were themselves draft dodgers, hiding behind privilege, influence, and escapes to Canada). When he asked the sobering question: "Why should I go half way around the world to kill a people who have never done harm to me, in order to protect **you**, who will not even speak up for my right as an American citizen to practice the religious freedom that you enjoy with impunity?" There was but one answer, and the resounding truth of that answer was the tide that began to swell until it washed away the stench of conscription which was poised to send thousands of additional young men off to die in an un-winnable war. The sad but true fact is that the well-meaning but misguided parents of those dear young men received their flag-draped coffins and marched to the funeral dirge of Taps, and suffered through the unfulfilled promise of "When Johnny Comes Marching Home Again."

- 13 -

It was Muhammad Ali that stood unflinchingly for the religious freedom, and the civil rights that every American citizen, and many who are neither Americans nor citizens enjoy today.

It is well to recall the wonderful moments relived on cable TV stations that show the master of modern pugilism at his best. It is well to remember the first rapper of our generation, when he accurately predicted in rhyme the round in which his opponent would fall. It is well to remember the greatest ticket hawk since P.T. Barnum, but it is noble to honor the man within whom a rare and compounded genius resides. Would that the nation of Great Britain were so magnanimous, brave and truly noble and make him a foreign born "Honorary" Knight. Although he is not a British national–as required, we could easily think of him as "Sir Muhammad Ali."

Is it an accident, is it luck, or is it coincidence that his surname begins with the letter A? For in keeping with the title and the theme of the book, I am compelled to place his name at the front and to honor him first. Therefore, dear Sir **Muhammad Ali,** we honestly, respectfully, and publicly extend to you **A Simple Thank You,** from the bottom of our collective hearts.

Chapter

B

Harry Belafonte

Harry Belafonte has been a favorite among an almost equal number of Back, and White fans. He burst on the scene as a gifted and versatile performer in the Fifties. In the Sixties he had already established himself as a successful singer, and was the first black entertainer to become a "crossover" heartthrob as an actor. His striking good looks translated 100% man to his fans, male and female alike. As a black teenager aspiring to be a singer, I knew most of his songs, and could do an acceptable impression of him. At that time, his was the quintessential image of intelligence, class, and urban cool with the "island" flavor. This was at a time when many black men and women in this country were not allowed to vote. His artistic success alone was enough to make him adored by black people, and believe me most black people, "Negroes" back then, had Harry Belafonte posters on their walls whenever they could find them. He could have rested on his laurels, so to speak, and remained content to be the token black singer turned cutting edge movie star, but he chose to do something more substantive with his life.

The Sixties is the decade that spawned the most radical change of the Twentieth Century in America. The Sixties is the decade, especially in the south, when the hidden hand of slavery was actually abolished for many blacks with the passage of the voting rights bill in 1964. It's when, for the first time, black men could apply for jobs as postal carriers, municipal bus drivers, meter readers, etc. in some areas of America. Philmore Peterson was the first black truck driver for "Sanger-Harris" a department store in Dallas. The Sixties, with all its social turmoil, was the most uplifting decade for our human awareness. The decade of the Sixties moved us forward toward a more humane and equitable society.

During a network TV variety show, in which Harry Belafonte and Petula Clark (a famous singer from England) were starring, in one of the show's segments, she reached over and touched Harry's arm. The phone lines lit up in protest from across America; whites were calling to ask the network: "How dare you allow that white woman to touch a nigger!" and declare, "I'm never watching this channel again." That single act exposed the deep-seated bigotry that existed in America, and one of the truly malevolent racial issues was brought to light and exposed to the whole world. Harry could have bowed his head low as was the custom at the time. Whenever a black man in television--and there were very few at the time--was chided (unfairly or not), as a rule they would have bowed low and knuckled under to the network bosses' pressure. The notable exception had been

Nat"King" Cole. Instead of buckling, Harry also took a stand like Nat had done and risked being black-balled by that network. His courage inspired Petula Clark to stand with him against the ridiculous unwritten "rule" that a black man could not so much as be touched by a white woman.

I referred to the late great Nat Cole, because to my knowledge he was the first black entertainer since Paul Robeson to take a stand against the seemingly intrinsic injustice that prevailed in the entertainment industry and nearly every walk of life against black people in America at that time. This certainly is not to say that there were not countless numbers of decent white people who were opposed to the blatant racism that was the order of the day in many American cities, towns, and hamlets during that era. In the late Fifties and early Sixties, Nat Cole was the biggest male singer in the U.S.--bar none. However, when Nat appeared on the Ed Sullivan Show, he was told what song to sing. When he refused, one of Ed Sullivan's staff immediately informed Sullivan of Nat's refusal to be told what song to sing. Sullivan stormed onto the set and informed Nat that "This is not a request but a demand." Then he proceeded to give Nat Cole an ultimatum: "You'll either sing what I tell you to, or you don't do my show, or any other TV show tonight or ever."

Nat Cole's stand against the slave owner mentality of Ed Sullivan may have been the inspiration for Harry Belafonte's activist awareness years. Belafonte is respected as an American treasure. He stands at the fore-front of any fight against injustice for black people and people of color everywhere. Until this incident, every other black person who appeared on Ed Sullivan's show, which was the biggest TV variety show in the world during its run, had acquiesced to the notoriously egomaniacal Ed Sullivan and his demands. As far as I can tell, Paul Robeson, Woody Strode, and Nat Cole, were the only black performers prior to Belafonte that stood up to the all but legalized bigotry that so many African-Americans faced in every segment of the media.

I first met Harry Belafonte in the spring of 1965. I was a singer on the rise with a duo called "The Pair Extraordinaire." My musical partner at that time was Marcus Hemphill--may he rest in peace. We were appearing in New York at "THE BITTER END," a famous coffee house/showroom type of club in Greenwich Village. One night at the end of our first set, a guy came into the club and said he'd just seen Harry Belafonte and Sidney Poitier standing outside. I'm sure a lot of people (myself included) thought: "Oh yeah, right--Harry and Sidney standing out front." Well the guy was right; at the end of the first song in the second show, the waitress seated Harry Belafonte and Sidney Poitier right up front in the second or third row. They stayed for the whole show, came back stage to hang out during the intermission, and stayed for the third show as well.

Harry had recorded a new album titled "Quiet Room." It was instantly one of my favorite Belafonte albums because it is an album of ballads. I love to hear Harry sing anything, but I especially like to hear him sing a ballad. I had bought five copies--all the copies in the store--and had given them as gifts to friends the previous Christmas. I also have in my Belafonte collection what is no doubt a rare find among Harry Belafonte memorabilia collectors. The name of this rare work is: "Belafonte Sings the Blues." It's a complete album of Harry doing blues songs, and he is singing some *soulful* and *funky* Blues.

The night I met him and Sidney, I was delighted that they were so cool and not phony, and I know for certain that they had a great time, based on their applause and the fact that they hung out with us through the intermission and stayed for the third show.

I indicated earlier in this chapter, that Harry Belafonte's dedication to the civil rights movement is well documented. It should solidify his place in history as not only a great artist, but as an unelected statesman as well. Although (to my knowledge) he has never run for a political office, the work he's done, and continues to do, for suffering people here and abroad speaks for itself.

I saw Harry in LA a few days after he performed at the Greek Theatre. I told him that I saw and enjoyed his show on opening night. He was genuinely ticked off when he asked, "Why the hell didn't you come back stage and say hello?" I told him the truth: I had to leave right after the show to take a friend to the airport. His eyes softened and he seemed pleased that I had an acceptable reason. I cannot say enough to adequately express my respect and appreciation for this giant of a man. In my humble opinion, it would be a crime if the whole world were not made aware of the stand that he has taken against injustice throughout his adult life.

This is **"A Simple Thank You," Harry Belafonte,** for all you have done to make us sing, pray, and reach out to those who suffer injustice, and for being so real through it all.

Miss Billie
Personal Hero

The first bit of true magic that touched my life came to me in the human form of Mrs. Billeia Montgomery--known to all as **Miss Billie.** She understood about that innate strain of genius healthy kids are born with. She also understood that in order for that genius to blossom in whichever child it chooses, the children must become aware of their capacity and their ability to learn. When you're working third grade level math problems in preschool, you come to understand that you can learn. I hasten to say that I was not unique in my ability to learn those things; every child in Miss Billie's school—when I attended could do the same things I could do, and maybe better.

It is well known that the people that have an effect on our lives in our formative years can often leave a permanent mark on the direction of our overall development. Generally, our parents, siblings, and certain family members have the most direct access to our mental growth. In my case and much to my good fortune, in addition to my dear mother Miss Billie had the most lasting influence on me. The values she instilled have been an active part of my life throughout the years.

In the 1980's, a book came out. Its premise was that just about everything he needed to know about life, he learned in kindergarten. As far flung as that statement may be, I can relate to it. I'm not the only one who can relate to it. I believe--no, I know--that every child that ever completed Miss Billie's Kindergarten School can relate to that statement. Thanks to God there are still a number of us around to validate what a remarkable human being this great and gracious woman was. She understood that all healthy black children are born brilliant, or, are brilliant by nature. By no means is this statement meant to suggest that black children are genetically superior or more intelligent than those from other racial backgrounds. It simply means that a healthy black infant is innately endowed with a gene structure that makes that infant capable of becoming brilliant. This is in stark contrast to the misguided notion held by some that black babies are born with less aptitude than whites.

Miss Billie gave us simple but lasting principles such as: "singing while doing chores will make it easier for you to finish more quickly." This has always and still does work for me. When my space sometimes becomes so cluttered with "stuff" that are things I don't want anybody else to touch, I have to bite the bullet and "de-clutterize." When I sing as I work, it definitely makes a difference. Sometimes, a glass of Gamay Beaujolais along with singing or listening to Marvin Gaye, Aretha Franklin, Andrea Bocelli or Norah Jones makes it easier still--although that's not one of Miss Billie's suggestions or rules.

She taught each and every child in her school how to read and write cursive legibly by the age of four. We knew our timetables, could read at a third grade level, and knew roman numerals up to twenty. And very importantly, we knew how to get along with each other. Once a year, she would take our preschool class across the street to N.W. Harllee Elementary School and put on demonstrations in math and spelling to third graders.

Miss Billie stressed good manners and punctuality. Her motto was: "If a job is great or small, do it well or not at all." Her disciplinary tactic was: every morning after reciting the pledge of allegiance, she would play the introduction on the upright piano, and the children would sing "The eyes of Texas are upon you all the live long day, etc." Then she would ask a series of question: "What is the state flower?" All the children answered in unison, "The bluebonnet." Next question, "What is the Texas State Motto?" Answer, "Be Friendly." Then she would ask, "What is the golden rule?" The final question she asked was: "If anybody doesn't pay attention, or misbehaves in class, what will Miss Billie do?" Again all the children would respond in unison: "Miss Billie will make your feathers fly high and high." This threat was sufficient to make us behave because we were terrified of being spanked (which was acceptable back then) and made to cry in front of the other children. It worked on the whole class because none of us can remember anybody getting spanked. If she had ever made anybody's feathers fly, I'm sure we would remember because it would have been a standout moment.

One of the brightest kids in my class at Miss Billie's Kindergarten was **David Lee Perry**. We graduated from Lincoln together and after serving in the Air Force, he went on to do great things in his life. Growing up, he was very easy going; he always had a hint of a smile on his face, he laughed easily, but was a rough and tumble kid. You might not want to take that little smile as a sign of weakness. David Lee could scrap (fight) with the best of them. Like many Miss Billie alumni, he became a trailblazer, as the first African-American to be elected to the city council in Plano, Texas, having run four consecutive campaigns--which was a record. During the fourth campaign, Councilman David Perry set a record in Plano by winning 68% of the vote in every precinct. As a result of that strong showing he never had another challenger. According to Mr. Perry, he persevered because he never forgot another one of Miss Billie's daily sayings, "Never give up". He was one of the few Council members, or Mayors, to be voted unanimously to the board of directors of the National League of Cities—the largest constituency group in the United States which affects congressional decisions. He became Deputy Mayor Pro-tem, and Mayor Pro-tem. He ran for Mayor of Plano, loosing by a narrow margin to an opponent with deep pockets who probably outspent David

Lee by double digits. He was the principal partner in an oil drilling company.

Among other things, he was one of the developers of the world's largest privately funded solar power plants at Warner Springs, California-- supplying peak power to San Diego Gas and Electric Company. It is significant to note that he was the first African-American to hold those coveted positions at the time and places cited above. He is also the cousin to one of America's great scientist, the late Dr. John Hopps Jr. who was also a student at Miss Billie's kindergarten school, and about whom you will learn more in this chapter.

David Lee and his beautiful wife Marie have been married for thirty-five years; they are highly respected within as well as outside of their community. Like all of the good and faithful wives of the men in this book, Marie has been an irreplaceable source of strength, support, encouragement and companionship for David. And again, like the other couples mentioned, Marie and David Lee's marriage and partnership are spiritually based and these marvelous women continue to stand by their husbands every step of the way.

Leon King is another Miss Billie-ite who became a man of distinction. He was a star football player (wide receiver). He and the great NFL running back Abner Butch Haynes were the first black athletes to break the segregation barrier at North Texas State University, now UNT. He is in State College of Texas' Football Hall Of Fame. Like most of the others I've mentioned who attended Miss Billie's Kindergarten, he has been married to his wonderful wife and high school sweetheart, Claudia, for fifty years.

Earl Shelton Riggs also attended Miss Billie's school. He was smart, athletic, and extremely popular in high school. After graduating from Texas College Earl married his lovely wife, Telesta, and they moved to Washington, DC. In the Nation's Capitol, Earl became an innovative and successful insurance executive. His creativity and the work ethic that Miss Billie instilled in all of her students helped Earl Riggs to increase his company's bottom line in a legendary fashion. He was later recruited by the R. J. Reynolds Tobacco Company from which he retired as Executive Vice President. He is currently president of the Washington-Lincoln Alumni Association of Dallas (WLAA). Earl and Tee (as she is affectionately called) have been married for forty-two years. They are yet another example of a husband and wife who are a team in every sense of the word.

L.G. Slider is a retired postmaster. L.G., James Freeman, and Harry Page were among the first black under-graduate students to attend the previously segregated University of Texas (UT) in Austin. L.G.'s sister, Bessie Slider Moody, a retired educator, is Executive Vice President of

Maurine F. Bailey Cultural Foundation Inc. (MFBCF). Bessie and her husband, Paul Moody, first met at Miss Billie's, and you might say they have been together ever since. Paul is a retired and still very much sought after mathematician and teacher. Bessie and Paul, a strikingly youthful couple, have been married almost fifty years. Paul Moody would've been the child most likely to have given Miss Billie cause to make his feathers fly.

Every single day, Paul would refuse to come into the classroom after recess. Miss Billie would finally ask the class: "Boys and girls, if Paul does not come into the classroom, what is Miss Billie going to do?" We would answer in unison: "Miss Billie will make his feathers fly high and high." Then she would go outside, gently take Paul by his hand, and lead him back inside. Paul would go to his seat and be the perfect student. Miss Billie's magic worked on Paul just as it did with the rest of us. Her patience, nurturing, and guidance gave him a love for math that has served him well.

Philmore Peterson, a graduate of Miss Billie's Kindergarten School, and his lovely wife Ruby own a landscaping service and beauty parlors. They are just a few of the many successful and respected people who attended Miss Billie's Kindergarten, and I could go on and on.

This is not to say that only children who attended Miss Billie's school turned out to be achievers. There are countless examples of young people who did not attend her school that were brilliant. Not the least of who is Joe Louis Atkins. As a senior at Lincoln High in 1955, he filed the law suit which became the test case that ended segregation at colleges and universities in the state of Texas.

Burlyce Sherrell Logan, Lurlene Bradley Jackson, along with the afore-mentioned, Joe Louis Atkins, Abner "Butch" Haynes and Leon king were among the first eleven black students from Lincoln to integrate UNT. Young Mr. Atkins attended another College –University of Texas, El Paso, no doubt because of security concerns. You can only imagine the horrors the other eleven had to endure. Someday their story will be told as a reminder of what America was like for black people as recently as the 1960s and 70s.

James Freeman and his wonderful wife Darlene, own Freeman's Custom Catering and Darlene is a department head with the HUD program. Rev. Joe Patterson was a very smart student. Rev. Patterson and his charming wife, Lynn are Pastor and first lady of the Greater New Zion Baptist Church, in Dallas, TX   Louis Rhone recently retired from Dallas Independent School district (DISD), and Gloria Trammel Mitchell was also brilliant, gifted and beautiful, as were Mary Lois Sweatt, Peggy Meshack King, and many others.   These are a few examples of very bright kids who did not attend Miss Billie's Kindergarten School. I remember that Clarence Robertson carried himself like a young "Knight" ever since he was six or seven years old. He along with Robert "Puggy" Woodard, Elijah Walker, Abner Haynes, Reed Epps Philmore Peterson, James Grey, James West, Earl Riggs, and others became super athletes and good students. Clarence had the same dignity and poise then as he has today.

In high school, our beloved music teacher, Mrs. Maurine F. Bailey always addressed him as Mr. President. True he was the president of Mrs. Bailey's Harry T. Burleigh Choir, but I think it was her way of instilling in him that he had those leadership qualities, and he still does.

Pastor Robertson and his dear wife Mable have built a loyal congregation in the church he pastors in Terrell, Texas. Their international outreach ministry serves hundreds of thousands of followers as far away as Ghana, Sierra Leone, Ivory Coast, Zambia, Kenya, South Africa and others countries. Rev. Robertson is a founding member of the MFBCF Advisory Board.

Pharmacist Gary Abernathy did attend Miss Billie's school. He and Clarence remained in close contact with Dr. John Hopps—the previously mentioned scientist, educator, politician and former student at Miss Billie's kindergarten who was an important member of the scientific team that advanced fiber optics and developed nanotechnology, bringing them to their current state of global application and prominance. The three of them were inseparable during their boyhood days at N.W. Harllee elementary school, and remained close friends until Dr. Hopps' untimely death in May of 2004. Clarence and Gary attended the dedication of a $8,000,000 structure on the Morehouse College campus in Atlanta, GA— John's Alma Mater, where he served as Provost for three years. The building was named for Dr. John Hopps Jr. in May, 2006.

According to Pastor Clarence Robertson, the kids that attended Miss Billie's kindergarten would come home from school and teach him and other interested kids everything they had learned at Miss Billie's. Sharing was another trait that we learned from her and here is a perfect example of its practice.

Dr. Hopps was not only one of Miss Billie's students, but he became one of the brightest stars in America's scientific community. John enrolled in Miss Billie's school a year behind us and he graduated from Lincoln High two full years ahead of us. Take a look at who this great American turned out to be. The contributions he has made to the world of science as a member of the research team that developed fiber optics, is just the tip of the iceberg. He was a highly valued member of the National defense team.

In 1992 John Hopps joined the National Science Foundation. President Bill Clinton appointed him Director of the Division of Materials Science.

In 2001 President George W. Bush appointed Dr. Hopps, Deputy Under Secretary of Defense for Laboratory and basic Sciences.

The following is an excerpt taken from the Biography of Dr. Hopps.

Dr. John Hopps Jr. was an African-American physicist and politician; he attended Miss Billie's kindergarten school, was a graduate of Lincoln High School –also located in Dallas, Texas- at the age of sixteen. He was extremely successful at his studies, and excelled in his college admissions examinations.

Dr. Hopps spoke fondly of Miss Billie, Lincoln High, Mrs. Maurine F. Bailey and his experiences under their direction. Although Miss Billie passed away before he made his mark, he kept in close touch with Mrs. Bailey. He recognized and introduced her before a distinguished panel of physicists at a convention over which he presided in Dallas while she was living. After graduating from Lincoln in 1954, he enrolled as a Ford scholar at Morehouse College, in Atlanta Georgia under the leadership of Dr. Benjamin Mays. Upon graduation from Morehouse, he enrolled in the Massachusetts Institute of Technology (MIT) in Cambridge, Massachusetts, and received his Doctorate in Physics from Brandies University, in Waltham, Massachusetts.

John was a member and Basileus, of Gamma Chapter of the Omega Psi Phi Fraternity. In 1971 he joined the faculty at Ohio State University, and later accepted a research position in nuclear engineering, and served in a leadership capacity at the Charles Stark Draper Laboratory in Cambridge, Massachusetts.

As if being Provost at Morehouse College, Director of the National Science Foundation, the Deputy Director of Defense Research & Engineering, and Deputy Undersecretary of Defense, etc. etc. etc. were not enough to make Miss Billie proud, John was an avid sponsor and coach of Youth football programs in the cities where he lived and/or worked. His beloved wife of forty-one years, Dr. June Gary Hopps, is Primary Professor of Public Policy at the University of Georgia in Athens, GA. It is well known that they adored each other and John often referred to his "June-bug" as the wind beneath his wings.

Dr. John Hopps Jr. not only made Miss Billie proud but he made all of us walk a little taller simply by knowing who and what he was, and from whence he came. For that alone, he along with the others mentioned in this chapter has more than earned a big **Thank you.**

(See: Miss Billie's photo pages 240-241)

The above is approximately one fifth of Dr. Hopps' distinguished record. His lengthy and extraordinary resume is available (at no cost) upon request from the Maurine F. Bailey Cultural Foundations, headquarters in Dallas Texas.

Another point that is noteworthy about **Miss Billie's Kindergarten School** is that, none of us can recall any one of Miss Billie's students going to the penitentiary. This is a remarkable statistic, given the almost constant parade of young black men that we grew up with who went to jail for various offences.

Miss Billie made the playing field level by putting us ahead of the game academically. She understood the importance of music and taught us how to sing and appreciate music. Her school was the archetype of what the perfect "Head Start" program looks like.

Dehumanization of our youth

Miss Billie's penetrating insight caused her to emphasize music and art as a main component of her approach to instilling humanitarian values to the young people in her charge. Were she with us today, I believe she would have recognized and pointed out the well disguised scheme, by certain interest groups, to under mind our youth. One of the most subtle and dehumanizing tactics currently being used by the "Anti-progressive" conservative elite is to eliminate the middle class. The opportunities that were made available to middle and lower-class children in the past, by sensitive and aware policy makers, are under fierce attack. The most direct assault on our children's development is the removal of music, art, and other subjects of the humanities from the public-school curriculum.

The elite promote the concept that the lack of money is the reason for the demise of those subjects in our schools. Short-sighted bureaucrats and self-serving politicians, buy the manipulation hook, line, and sinker.

We the public watch the dehumanization of America's youth year after year, as evidenced by the lack of humanity and compassion that has become the acceptable attitude among many young people today.

Using the pandering media, these same elitists, make scapegoats of the disenfranchised communities by pointing to reckless behavior. **While I do not condone nor excuse that behavior,** I fully recognize that it is spawned by an absence of meaningful and healthy outlets for young people before, during, or after school. The traditional alternatives such as music, art, dance etc. and other after-school activities are systematically being removed as options for our children.

True, the lack of funds is a reality, but some of those who would undermine and destroy the middle class have access to the funds that could easily remedy the situation. Likewise, there is much that could be and should be done by the parents of the children who are targeted and destined to become the under paid household servants of the elite. Unfortunately, some seem to be to unaware to know, and others too tired and/or too defeated to care.

There needs to be a district-wide outcry whenever a school considers dropping humanities-related subject from the curriculum. Otherwise music, art, and dance etc., will be available only to the children of the "top hat and tails" stuffed shirt Americans, the way it was before President Franklin Delano Roosevelt established the Federal Theatre Project in the 1930's, and made theater-going available to working-class people.

A World without Music Would Be a Mistake

The common thread that runs through much of my text is that many of the people that I write about are musical people. This was not by design; in fact I only became aware of it when I started doing the rewrites on this book. For me, music began with my mother and *then* came Miss Billie, but it was at Miss Billie's Kindergarten School where I first felt the magic. It has ordered the direction of my grateful and fulfilling life.

We can help revitalize our humanity by reinstating and revitalizing the humanities subjects in our schools. To some this statement might seem simplistic, but, just as academics massage and expand our minds; the arts caress and uplift our spirits, and music is the most accessible pathway to our peace-seeking souls.

Yes, it is true that some of the most important things I learned about life were learned at Miss Billie's Kindergarten School. In hindsight I see that she was motivated by her love for the children, and her commitment to their mental and physical advancement towards the total well-being of each child.

The fundamental principles she imparted were sustained and potent and I can still call upon them from time to time with good results. Miss Billie started us on the right track, gave us a head start, and put us in touch with the best in ourselves. She awakened in us the realization that we could learn, and would be rewarded for learning. Before our minds were tampered with by the rules that governed a pre- Civil Rights Act society, she captured our attention, and filled our minds and imagination with easily absorbed self-affirming qualities and habits.

Those lessons were simple enough for a four year old to grasp and practical enough to bring instant dividends when practiced in a forthright and timely way. For example: having good manners and using them appropriately, pays one of the most important of all social dividends, which is a way of being accepted in a group or community. Being punctual, finishing a task, finding a way to enjoy the chores or work that you have to do, and never giving up, are simple and straightforward principles that will well serve who ever applies them. The fact that we were able to read, write, spell and count coherently, and with comprehension at four years old, could be said to have been the fuel that propelled those principles into concrete, and lasting value.

One of the most important of the many bonuses we received by being in her presence was indeed the music that began each day at Miss Billie's. In the photo, (See Billie's photo pages) there were 53, three, four, and five year old children in her class. Miss Billie didn't have an assistant or a teacher's aide, yet she managed all those children without breaking a sweat or raising her voice. The school bell that she rang to begin and end the day was kept on her desk. If the room got too noisy she would ring that bell until we quieted down; it didn't take long. The sound of that bell in the small classroom got your attention fast.

A quest for knowledge and a passion for learning is the result of her enduring influence, and even today it colors everything good or worthwhile that I undertake. Because of the life affirming, esteem building qualities she instilled in us at the tender age of four, my thoughts and memories ascend towards the heavens on the wings of prayerful gratitude, sending forth… **A Simple but special… Thank You** to the one and only Mrs. Billeia Montgomery. We want the world to know, Oh how we loved, trusted, honored and obeyed our dear **Miss Billie;** May she forever rest in peace. (See Miss Billie's photo pages 240-241)

Maurine F. Bailey
Personal Hero

Maurine F. Bailey is the primary reason that this book was written. She was my high school music teacher who took an interest in me at a crucial time in my life. I decided that I wanted to be a singer at the age of eleven or so. I always had loved to sing, and briefly thought of becoming a singer when, as a small boy, I met the great blues-singer and guitarist, T Bone Walker. Although that fantasy was relatively short lived I continued to sing at every opportunity.

The thought of becoming a professional singer became my passion one day while I was trying to high jump over a rope that I had tied to two broomsticks. We had a radio that I would turn towards the window so as to hear the music playing when I was in the back yard high jumping.

On this particular day while in the back yard listening to the radio, the disk jockey played a song by my favorite singer, Billy Eckstine. The name of the song was "I Apologize." I knew the lyrics to the song because my mother had a 78 rpm recording of it that we listened to a lot. I sang along with the record, fantasizing that I was Billy Eckstine. At that time, I could not do a very good impersonation of Mr. B. because I was a boy soprano in Mrs. Dixon's chorus at N.W. Harllee Elementary School.

I had only seen photographs of Eckstine at that point because TV had not yet been invented as far as we knew. I imagined that I was Mr. B and sang along. When the song ended, the DJ said that Billy Eckstine would be appearing in Las Vegas, and he would be paid two thousand five hundred dollars a week. I could not comprehend such a thing. I literally did not know that anybody, not even the President of the United States earned $2500 a week. When I told my friend Gip about it, he started laughing and said I was making up the story. When Mudear came home from work, I told her what I'd heard on the radio about Billy Eckstine singing in Las Vegas for twenty-five hundred dollars a week; she said that she'd once read in a magazine that the Mills Brothers made $3,000 a week in Las Vegas.

This was at a time when my mother was earning $9.00 and carfare per week. I dreamed about Billy Eckstine three nights straight and the $2,500 a week occupied my mind for weeks. That night I prayed and asked God to let me be a singer like Billy Eckstine, and by the time I enrolled at Lincoln I could do a perfect Eckstine impersonation. In fact, Eckstine was the only nickname I ever had that stuck. I was a good singer, but I wanted to be a *professional* singer and I sang ALL THE TIME. Still, I did not know that it could really happen until Mrs. Bailey took an interest in me and made me believe that I had the talent and could make it as a singer. By the time I was in the eleventh grade I started getting hired as a professional singer around Dallas.

Ma Bailey convinced me to join the choir; she trained me to breathe and phrase correctly, and she taught me to always have good diction. I remember her saying to me, "You can have the best voice in the world and it means nothing if people don't understand what you're saying." She pointed out that great singers like Nat King Cole, Ella Fitzgerald, Frank Sinatra, Billy Eckstine, Lena Horne, Cab Calloway and others, all have good diction and you can understand every word they sing.

She worked with the school counselor, Mrs. Mable Chandler, and got me a music scholarship to Huston-Tillotson College, now known as Huston-Tillotson University, where I majored in music. I loved it because I got to sing the great classical arias and quickly became baritone soloist because Mrs. Bailey had taught us complete cantatas like Verdi's Requiem, Handel's Messiah, and other great classical music favorites. Nights and weekends, I sang blues, jazz, and popular music at local night clubs with my band that I named "The Steppers."

Maurine F. Bailey also instilled in us that life is no flower bed of roses, and that being successful at anything requires dedication and hard work. She said that it's easy to work hard at something that you love doing. She used to say, "Be clear-minded, and with God's help, that's the ticket to success." She was the most poised, elegant, and straightforward person I have ever known.

Ma Bailey, more than any other person, opened up the doors for black kids to be accepted across color lines in the city of Dallas. Often, she took us places where no black students had ever been invited, and she would remind us that: "You are not here just to sing; you are here to be remembered and respected." As a result of her wise counsel, and gentle but firm leadership, our performances were flawless, and our behavior was impeccable. When our host and people from the audience spoke with us after our performances, what they encountered were black high school students who were indeed clear-thinking and talented individuals. She groomed us to become successful ambassadors for racial harmony, and we were

One of the truly great moments in my life was in 1971 when I was on tour with Bill Cosby and we appeared at the Fair Park Music Hall. It was a typically icy winter in Dallas. The streets were all but impassable. I tried to convince Mrs. Bailey not to drive; her husband, Mr. Sterling Bailey refused to drive in such conditions. My own mother rode to the concert with my siblings and I thought, since Mrs. Bailey's husband was not coming, she would not risk driving that night, but to my surprise she drove anyway and showed up at the show. Lots of people braved the weather that night because the Music Hall was sold out and we played to a packed house.

Halfway through our portion of the show, before Cosby came on, I asked that the house lights be turned up full. I had not planned to do it, but when I realized that Mrs. Bailey had come out in that weather, I was so moved that the two great ladies in my life were sitting side by side in the auditorium, I could not resist.

When the house lights came up I told the audience that: "I have a special treat that I want to share with you." I told them that the two wonderful women that were directly responsible for my being on this stage performing with Bill Cosby are here tonight. I introduced my mother, Mrs. Nathalie Mathis. She stood up and the spotlight was on her and the audience applauded for about fifteen or twenty seconds. But when I introduced Mrs. Maurine F. Bailey, my former music teacher at Lincoln high school; she stood and the spotlight hit her, and the auditorium exploded into applause. Mrs. Bailey was wearing a full-length mink coat, and a diamond necklace that sparkled like dancing flames, reflecting in the spotlight. The applause was extended and continued for about five seconds after she sat down. It was wonderful.

The following day I went to Mr. and Mrs. Bailey's house on Magna Vista Dr. She was floating on air that I had introduced her at the concert in the Fair Park Music Hall-the city's most important music venue. She made a special lunch which she, Mr. Sterling Bailey, and I enjoyed as we visited for about three hours. He said that he would like to have attended the show, and that he had been worried about Maurine until he heard her car pull into the driveway.

As I was leaving, I asked them if I could get them something before I went back to California; they said no. When I asked her if I could buy her anything at all, she insisted that she had everything she needed. Then she said, "If you really want to do something for us, you can promise me that someday between now and the day the Lord calls you home; you will help ten young people improve their lives, and require that they in turn will help ten, and each ten will help ten and that way we can "uplift the human condition." I promised. The promise I made to Mrs. Bailey that day is the reason I started working with young people years later in Los Angeles. I was co-founder of the successful after-school youth intervention/anti-gang program, Living Literature Colors United.

I am grateful to be able to say that in the year 2000, after the passing of dear Ma Bailey, the Maurine F. Bailey Cultural Foundation was formed in her honor, and each year since its inception the Foundation has given college scholarships to deserving under-privileged students, and we look forward to continuing with that as well as with other philanthropic endeavors. The Bailey Foundation also presents a community service award to outstanding citizens from the community each year as part of our mission. The awards are presented at the Maurine F. Bailey Cultural Foundation's Annual Awards Banquet held every August in Dallas, Texas. With the help and cooperation of Dallas City Councilman Leo V. Chaney, the Bailey Foundation has had a street named MAURINE F. BAILEY WAY in her honor. Her name is also installed on the South Dallas "Walk of Fame," and recently she was inducted into The African-American Museum of Dallas as an outstanding educator, and for her overall contribution to youth and community. In 2005 a resolution was passed by the City of Dallas proclaiming her birthday, August 13th, Maurine F. Bailey Day.

In 1976 my beloved mother Nathalie Mathis passed away. After her burial, I went to Ma Bailey for solace. She and Mr. Bailey were wonderful to me. Ma said to me, "Its official: I am your mother now." Mr. Bailey concurred and from that day forward I called her Ma. What a blessing for me to have been so honored. Mrs. Bailey's beloved husband, Mr. Sterling Bailey preceded her in death; he passed away in 1986. A few days before my birth mother passed she and I talked by phone for more that two and a half hours. I was in the middle of taping the "Flip Wilson Special," with Sammy Davis Jr. and Helen Reddy. Toward the end of our lengthy but moving conversation, my mother said to me, "I'm tired and I want to go home." I told her that I was leaving the show and coming home tomorrow. She said, "No you don't"; she insisted that she was not going to interrupt my work. One of the last things she said to me was, "Honey, you take of Mrs. Bailey; she's a wonderful lady." I promised that I would. As always, but especially at that moment, her wish was my command. I kept that promise and I know that Ma Bailey was pleased with me because before she died, she told me that I had been a blessing to her. I reminded her that it had been mutual. When visiting hours ended at the Methodist Hospital and I had to leave her bedside where she lay unconscious, I got close to her ear and sang "Ingemisco," her favorite aria from Giuseppe Verdi's Requiem. To my surprise, when I finished the song she turned her head ever so slightly toward me. I know she heard the song, and I know she loved it. I gave her a kiss on her forehead and said, "Goodbye, Ma. I love you." The next morning, July 19, 2000, I got the call from the hospital; Ma Bailey was gone.

Maurine F. Bailey is in Heaven with her dear husband, Sterling, and I know my birth mother was there to welcome her. To one of the most wonderful women I have ever known: I am fortunate to have shared almost fifty of your ninety-nine years on Earth. For all you did for me and so many others, by the golden cord of gratitude, I attach these precious words floating on a celestial melody they bring to you...**A most gracious Thank You**. (See Bailey photo pages 238-239)

Jeff Bridges
Great Actor-Musician- Family Man

When people recognize me for my role in "Seabiscuit," invariably, the first question out of their mouths is: "What is Jeff Bridges really like?" Of course they inquire about each of the stars in that film but 100% of the time Jeff is the first one they ask about –except of course those energetic young Toby Maguire fans. What sets Jeff apart from a lot of other celebs is that this question is regularly asked by other musicians and artists. Even if they have never met him there is a cordial respect and obvious admiration for Jeff's work as an actor, and to a person, they say they would like to work with him.

Most of the people I've met and/or worked with in the entertainment industry have been nice people, but on rare occasions I have encountered a jerk or two. When someone asked me about those kinds of people, I generally give my stock answer, which is: "I did not spend much quality time with that person." But when asked by another artist I'll say, "I did not have a pleasant experience with him/her." If I'm asked by my friends I simply say, so and so was a jerk.

When I hear negative information about a person from someone who heard it from someone else, I consider that gossip and will not repeat it. Gossip stops when it reaches my ears, and there are few exceptions.

Jeff Bridges is one of those rare people that seem to leave a good impression wherever he goes. In that sense he is like a Jack Lemmon or Dennis Weaver--universally admired and I might add, for all the right reasons. His body of work is indeed impressive; He has done a variety of roles that prove that his range as an actor is enormous. I do not claim to have seen every film he has made, but I've probably seen most and I have never watched a Jeff Bridges film in which he was not believable and his characterization not well-rounded. Every actor knows that some scripts will be better than others, but my opinion is that he has made even those few projects better. Proof again, is the fact that every actor I know wants to work with him and I understand why. He is a solid professional and a natural talent that makes the work seem easy. He gives the actors in the scenes with him different angles of the character he is playing, and every nuance and cinematic gesture triggers a spontaneous response that makes the actors in the scene with him better as well.

He is fun to work with, has a thorough understanding of film making and off the set he's not afraid to let you know who he really is. I could go on and on about how actors in particular (and people in general) feel about this man, but instead, I will share an incident that validates my point.

I was talking with Morgan Freeman at an affair in Beverly Hills recently. I told him about this book I'm writing; he listened politely, but when I mentioned that Jeff Bridges had agreed to write the foreword, Morgan became interested and wanted to know more about it. He listened with more focused attention. I gave him an idea of what the book would be about—purposely not mentioning that he (Morgan) would be in this book. When I finished giving him an over-view of the book, the only comment he made was, "I love Jeff Bridges." Those are exactly the words most often used to describe how people feel about Jeff. This proves that he is by consensus one of Hollywood's finest actors and people.

There is no way that Jeff Bridges can possibly know how much he is appreciated, admired, and loved. He is solid in his industry, he is adored by his fans, and he is loved by those who have the good fortune to know him.

I met Jeff when I was hired to play "Sam"--Seabiscuit's groom. I went to Universal Studios to be camera-tested. I was escorted to make-up and when I entered the make-up trailer, there was one open chair. The chair next to the vacant one was occupied by an actor having his make-up applied. I sat in the vacant chair and recognized that the actor next to me was Jeff Bridges. I said to the make-up artist, making sure that Jeff could hear, "Is that who I think it is?" Jeff opened his eyes, turned his head towards me, extended his hand and said, "Jeff Bridges." I shook his hand and said "Kingston DuCoeur, nice to meet you." Jeff replied, "Kingston… That's a cool name, and easy for me to remember." He did a surprisingly good Caribbean accent as he continued, "Ya Mon, like Kingston, Jamaica. Ya, Mon?"

We spoke for two maybe three minutes and he was gone; one of the AD's (assistant director) came to escort him to the set for his camera test.

We didn't meet again until two weeks later on the first day of shooting--in Saratoga, NY. It was cold, early November; the focused hustle and bustle of the first day of principal photography is always a time of heightened anxiety and efficiency. This is when the real deal goes down. The prep time is essentially over, and there's no place for an actor to hide—except on the cutting room floor. It's when a different phase of the same work begins for most actors.

Jeff walked onto the set accompanied by his personal assistant and stunt double; his hair and makeup artist followed closely behind. Gary Ross, the director approached him; they conferred and shortly thereafter, came the 1st AD's call for rehearsal.

That first day, like most of the days that followed went well. On my way back to my dressing room, I passed by Jeff's dressing room. The door was open, and I peeked in. There was no one in the front room so I did not stop, but I noticed a guitar on the couch. A couple of days later, I passed by; the door was closed but I could hear someone softly strumming on the guitar. I knocked and Jeff answered the door, guitar in hand. I said, "Is that you playing?" JB: "I'm just fooling around." I asked if he would mind if I came in and he waved me in. There was a Motown songbook on the coffee table. We talked about a feature documentary about the Motown R&B band, "The Funk Brothers". They were the incredible musicians responsible for nearly all of the early Motown hits. Jeff had already seen the documentary. It was on my list of films to see and because he dug the movie so much when telling me about it, I became more excited about checking it out. I did see it later that week and it was great. I told Jeff that I'd bring my portable keyboard and we could play some music. He was all for it. I started bringing my keyboard and between takes Jeff and I passed the time with Motown, the Beatles, and the Blues. We would spend time fooling around with music in his or my dressing room between takes and soon discovered that Robin Bissell was a musician and singer, and that Chris Cooper had also been a singer during and just after college. Jeff said jokingly that we could form a band and call ourselves, "The Seabiscuits." After the laughter died down, he and I continued to play around with the music.

I suggested to Jeff that we really should form the "Seabiscuit" band and surprise everyone by playing a couple of songs at the wrap party. I don't think Jeff was too keen on the idea at first, but day after day of passing time together, he finally agreed that it would be a lark to do it. I told him that I would see if Toby Maguire, Chris Cooper, Elizabeth Banks and Robin Bissell would be up for joining the "The Seabiscuits." I approached Toby and he said he was not sure that wanted to embarrass himself because he did not consider himself a singer or musician by any means. My response was that he did not have to sing if he didn't want to, that he could play the tambourine. Again, he was sort of unsure, but seeing that he had a mellow vibe on the set, I was able to assure him that he would be a good tambourine player because he has natural rhythm. I knew this to be true because when we shot the church scene I was seated next to Toby and as we sang the hymn in that scene, I picked up his rhythm and matched my rhythm to his. I would have *never* done that if his rhythm had not been right on.

I talked to Chris Cooper and he was game for the idea, and so were Elizabeth Banks and Robin Bissell. Jeff had written and recorded some nice songs on his CD titled, "Be Here Soon." His songs are well written and would be easy enough to learn. Everyone agreed that we would only need one rehearsal to pull it off. The trick would be to keep it a secret so it would be a surprise when The Seabiscuits took the stage at the wrap party. The idea gained momentum with Jeff, Toby, Chris, Robin, Elizabeth, and I was excited. Every time I thought about the idea of The Seabiscuits rocking out at the wrap party, I chuckled with delight. I checked the shooting schedule for a day that we could get together for an hour and rehearse. Jeff supplied some copies of his CD so each of us could learn the chosen songs beforehand. Everybody was enthusiastic about the "gig."

While I kept an eye on the shooting schedule, life went on smoothly, on and off the set until one night well after the days filming was over and the cast and crew had turned in for the night, unbeknownst to me, a terrible storm struck. I had an early call and was scheduled to shoot my first scene around 7:00Am. This meant that I needed to be on the set ready for make up, wardrobe and breakfast by 5:30 AM. I had requested a 4:30AM wake up call because the driver would be in the hotel lobby at 5:00AM. The phone rang and a pleasant voice on the line said, "Good morning Mr. DuCoeur, this is your wake up call; have a nice day sir." I got up, washed my face, brushed my teeth and got dressed. It was a cold day and I decided to wait and take a shower in my dressing room when I got to the set.

I got into the SUV with some other actors who also had an early call time. That's when I discovered that the storm that hit overnight had literally destroyed the set. The driver explained the extensive damage it had caused. He painted a pretty dismal picture of the destruction, and he did not exaggerate. The devastation was apparent as we drove past scores of fallen trees, downed power lines, over-turned cars, damaged roofs and so on. When we arrived at base camp, evidence of the storm's force was everywhere. I was sure that we would lose at least a day's shooting based on what I had seen on the drive in. I changed into wardrobe and had my makeup applied, ordered breakfast and then I went to the set to view the damage.

The storm had damaged Toby Maguire's trailer but obviously Toby was long gone and no where near the set when the storm hit. Toby being the extremely focused and hard working professional that he is, was probably sleeping like a log when the storm came thru well after midnight.

One of the reasons that Seabiscuit was such a success is because the cast also included such pros as previously mentioned, Chris Cooper, Elizabeth Banks, Eddie Jones, Sam Bottoms, plus a crew to die for. Add to that John Schwartzman, DP-director of photography, under the leadership of Gary

Ross, and with the support of Robin Bissell and others, in my opinion you have a real cinematic dream team.

I also spent some time with the professional jockeys that worked on the film, such as Hall of Fame Jockeys Chris McCarran, so for real and smooth he could run for Mayor. The great Gary Stevens did a heck of a job in the role of George Woolf. Gary Stevens is a natural actor who has a future in the movie and TV business should he choose to pursue it.

Other jockeys that I got to know such as Luis Jauregui, Ricky Frazier, Kevin Mangold, Joe Stein, Paul Atkinson, David Neusch, Alan Patterson, Michael Hunter, Mark Munoz, Gallyn Mitchell, Cory Black, and Bobby Coltan, also did their jobs extremely well. These guys are **real men** and fun to be around and one of the things we have in common is that we all dug being around Jeff Bridges whenever time and circumstances allowed.

I changed into my wardrobe, went to makeup, finished my breakfast and the driver picked me up at base camp and drove me to the set. To my complete surprise, the set had been fully restored. Kathleen Kennedy, the producer of the movie was in complete control. Working with the production designer Jeannine Oppewall and the crew, she had worked a miracle. As far as I could tell, the entire set looked the way it had looked the day before the storm hit. It was amazing. I had read somewhere that if you want your film project to be successful, get Kathleen Kennedy and Frank Marshall involved. Watching them work--Frank was second unit director and Kathleen was the producer. I concur, wholeheartedly, with the statement confirming their film making savvy and unchallenged commitment to the success of the project.

At lunch that afternoon, one of the actors at the table commented on the unbelievable condition to which the set had been restored. The conversation progressed and someone mentioned what remarkable work had been done to get the set restored in such a short time. Then Jeff Bridges' name came up when one of the actors said he had a scene with him later that day and said that he always looked forward to working with Jeff. I sat quietly and listened as every actor commented and/or agreed that they enjoyed being around him. The general feelings that were expressed confirmed my good opinion of Jeff Bridges, because they all considered him to be a genuinely "for real" guy, whose talent and skills rate with the best.

Nearly all evidence of the terrible storm that had claimed thirty-eight lives across six states was gone and the days shoot went without a hitch. I continued to check the shooting schedule for a suitable day and time for the "Seabiscuits" to rehearse.

Alas, during the whole five months I worked on the movie, there was not one day when the shooting schedule would allow for all of us to get together and run through the songs. Perhaps it was just as well because I spoke with Jeff at one point near the end of the shoot, and he informed me that the wrap party was going to be bigger than either of us had expected. This meant that it would not be just the cast, crew and guests that the "Seabiscuits" would've played to as originally planned. He was correct. It was so huge that it was held at Union Station in downtown Los Angeles, and the entire pavilion was packed with a cross section of Hollywood partygoers. I had a great time, but was I glad that we did not attempt to jam for such a large and diverse crowd. It was a great party and everybody had a fabulous time. Jeff Bridges is an actor for whom the best is yet to come.

One day Mrs. Dorothy--Jeff and Beau's dear mother-- came to spend the day on the set. She is an adorable lady who beams with pride when she talks about her children. There are always two or three people around her enjoying her presence and keeping her company. It is true that the Bridges clan is all about family. We also had the pleasure of meeting Jeff's lovely wife, Susan. She too has that same sense of ease, the "real people" type of personality that must be the family trademark. When Jeff talks about his brother Beau, you can tell that they are also best friends. When I met Beau, my impression was that the Bridges boys were raised right; you feel comfortable in their presence.

Aside from being a well established and highly respected actor and a good singer/ songwriter and musician, Jeff is also a first rate photographer. He took candid shots on the set and generously presented the cast and crew with a complete photo journal of the entire "Seabiscuit" experience. I will cherish my signed copy forever- as will the other cast and crew members, I'm sure. There is an even more impressive photo journal that he put together of photos he took with his "special" camera. This is a camera that seems to take pictures around a corner. I had never before seen one like it. One afternoon, Jeff was looking through the final mock up of his soon to be published photo journal. It consists of candid photos from just about every film he has ever appeared in. The title is <u>Pictures by Jeff Bridges</u>. The cover of this beautifully constructed coffee table book features a shot from his favorite film, "The Baker Boys." The cover shot also features his favorite co-star and friend who happens to be his brother, Beau.

As he thumbed through the pages, he said: "Kingston, take a look at this." He was looking at a photo of his father, Lloyd, and his mother, Dorothy which was taken when his parents were younger. There was such excitement and joy in his voice when he said: "Look at how he's looking at her." I hope Jeff won't mind me saying that I think looking at that photo made him a wee bit teary-eyed. It is indeed a touching photograph and I see why it is special to him.

I attended the opening of his photo exhibit at a gallery in Santa Monica when this magnificent book was released. There were throngs of celebrities, Industry people, friends, and supporters at the opening; stacks and stacks of books disappeared from the table as people were buying them two and three at a time. All of the proceeds from the sale of that book go to one of Jeff's favorite charities, "The Motion Picture and Television Fund. At his photo exhibit I was introduced to his very talented brother Beau who has that same understated confidence and ease. What a guy! What a family! They are good people and its fun to be in the same room with them. Jeff is obviously someone for whom I have great respect and admiration. He is a powerful man, with a mild manner and a good heart.

When I committed to writing this book, I knew that I would ask Jeff Bridges to write the foreword. I think that the life force that runs through him is compatible with the true meaning of gratitude. Our discussions about a few different subjects revealed a man who is of a thoughtful mind and a clean spirit. I am grateful that he agreed to lend his good name to my effort.

Mr. Jeff Bridges: for your gracious words, your friendship, and for making my work on Seabiscuit such a fun and memorable experience, please accept… **a Simple Thank You**. (See Bridges photo pages)

Jim Brown
American Icon

Jim Brown. In the 1955 football season in Texas, no one heard much about football outside of the local high school teams. No matter what the team's name, mascot, coach, or star player, they all had one thing in common. To varying degrees, they each had the dream of winning a championship. The NFL was coming into its own with star athletes such as Bobby Layne, Otto Graham, Marion Motley, Tank Younger, the great Johnny Unitas and the likes.

College football stars were known only to regional, state, or area rivals. Unfortunately I'd not heard of Jim Brown until about a week or so before the game between Syracuse and Texas Christian University (TCU), at the Cotton Bowl. Word got around in the community that there was a great running back on the Syracuse team, and he was black. His name was Jim Brown. Not many black people in Dallas attended Texas Longhorn, or TCU games because, like most "white" schools in the South, they did not allow black players on their teams. We were more into Grambling and Southern University, or Prairie View A & M, and Texas Southern University (TSU).

Jim Brown ran with such power and grace that day at the Cotton Bowl, he became a living embodiment of a "real man" to many black people in America. This was the beginning of my awareness of Jim Brown. He went on to conquer the sports world by setting records that were so amazing it was believed they would, or will, never be broken. Jim's 5.2 yards per carry average might never be broken. Although the fine San Diego Chargers Running-back, LaDainian Tomlinson, seems to be on course to set new records, (at this time) the closest player to Jim Brown's average is, the great Barry Sanders, who averaged 5.0 yards per carry. All the other running backs including the great Gale Sayers, Emmitt Smith, O.J, Thurman Thomas, to name a few, are in the 4 plus yards per carry.

Jim Brown's record for most touchdowns in a single season stood for 20 years until the great Walter Payton of the Chicago Bears broke it in 1986. The difference being, that the first three years that Jim played there were only 12 games per season. When Walter Payton played there were 14 games per season during his first three years, and 16 games per season for the remaining ten years that he played. Therefore, Walter --great though he unquestionably was, had two more games per season to score touchdowns, for three years, (a total of six more games). For ten years thereafter, he had four more games per year, (forty games more) than Jim. That means that Walter, as great as he was, had a grand total of forty-six more games, which breaks down to, 184 more quarters of playing time than Jim. Assuming that Walter averaged 20 carries per game (a low estimate), that would mean that he had a minimum of 920 more carries-or opportunities, to score touchdowns than Jim Brown.

When Hall of Fame Running back, Emmitt Smith, came in to the league in 1990, the sixteen game seasons were in full force. This means that Emmitt had more than double the number of carries-or opportunities to score more touchdowns than Jim or Walter.

These facts are not intended to diminish the outstanding careers of Emmitt Smith and Walter Payton. **They are great in their own right**, and will be rightfully celebrated for their accomplishments, and the many thrills they gave to football fans the world over. The purpose for sighting the statistics is to put into proper perspective, the man for man comparison of three of greatest running back in football history. Jim Brown is indisputably head and shoulders above the rest.

Jim Brown is in a league of his own

Jim Brown is in three different Halls of Fame: 1. College Football Hall of Fame, 2. NFL Hall of Fame and 3. The College Hall of Fame for his unequaled ability as a lacrosse player. Jim's lacrosse coach at Syracuse is on record as saying that Jim Brown was the best lacrosse player he has ever seen. How many athletes in the history of sport can you name who have earned such distinction? Not even the great Jim Thorpe, the great Native-American athlete is in this unique category.

What goes largely unnoticed is the little known fact that Jim Brown was also highly successful academically as a student at Syracuse. This comes as no surprise to me because unlike many in our society, I have never held the stereotypical belief that athletes are by nature dumb. This is a flawed generalization that never took hold in the black community in Dallas where I was raised. Most of us recognized the fact that the star players on our high school football, basketball, and track teams were usually among the best students academically.

 Perhaps,-although I have no evidence to prove it, the "dumb athlete" myth might have taken hold at the college level. Often times, and in some colleges and universities, star players are given a "free ride" where their studies are concerned, because their value to the prestige and the economic bottom line of some educational institutions trumps the requirement to excel in the classroom.

The fallacious notion that all athletes are incapable of learning at a higher level can be easily disproved. In addition to Jim Brown's academic excellence, there are others like Bernie Casey, Fred Williamson, Carl Weathers, Fred Dryer, Walter Payton, Jackie Robinson, Elston Howard and others star athletes who became successful as film and TV actors. I worked closely with Bernie Casey on the National Board of Directors of Screen Actors Guild. When I was elected to the SAG Board, he was Chairman of several committees. I heard him make speeches that were brilliant. I also saw his effectiveness in the board room. Not only is he a brilliant thinker, but he is also, a world-class fine artist whose paintings are sought after and commissioned on a global scale. He is highly intelligent and genuinely concerned about the pitfalls that capture and trap our young men and women. Those traps are set and baited by the urban street-speak that promote the rather hideous misconception that students who strive to achieve academic excellence are "sell outs". Worse yet, they are often accused of "trying to be white." That is perhaps the most crippling and self defeating indictment of all.

 Jim Brown and others have proven that an education is worth having even if you are gifted in sports. For example Minnesota State Supreme court Justice, Allen Page, All pro Lineman for the Minnesota Vikings, was academically sound during his college years at Notre Dame. Another great running back, at Kansas State, and with the Chicago Bears, Gale Sayers is listed among the top fifty African-Americans who drive innovation in Industry, Government, and Academia. Mr. Sayers is Founder and CEO of Sayers Group, a hardware and software distribution company headquartered in Mt. Prospect, Illinois. There are others, too numerous to mention.

Jim Brown retired from professional football in 1966 while he was on top, a fact that speaks to his savvy, as far as his own marketability and ambitions were concerned. He went on to destroy stereotypes by the roles he played in movies. He never played a weak subservient role. Instead, like Woody Strode, William Marshall, Sidney Poitier, Denzel Washington, Bernie Casey, and a few others, Jim played strong, courageous, and purposeful characters.

He starred in "A Hundred Rifles" with Raquel Welch and Burt Reynolds—two of Hollywood's hottest stars at the beginning of his acting career. He was dominant in the film, and he got the girl. He went on to do "The Dirty Dozen", "Ice Station Zebra", and more than forty other movies.

Jim Brown is a man who has always stood for a black man's right to dignity. In the 1960s he helped form the Negro Economic Union, to assist black-owned businesses. Like some, and more than other successful and famous black men, he has been consistently targeted by the haters with the: "That nigger's too big for his britches" syndrome. He has stood up against every false and trumped up charge and the orchestrated setups that were designed to entrap, discredit, and humiliate. As a community activist, Jim is the most courageous of this generation.

I believe Jim understood something way back in the Seventies and Eighties when he started to work with black kids in Watts, and studied the Spanish language in order to relate to Latino kids in East LA. This was at a time when the mean streets of South Central Los Angeles, were becoming as dangerous for a stranger as they were for the people who lived there. The gang infested areas of East LA were strictly off limits to a black man, JB walked the walk and talked the talk and did a lot of good by way of example.

Founded upon the promise I had made to Mrs. Bailey, it was his example that encouraged me to finally take the plunge and work with disenfranchised, physically, and emotionally abused young people. Often these are the ones that help make up the core group of gang members. I started by working for a home for troubled kids in Altadena, CA where I lived, and became a member of the Town Council.

In 1992 Jim was the Grand Marshal in the parade that kicked off the WATTS FESTIVAL–an annual event that is held in South Los Angeles. We had a group of students named "Colors United," from Jordan High School, in the parade. I had not seen Jim in person for quite a few years. He sat in his brown convertible Mercedes-Benz, surrounded by a group of reformed gang members, who were working with "AMER I CAN." This is an organization that Jim started in 1988, for the purpose of helping uplift the community by focusing on creating jobs, and working for peace. I reintroduced myself and when I mentioned that I was the former singer with "The Pair Extraordinaire" he remembered me.

We waited for the parade to begin, and talked about the work that we were doing in Watts. I remember that Jim was pleased that I had chosen to join the fight to help stop the all-too-frequent killings and violence among youths. As I stated before, in 1989, 90, and 91 we were losing approximately three to five young men per day to drive-by shootings in the communities of Watts, Venice, Compton, and East LA.

Jim Brown and I had originally met in the late Sixties through a mutual friend with whom I was studying acting: Fred "The Hammer" Williamson, an ex-football player who like Jim had turned actor. Fred was also his own man. He was the actor who wrote, found financing, and made his own movies. He may have been the inspiration for Spike Lee who I believe was the first African-American film maker to make successful movies that opened with "wide release", and played in "mainstream" theaters in America and abroad.

At the time, Jim Brown the actor was also instrumental in the discovery of the R & B musical group "Friends of Distinction" (whose hit song was titled, "Going in Circles." He also helped the, as yet undiscovered, R & B group from Chicago: "EARTH WIND AND FIRE," break into the business.

I was a singer at the time and had not yet ventured into acting as a profession. When I was in town, occasionally I'd run into Fred, and/or Jim around town. Sometimes, Jim would be with a beautiful woman, other times he might be solo or with the boys. Alphie's, a café on the Sunset Strip was one of the spots where black actors and musicians gathered during the day.

One afternoon a group of us were having lunch and talking. The conversation started out about sports (i.e. Muhammad Ali, Arthur Ashe, et al), and covered numerous topics. At one point when Jim was talking, I sensed that he seemed to know something back then that many people today are just beginning to understand. I believe Jim Brown understood that a man's dignity is primarily based on the outer and inner image he holds of himself. If a man can be made to act inferior, the world around him will accept, believe, and demand that he occupy that image with every part of his physical, mental, and spiritual being. In other words, Slavery's most subtle and a final stronghold is *Esclevage de l'esprit*, or in plain English, "slavery of the mind."

Although invisible to the outside world, this type of slavery is practised, promoted, and perpetuated primarily in our prison system. Therefore, it is not exclusively the black man's problem. Any person of any color, including a caucasian, who gets caught up, and does not have the resources to hire adequate legal representation, is apt to wind up in the penal system where the slave mentality seems to prevail on both sides of the bars.

There is one important fact that could perhaps help young black men who find themselves caught up in the legal aystem. That would be to learn how to conduct themselves, when appearing before a judge, or magistrate. A good start would be to simply pull up their pants, speak intelligently, and address the court in an acceptable manner. Obviously, this is not a cure-all for the ingrained prejudice that some officials might harbor. However, there are those officials, who understand the sometimes wreckless, but often restless pranks of youth, that are prone to be lenient. That leniency may be tharted by the young person's physical appearance, and lack of respectful and intelligent response to the court.

Anyone who gets involved with trying to help " save" young people from such a fate (the way Jim and others like him have done) gets to know the system first-hand. Unfortunately, young African-American, and Latino men are not made to realize this sad fact of what I call "*Le Nouvel esclavage*"–the new slavery- at an early enough age. Some never realize it until it is too late.

I believe Jim Brown understands that in certain places in America, there is a jail cell that is already waiting for every male black child. For an example, when, and where I was born, there was a jail cell that already had my name on it–so to speak. Luckily, by the Grace of God, and the type of community awareness and spirit of unity that was the norm when I was a child, I did not end up occupying that jail cell.

The African Proverb: "It takes a village to raise a child" has been trivialized by political spin doctors and the like. But it really does "take a village" to help the average under-privileged African-American child to succeed. Given the state of our current "every man for himself and everyone else be damned" mentality that seems to be the prevailing attitude in much of the black community, a village mentality would be welcomed.

In the 1940's, 50's, and 60's, black communities in general had that village type of mentality. Adults helped each other, informed each other, and looked out for each other's best inrerest. They were able to chastise and correct an errant child (not by physical means) without being assaulted by the misbehaving child's parent. Such is not the case today. Try to correct a child today–in any community—and you are likely to encounter the wrath of an irate parent, yelling, cursing and screaming, "It's none of your God Damned business!"

If a police officer happens to witness an incident and hauls the kid off to juvenile hall or to jail, then some parents, and often members of the community want to cry foul. I'm not talking about the needless brutality that a number of cops use all too often against certain minority groups. It was not always easy, but I beat the odds and stayed out of prison–thanks to caring people, the grace of God, and other reasons that I stated earlier.

I am not one who believes that all or even most of the problems in black communities are caused by policemen. In fact I am pro law enforcement. I fully understand that law and order, and a fair and balanced judicial system, are the foundation and guardians of a free and just society. I also realize that the penal system as it is today, and some (not all) of the people who run it, along with harded career criminals, are viewed as the founding fathers of *Le Nouvel Esclavage,* whether they wish to be or not.

It is a system that is perpetuated by the uninformed, and a significant number of uncaring politicians, citizens, and institionalized perpetrators. The prison system is a complete world unto itself, and contrary to popular belief it is accountable to no one. Not even the governors, the president, or the congress, seem to have the concern, the will, and therefore the ability to change or effectively reform it. An uninformed public is hunkered down in fear and resentment behind their well guarded (and necessary) safety doors.

I am not one who believes that violent, hardened or career criminals ought to be pampered, or coddled. I **do** believe that people with a drug problem should **not** be placed with those who are violent, hardened, or career offenders. The most convenient excuse is: "lack of space". True there are not enough facilities and probably never will be, to adequately house offenders as long as the new prisons that are built are used in the present manner.

Why is it, that more of the new prison facilities are **not** used specifically to separate those who might be drug abusers from those who are incorrigible or hardened criminals?

This book is not an attempt to write a treatise on race or racism. Still, it would be fraudulent and a lie to deal with the realities of the Penal Industrial Complex as it stands today, without establishing the back-drop against which a sometimes corrupt tapestry is woven.

Since Jim Brown, like others before him, has stood openly against racists and racism, I think it fitting to deal with it in this chapter. It is noteworthy to point out that Jim Brown, is a man who has been targeted and harrassed in the past. His self respect, and human dignity caused him to go jail rather than accept what he believed to be humiliating, and degrading redress, of a misdemenor offence for which he was accused.

Because of his genuine concern for justice he made the best of his time spent while incarcerated. Not only did he come out of jail a stronger (with more than just weight lifting strength) and a better man, but it is apparent that even those in law enforcement recognize that his approach to helping inmates become productive citizens (if given the chance) upon their release back into society has merit, and is proving to be effective.

This is evident in the fact that Mr. Brown (since his release) has worked to install a program in conjunction with the Los Angeles County Jail that would be sanctioned -if implemented, by Sheriff Lee Baca,--to Sherrif Baca's great credit. The program is no doubt based on the concept of Jim's "Amer I Can" organization that has a proven track record of helping ex-offenders find hope, dignity, and productivity upon their return to society.

It is not solely the "white man's" fault that racism finds favor in our world, or in our communities. Just as Jim Brown has designed and implemented an effective program for the prisons, we would do well to introduce curriculum into every school district in America, a required course designed to teach the naked truth, which is: to be imprisoned for a felony is to be a slave.

With the help of others, I am at present designing such a course. We need to better inform our youth by teaching them that to be a repeat offender is to become a bonified slave in America, for all but a privileged few. Emphasis should be placed on schools in districts where felonious assaults, drug related felonies, and teen/pre-teen pregnancies are most prevalent.

The prevailing lack of vision and pseudo-political concern are disguised as a lack of funds. Some folks declare that if those well hidden economic statistics on prisons were to be revealed, it would more than likely show that the overall prison systems in this country are one of the most lucrative industries in the world. Perhaps that is why the political lip service and half-hearted attempts at reform are promised to, and paraded before the electorate at election time. Here again, the smoke and mirror practices hide a situation of resignation that can degenerate into defeat.

It is a malady that has lulled the American people into believing that the only real problems are based on the images they see on TV shows such as "Cops," "Cheaters," and the evening news. Ninety percent of the time, these TV staples show black people at their worst. The counterargument has been: "If the unlawful acts were not committed, they could not be filmed and shown to the public." While that is obviously a valid point, it is still, in the final analysis, an out-of-balance distortion because criminal acts are committed everyday by all racial groups.

The destructive influence is created and perpetuated when many of the same acts are committed by other groups, including whites. While they may get some mention, the story is not replayed ad nauseum and constantly regurgitated upon a trusting and unaware public, unless it is a black person committing an unlawful act. It is this subtle racism that is practiced day in and day out by ultra-conservative media outlets that justify the fear and loathing that is spoon-fed daily to the masses.

The reason for this systematic distortion does not rest with the media alone. It is true that the broadcast media is the primary delivery system, as well as the most intrenched mechanism, used to exploit these unbalanced, biased, and racially-provocative images. The ease with which most Americans buy into this mass manipulation originates from a much deeper source. That source is a lingering concept that has followed us from the cotton fields of antebellum plantations to the auction blocks of New Orleans and other seaport in the Americas.

In my mind, I can hear the moans and groans of blacks and whites alike, saying, "Oh not again; is he really going to start with the slavery bit again? Doesn't he realize that Americans are tired of hearing about slavery and being blamed for something that happened over a hundred years ago? When will they realize that my generation was not living during that time, and that I had nothing to do with what happened way back then?"

I understand that point of view being expressed by many well-meaning whites and some mis-informed black folk as well. I feel regret that some blacks vehemently cling to such an attitude. I am embarrassed and saddened that the subject of Slavery still must not be allowed to disappear from the conscience of this nation, just as the Holocaust is not and should not be allowed to be forgotten by the world at large. It should be the task of every freedom loving human being on this planet and beyond, to resist the type of barbaric inhumanity that was perpetuated by slave-trading Europeans, as well as the twisted ideology of Adolph Hitler.

His vitriolic diatribes, and facist rhetoric were allowed to dehumanize and destroy millions of brilliant, and enterprising human beings solely because they were Jewish. The greater truth is that while the world should care,and remember, it is the the **duty** of every Jewish person alive, and the as of yet unborn, to make certain that such an atrocity in any way, size, shape or form is not to be repeated, nor forgotten. It appears that Jewish people everywhere, realize this vital fact. Therefore, their commitment to the slogan (or their call to arms, if you will) "Never Again" serves as an effective reminder for Jewish people.

If we are to learn from history, African-Americans need to draw on the wisdom of every people who have risen from the chains of oppression, and/or survived the evil finality of genocide, no matter what their racial, religious, cultural, or ancestral origin might be.

I too, did not live during those three hundred plus years before the Emancipation Proclamation was signed into law by a "white" president. It does not matter what his motives may have been, I am grateful for his actions and I am also grateful that it was ratified by a white Congress, regardless of how many slaves they may have owned at the time. It is not necessary for me to have lived during that dark and diabolical period in history. I do not need to have experienced the trials and tribulations of slavery in order to know what it must have been like for my ancestors who lived, died, and survived through it. I **do** remember the legalized injustice that was the bane of the "Negroes" before and during the 1950's, 60's, and early 70's.

I remember in my home state of Texas, when a "poll tax" and other forms of intimidation were the rules that precluded my parents from being able to vote. I remember being a pre-teenager who could not sit down on the city bus without moving the sign that read "For Whites," and the other side of the sign that read "For Coloreds."

Today—some fifty years later—as I write this chapter, the Voting Rights Act is under attack by what some see as a neo-fascist attempt to turn back the clock. It is my responsibility and my duty as a black man, an African-American, a negro, a spade, or whatever label certain people may try to pin on me. It is my sacred duty to remember to struggle against the well organized remnants of the post-emancipation injustices that are poised to be unleashed upon unsuspecting, politically apathetic, and economically disconnected blacks in America.

Just three days before I wrote this chapter, Hurricane Katrina struck New Orleans and other Gulf Coast communities. As I write this, I can hardly believe some of the comments I hear on talk radio programs, statements such as, "Why the hell didn't all those black people leave when they were told to?" This type of comment was voiced by caller after caller after caller. Finally to the credit of one of the dual hosts of the show (a white man) he tried to explain that some of those people had no way to leave and no place to go. The Super Dome shelter had not been announced at the time when the first warnings were given. Although I am aware of the kind of world we live in, I was shocked and appalled that so many whites have (or claim to have) no idea that some people in America actually do live, despite their best efforts, below the poverty line. Most of them are not deadbeats. They rely on public transportation and there was none available to them at the time. Many of the callers to the talk show, complained incessantly that all the looters were black. I have no doubt that the majority may have been. My question is: what would you do, having been stranded in a city eight feet below sea level with no way out, no food, and no response from a Federal Government that was distributing food and shelter six thousand miles away in Indonesia within twenty-four hours of that unfortunate tsunami disaster?

What would you do? Let all the edible food left in the abandoned stores rot on the shelf and watch your children starve? I don't think so. Even this type of misguided thinking is not solely the fault of the "white man"; we need to teach our own children the truth and stop perpetuating the lie that they are equal just because they were born American citizens.

Young people in the hood—you are not equal. You may have been born equal but you do not remain equal until and unless you achieve something that gives you equal status with those who have either earned, inherited, or otherwise captured equality.

An uneducated person in America cannot be equal in the meaningful sense of the word until he/she can do something that affords him/her a modicum of equality. No matter how successful you might become, there will still be those who will openly, or secretly, deny your freedom if they can. The one overriding reason is simply because your skin is black.

You must become educated and/or successful enough that no one can deny you what you know yourself to be capable and willing enough to earn, win, capture, and demand as true equality.

It is not wise for us to allow our children to grow up believing that a welfare check and food stamps allows you to be equal. I do not begrudge those who truly need that type of assistance. My mother was on welfare during a time when she had no choice. Welfare will not allow you to be equal to Bill Gates, Oprah Winfrey, or the guy who owns a successful "Fat Burger" stand or a shoeshine franchise. To continue to let our children grow up in America believing such a sham would be the height of folly, and a testament to our own lack of understanding.

In the spirit and image of Jim Brown, I have already suggested the need for a specific curriculum designed to teach our youth the subtleties of *esclevage de L'esprit* (slavery of the mind), which is the incubating fetus of *Le nouvel esclevage*-the new slavery. A far-fetched idea today could become a startling reality tomorrow, surreptitiously creeping into view, and followed by a muted chorus of "How did this happen in America!"

The new curriculum is long overdue. Sadly, such a curriculum and even the concept will not come to be, unless and until African-Americans begin to regularly attend PTA and School Board meetings. Parents must start to read more than Jet, Ebony, and People Magazines (no disrespect is intended towards those wonderfully successful, world-class publications). We hear all too often, "I'm a single parent," or, "I work two jobs," etc. So be it: once a month go to the meeting tired, and speak up. It should energize you when you realize that being too tired or any other excuse, empowers those whose agenda is to keep you tired and uninvolved. Our lack of participation allows them to justify teaching and spreading the belief that we are too lazy to care.

Until we open our minds, and refocus our mental, spiritual, and economic energy on things that inspire our youth to succeed in every area and phase of life, *the new slavery* will continue to creep into the American psyche. It will slowly overtake us by stealthily eroding the hard fought-for gains that previous generations of our people suffered and died for. It is happening every day before our all too myopic eyes and the proof is evident.

Based on a Jim Brown type of awareness, we need a special curriculum to teach our children, K thuough 12, that when a person goes to prison for a felony in America, guilty or not, he/she looses almost all rights that are afforded to other citizens. He loses the right to vote, the right to find a decent job (especially if he is black), and he loses the right to be forgiven for the simple, small, and sometimes unavoidable mistakes that are not considered serious when made by most other citizens. Too often our young men become institutionalized in prison, and when they return to society and try to lead a good life, they end up back in jail because many times, though not always, the reality that awaits them outside is harsh, entrenched, and ruthless. This is so because as black people, we are "victims" of our own indifference, and seeming lack of propriety.

The rate of recidivism among African-American inmates is disproportionately high for a reason. For example: When non-black inmates are released, they often go back to their community and, unless they are incorrigible criminals, they sometimes find work at a small business or enterprise that is owned by a relative, a friend, or somebody who can hook them up with someone who will give them a chance. Again, our lack of enterprise in our own community renders us void of a solid economic base. Ownership of small and medium-sized businesses would allow us to put even those that are truly rehabilitated, to work in at least the most basic "survival kit" types of jobs. This is another reason I respect and admire Jim Brown. He started such an enterprise that was designed to help employ young black men, including those who returned from prison. Most of them worked hard and stayed straight. He created and ran that program for the most part by himself, but what single individual could continue to do it alone? Year after year no meaningful, and little sustaining, help was forthcoming. Again, because we blacks own so few businesses, large or small in our communities, the haters of the world see and project us as shiftless, incapable derelicts. We have become insatiable consumers who are systematically targeted by those who shamelessly exploit our lack of enterprise.

We are indeed consumers in our own communities, and thereby allow others to become consumers **of** our communities. It is all too evident that too many of our people that "make it big" don't necessarily forget where they came from, but some of them seem to remember with disdain from whence they came. They do little or nothing to revitalize, uplift, or change the increasingly degenerating conditions.

Magic Johnson is one notable exception. It was believed by some that Magic's example of creating a successful and profitable enterprise within and outside of the black community would inspire others to become creative entrepreneurs who value the community. Like Magic they could profit wisely from their efforts. Who are they? Where are they? Has our cultural myopia led to this malaise that seems to be eating away the very spirit of our human and racial dignity? Or is it even more deeply rooted in a self hatred so pervasive that it appears to be essential if not in fact self-regenerating or, worse yet, inbred. **When the slave becomes the slave holder, the unborn children of freedom have no hope.**

Jim Brown has consistently resisted the subtle and not so subtle merchants and purveyors of degradation, and I believe he has done so sucessfully. He has stood against every attempt to reduce him to something less than what he knows himself to be—a man. In my opinion, he is a man of human flesh, spiritual light, and a man of psychological steel. He handled the latest attempt to reduce him with quiet strength and unyeilding dignity. The Court gave him a choice: he could either stoop below himself, be publically humiliated, or spend six months in the county jail. How many people would have bowed down, in order to avoid the peril, and discomfort of the County Jail? All his accusers wanted was for him to bow down. With that, he could have returned to his beautiful wife and family, his comfortable house in the Hollywood Hills, and he could have avoided doing six months jail time. Instead, he stood not only for himself, but for every black man who refuses to surrender to the tremendous pressure that a mostly unknowing, and largely uncaring, society places on men of color when they are arrested—often if there is no evidence to prove them guilty, and sometimes when there is ample evidence to prove their innocence.

Let me state emphatically, that **in no way am I attempting to speak for Mr. Brown.** He speaks for himself better than I or anyone else could. I'm writing about these issues in this particular chapter because, to me, Jim Brown has not wavered in his stance to resist the orchestrated efforts made to reduce him. Every person I write about in this book is special, and in some way is a heroic contributor to our young people and/or our community. Because of the consistently overt and defiant way he has faced his adversaries, Jim Brown is among those who I believe to be the most prepared African-Americans of his generation. He is cut from the same cloth as Muhammad Ali, Dr. Martin Luther King Jr., Malcolm X, and others that you may wish to name.

Jim Brown's knowledge of, and respect for, self can be a shining example to young African-American males. It proves that you can even survive incarceration without becoming an institutionalized repeat offender—a bona fide slave. Our call is to have something by way of basic jobs within our communities that can pay better than minimum wage to the ones who are willing to give up the "fast track" back to slavery. When they return looking for some legitmate opportunity for work, they need a job to begin to show that they can be productive human beings. They're not necessarily asking for an equal chance, because whether they know it or not, they have pretty much lost that right by being a convicted felon. God forbid that we should find ourselves with an imbalance of insensitive Supreme Court Justices. At some point, freedom as we know it could be just one sitting Justice away from becoming a quasi Fascist society.

Personally, I have no complaints, because as an African-American, I have had the best of it, but I have also known the fullness of the struggle to remain a self-respecting free man. Sometimes (even today) the struggle is on a day-to-day basis. I have come to a point where I rarely expect fairness in certain situations where race might be the determining factor. What I look for is an opportunity to show what I can bring to the table. The formula that has worked for me so far, is to be as fully prepared as possible and having a true but not fanatical belief in a higher power. It also helps to not overreact to seemingly unfair or hostile circumstances, have respect for myself and others, and know my acceptable relationship to those with whom I work and/or play.

One of the most valuable lessons I have learned is that it is easier to remain true to myself, when I have the courage to show a dash of genuine humility. The kind of humility I speak of is not feigned or contrived, nor is it overly pious. I enjoy being with people that know more than I do about almost any topic of interest. I believe the study of other languages has made me a better listener; I like to talk, but what I really enjoy is a good conversation in which I am inspired, and often compelled to listen. I could listen attentively to each person that I write about in this book.

Jim Brown: for what you have stood for and what you stand for today, more so than your outstanding accomplishments in sports and entertainment which are in themselves, clearly phenomenal and above the rim; I hope you will read this book and accept from me, the author… **"A simple and powerful Thank You."**

An afterthought

The following was sent to me by e-mail. I am encouraged to see that many of our young people are beginning to dialogue about the derogatory mind set that has been thrust upon, and accepted by our young men and women.

The episode in the e-mail took place in the women's dorm at an out of state college. Here is what she said happened.

"A friend of mine came to my dorm room just to chat while her laundry was drying. As we were chatting, two young freshmen came by. One of the boys wanted to "talk" to my friend (as in date). She asked how old they were, and both of the boys replied, 18. My friend and I both laughed hysterically because we are both 22 years old. After my friend left, the two young men were still hanging around and one wanted to know how he could gain her interest.

The first thing I told him to do was to pull up his pants. He asked why, and said he liked saggin' his pants. I told him to come over to my computer and spell the word saggin'. Then I told him to write the word saggin' backwards.
S-A-G-G-I-N
N-I-G-G-A-S

I told him the origin of that look was from prison. Men in prison wore their pants low when they were spoken for. The other reason their pants looked like that was because they were not allowed to have belts because prisoners were likely to try to commit suicide.

We as young black people have to be the ones to effect change. We are dying. The media has made a mockery of Black America. Even our brothers and sisters from Africa don't take us seriously. Something as simple as pulling up your pants and standing with your head high could make the biggest difference in the world's perception of us. It is time to do right by ourselves. We need to love and embrace each other. No one is going to do it for us. It all comes down to perception. What people perceive is reality to them. We have to change not only the media's perception of us, but we need to change our perception of ourselves. Remember, all eyes are on you Black Man. All eyes are on you Black Woman. All eyes are on you Black Child. People are waiting for us to mess up. We have let not only the media but the government and the world taint the pure essence of us. They have stripped our culture down to the point where we only believe we can become rappers and athletes. We are so much more.

TO All MY BLACK MEN:
It's time to stand up. There are billions of Black Women who want to do nothing more than worship the ground that you walk on. We are so in love with your potential. We want to have your back. We want to love, and support every ounce of your being. But with that you have to show that you want to be the head of our households. You have to prove

yourself worthy of our submission. We need you to be hard working…not a hustler. We need you to seek higher education, to seek spirituality. We need you to stand! And trust us; we will have your back. We know that it gets hard. We know that you get weary. Trust and believe that there is nothing that a Black Woman and a Black Man can't handle with God on their sides.

TO All MY BLACK WOMEN:
It is also time for us to stand up. It is time for us to stop using our bodies as our primary form of communication. It is time to be that virtuous woman that Proverbs spoke of. We can not sit by the wayside while our men are dying by the masses. We are the epitome of Black Love. It starts within us. We need to speak with conviction to let not only our Black Men know, but let the world know that we are the mothers of this world. We are so powerful. We are so beautiful. We need to love and embrace every blessing God has given us physically, emotionally, and spiritually.

TO All MY BLACK CHILDREN:
We need to love them. We need to teach them. We need to stand up for them. We need to protect them. We need to show them that there are no "get rich quick" schemes. We need to tell them that they will die trying if they submit to a life of crime and deceit. We need to teach our children that no one will love them the way we can. And being a basketball player, a rapper, or a drug dealer is not reality. It's not reality and only a small percentage of people ever make it as a rapper or a professional athlete. We need to teach our children that we can be more than rappers and athletes. We can be owners of these sports teams; we can be CEOs of our Fortune 500 companies. We need to believe in literacy. I am almost certain if we were to look back to the 1930s and 40s, the literacy rate for Black American children was probably proportionately higher than it is today.

OK…I am stepping off of my soap box now. Pull up your Pants!"

In my opinion, this young lady is not making a statement about fashion. We understand that fashion is simply fashion. This is about lifestyle; this is about image, and perception, this is about survival. You cannot play basketball wearing skiing gear. In other words, if you like "saggin" with the Homies, that's one thing, but if you have to go before the judge, dress appropriately. To do otherwise, is to risk unnecessarily harsh consequences because most Judges have good-sized egos. Many feel disrespected, even insulted when you appear before them "saggin."

When you go to a job interview, dress in a manner that makes you appear eager to be part of the team. It will show the employer that you respect the company's culture, and are willing to represent the image that the company has established.

Your choice of fashion is an expression of your personal tastes and preference. It is not to be thrust upon people in authority for the sake of "keeping it Real." The true meaning of "Keeping it real" can be found in Shakespeare's words:

"All the *world's a stage, and all men and women merely players. They have their exits and their entrances; and one man in his time plays many parts.* "

That's keeping it real. You can not be on a basketball team wearing a Hockey uniform. Let's teach the children to know what stage they're on, at a given time, and how to dress, and act accordingly.

CHAPTER

C

Bill Cosby
American Icon

Dr. William H. "Bill" Cosby Jr. is and has been one of the most honorable and influential men in America. I did not say one of the most honorable and influential *black* men, but one of the most influential and honorable *men* in America, period. Most people have no idea what Bill and his wife Camille have done to try to uplift the human condition. They were supporting black people when most black folk were not supporting them. I know this to be more than mere fact. I know this first-hand and without a doubt to be the truth. You may ask how I know this to be true. I know because I first met Bill Cosby at the beginning of his meteoric rise to stardom, after his break-through comedy album "Wonderfulness," and during the second season of "I Spy."

Exactly two weeks from our first meeting, we began touring together. We toured almost exclusively together for about three years, and after that off and on up to the time Cosby enrolled in the University of Massachusetts to begin work on his Ed. D. Because of Bill's generosity my musical partner, Marcus Hemphill and I toured the country as co-headliners with him, though this does not mean that we were paid the same amount of money as he. He was our employer, and what fun it was to work with him. Up until then, if you were an opening act, you remained an opening act for as long as you worked with that particular headliner.

After about six months, Bill told the promoters to give us more marquee space, and he instructed his personal manager to give us a substantial raise in pay. He wanted us to be billed as co-headliners and insisted that our name appear larger on the marquee than it had been. To my knowledge, he was the first to promote his opening act to co-headliner status. Year after year we appeared in Las Vegas, Lake Tahoe, and Lincoln Center's Philharmonic Auditorium, colleges, and municipal auditoriums across the US and Canada. Sometimes we did as many as twenty-five consecutive one-night stands which, unlike today, were considered a lot. You get to know a person pretty well under those circumstances and we became friends.

I am giving this background in order to validate the statement I made earlier when I said not many black people supported Bill Cosby early in his career, not nearly as much as he supported them. Night after night, we performed at sold-out arenas, nightclubs, auditoriums, and concert halls; you could count the African-Americans in attendance on two, and sometimes on one, hand. Until I met Bill in person, and began to appear on stage with him, I myself had not owned his albums. I, like most black people back then, grew up on the comedic style of Red Foxx, Moms Mabley, Nipsy Russell, etc.

When I started working with Cosby night after night, I began to see the completely fresh expression and original genius in what he created. The blacks who did attend his shows always enjoyed him as much as anyone, it's just that not many supported his act the way they supported the afore-mentioned comedians. I go on record when I say to all the hyper-erudite, pseudo-intellectual, pundits, and the barbershop philosophers who criticize Bill Cosby for his true and straight-forward comments about the state of the black community in the 21st Century, and what we as African-Americans need to do to help change it. **"Please, SHUT UP, AND LEAVE DR. COSBY ALONE"!**

Ask them how many Bill Cosby Comedy albums are in their collection. Ask them how many tickets they bought to his concerts or other shows. Ask them how many Bunion Bradford albums they bought. Bunions Bradford was one of the best Avant Guard jazz type bands of its generation. It was none other than Bill Cosby, who wrote some of the material, hired the best jazz musicians to perform it and put this excellent band together. Often he would hire two or three musicians when the gig only called for one player on that instrument. He did this simply to give those great musicians work, (and maybe to hang out a bit). The music Bill wrote and recorded with this band was good music. Most people have no idea that Cos is a good jazz drummer, and can play a decent bass fiddle. Even when we played Vegas, you could see black folks going to see Tom Jones and Liberace. I happen to think that Liberace was one of the best entertainers to appear in Las Vegas. I also **know** that Bill Cosby is a rare and genuine gift to all of mankind, and one of the finest ambassadors for equality and African-American dignity, since Dr. Martin Luther King, Jr.

His presence on Earth is one of the truly profound reasons that many of the ingrained and hideous stereotypes about black people being inferior were destroyed. The only way those degrading lies and myths (that became the demoralizing propaganda that is still prevalent today) will remain broken, is for the black community to recognize the truth in what Dr. Cosby is saying.

I believe that part of Bill Cosby's genius lies in the fact that he has always recognized the subtle and not so subtle racism that is the underbelly of American society. Another part of his genius is that he developed one of the most potent remedies for change–his humor. It effectively points to what we as people, black and white alike, have in common. His stories show all of us that we are more alike than we are different, and he does it without judgment, criticism, threats, or preaching. I saw America change for the better because of Bill Cosby. America was a different place for Black-Americans before Bill Cosby's contribution, and again I say America became a much, much better place, where race relations were concerned, because of his success and the way he lives.

He is a consummate trendsetter who changed the course of television. Bill was the first television star to demand that his shows hire black directors, and other black people behind the cameras. He and Camille have given millions of dollars to black institutions and often forbid anyone to talk about it, because they were not giving to be publicized, but rather, giving from the heart.

Bill has never been a hypocrite. He has always believed in education. He was a major star when he went back to get his doctorate. He could have easily accepted and settled for one of the many "honorary" doctorate degree from his Alma Mater, Temple University, or any number of universities that would be honored to have his name on their list of distinguished associates. Instead, Bill Cosby became Dr. William H. Cosby Jr. because he actually enrolled in U Mass.   He was a serious student who worked his behind off. He refused to be a comedian in the class-room. He was no joker, and he did few, if any, "funny" routines or comic bits. He was there to study and earn his degree and he did just that. I understand that he was in class and on time as a matter of routine, did his homework at night, and turned in his assignments on time. That's why he is taken seriously by thoughtful and intelligent people. Not "intellectual hustlers," whose criticism of Dr. Cosby seems to be self-serving, to say the least.

Many people believe that those who make condemning remarks about Cosby's message to African-American parents appear to be an attempt to gain fame by opposing the legitimate concerns of Dr. Cosby. He is a sincere African-American, and has more than earned the right to call it like he and many other black people see it. Is the criticism of Dr. Cosby being levied by someone who is still waiting to receive forty acres and a mule? Like most black parents, I do not want my children waiting for some handout, be it a welfare check, a bag of rocks, or the long and unfulfilled promise of "forty acres and a mule." Forty acres would be a welcomed acquisition, because the new definition of perpetual motion is: "The average black man driving his Cadillac until he comes to some land that he owns."

Should it come to pass that I'm granted forty acres and a mule all the better, but I won't stand still and wait for my life to improve in the meantime.

I respect the "in your face" challenge that was courageously issued by Bill Cosby. At least we know he did not do it for fame or fortune because he has, and has maintained both for longer than most.

Cosby's TV show was not cancelled. He walked away on his own terms. I believe that he did it because he realized that as a black American he wanted to contribute something more than the millions of dollars he and Camille have given to causes, that serve blacks as well as other Americans. So why be surprised when he calls black parents to task for buying their kids super-expensive sneakers to hang out and cut school in?

Bill and Camille were giving to help black people long before "The Cosby Show" hit the air waves, which is when many of the Johnny-come-lately black supporters and detractors joined the bandwagon. Cosby was a trendsetter in the 1970's, 80's and the 90's. His was the first TV show that allowed kid stars to age and grow up on the shows. Before "The Cosby Show," if a child star got to be too old, or outgrew the physical character, the show was usually cancelled. He changed that. He was never jealous of the actors he hired—he taught them the craft and allowed them to develop, just as he had allowed us to be co-headliners with him back in the day (and yes, we deserved it, but he did not have to do it).

Bill Cosby is a man of character and one of the brightest people around, but he never flaunts it and I believe he even plays it down. I know him to be generous and loyal to the people close to him, but woe to the person that betrays him. I personally know of two people who mistook his kindness for weakness. One was a cook who he trusted. This guy could have asked Bill and Camille for almost anything and I believe Bill would have considered it. Instead he was caught stealing. He cried, crawled, and begged for forgiveness. I never saw that guy again. Another was one of Bill's longtime personal assistants. As some PA's are known to do, her head got a bit too big for her hat. We could see it coming. Cosby gave her enough rope to hang herself, and like the foolish cook, she begged and cried to no avail.

In case you have not figured it out yet, I have more respect for Bill Cosby than any other person I've worked with, bar none. His name and Mrs. Maurine F. Bailey's are two of the few names that might reoccur throughout this book because they made such a positive and lasting impact on my life.

Although we are about the same age, I learned valuable lessons just by being around and observing him. One of the lessons that caused me to mature was Cosby's complete coolness about things.

He does not have a "prima donna" hair on his head. He just expects you to be professional and decent. He will not stand for anyone in his employ or entourage, mistreating another person just because one has a bigger title or higher paying position. When we first hooked up, I must admit that I had almost no patience about anything. I thank God that my patience changed many years ago, but not because of anything that went down between Bill and me. I can honestly say that in all the years we worked together, there was never a cross word between us. (My former partner in "The Pair", Marcus would have responded to this remark ("never a cross word between us") by injecting his own style of humor and saying: "Wow! That must have been puzzling." Bill would have rolled his eyes toward the sky, and I might have said "burump bump." It's true—the three of us got along well. From the very beginning we had a ball on stage and off. As I said, Cosby was so cool about almost everything.

During those early years, when being a big-time celebrity was new to me, I saw Bill handle certain situations that might have caused many celebrities that I knew to explode. They would throw tantrums, and try to get people fired for a simple mistake, or an honest oversight. Certain entertainers were notorious for this type of behavior. Let's say, for instance, that if they arrived at a hotel and their rooms were not quite ready, they would raise holy hell. Over the years that we worked with Cosby, this happened to us on a couple of occasions. I must admit I was ready to express my indignation to management. Bill would always handle it almost matter-of-fact. He asked the person at the front desk, "About how long do you think it'll take before the room is ready?" The desk clerk nervously replied, "Right away, Mr. Cosby, right away." Bill would say: "We'll be in the lounge. Would you let us know when the rooms are ready?" The three of us would go into the lounge and kick back for a few minutes until the rooms were ready. If a fan approached us, Cos would be gracious, signing autographs and chatting with them and so did we.

I have never seen Bill Cosby treat anyone with haughty self-importance.

Cosby was cool with everybody. However, if someone should approach him with less than a respectful attitude, they will feel the freezing cold sting of dry ice in Cosby's eyes. I recall one such occasion. we were appearing in my home town of Dallas. Bill and I were standing in the lobby of the hotel waiting for Marcus to come down. Our routine when touring was, we would go shopping in the afternoon to pass the time. My mother worked for Herbert and Stanley Marcus, the owners of Nieman Marcus Department store. For more than twenty years, she was the supervisor of staff (a fancy title for: head maid) in their Highland Park home. Marcus told me that he had suggested to Bill that we go shopping at Neiman Marcus today. As you might imagine, the staff that worked with my mother would have gotten a kick out of knowing that we were shopping with Bill Cosby in Neiman Marcus.

Marcus got off the elevator in the lobby to join Bill and me as a guy walked up behind Bill. He was wearing a sport coat and tie, and was carrying a cigar box. He tapped Bill lightly on the shoulder and he spoke with a slight Caribbean accent. When Cosby turned around to see who tapped him, the man said in a somewhat bossy tone: "Bill Cosby, listen! I want to invite you to come to my house after the show. I have a few friends waiting there to meet you." Bill looked at him with a look of consternation but did not speak. The guy continued confidently, "I know you like to smoke cigars: I brought you these."

By this time Marcus had joined us and this fellow extended the box of cheap cigars to Bill. Marcus took the cigars and when he and I made eye contact, it took everything we could muster to keep from laughing out loud. Bill just stared at this guy and slowly shook his head. I imagine he was thinking his favorite word in which he'd pronounce every syllable. Whenever someone did or said something really stupid, Cos would say "Pit-ti-ful." I'm sure he was saying it in his mind right then. Marcus and I could not hold it any longer, so we politely turned away and could not stop laughing. Bill saw us cracking up, and said to the guy, "We have other plans after the show." The guy looked disappointed, and then he said, "I'll leave my address at the front desk in case you decide to come." And without another word the guy rushed towards the front desk, reaching into his inside coat pocket for his pen, while Marcus, Bill and I proceeded to the front door where the limo was waiting.

When we entered the limo, my partner and I could not stop laughing. We were like two kids in church that can't stop laughing. It must have been contagious, because Cosby started to chuckle softly along with us. Bill was seated in the front seat of the limo, when we finally stopped laughing he turned around, looked at us and said, "That guy is Pi-ti-ful." The laughter started all over again. To this very day, when Bill Cosby and I meet, not having seen each other in a long time, the first words out of either of our mouths are likely to be: "Listen! ...to your cheap cigars." With that, we proceed as usual.

On stage, there was *never* a night when we didn't cook. The three of us were great on stage together. When you do a series of one-night stands sometimes you don't really feel like going on. One night Bill came into the dressing room and asked:" Anybody got a stamp?" I replied, "I got stamps at the hotel." Bill said: "I need a stamp now so I can mail in tonight's show," but once we got on stage we didn't want to get off.

I can honestly say, and I believe Cosby will confirm, that in all the years we worked together, we never once did a bad show, always had fun, and never came close to letting the audience down. For me, that will always be a huge source of pride.

We had fun off stage as well. When we toured, we traveled in Cosby's Learjet. To pass the time in flight, sometimes we would play various games. Marcus and Cosby were master chess players, and competitive gamesmen in general. I was just learning to play chess, and was not in the same league with either of them. My game was dominos, which they both loved as well. In fact there was hardly a game that the two of them could not play well, be it chess, backgammon, dominos, poker, pity pat, Tonk; you name the game and most likely Cosby and Marcus could play it. My strongest game was dominos. Sometimes on the plane we'd play for the city in which we were performing that particular night. In other words, the winner would get to call the shots after the show, i.e. where we would eat, or what show we'd see, etc. As I stated earlier, Bill Cosby is the master of cool. He does not let petty things ruffle him. In fact, one of the rare occasions when I saw Cosby seriously ticked off, happened one night when we were on tour.

On the flight to Cleveland, Ohio, we played dominos, and Bill won the city. After our show that night he said: "Tonight we're going to see Ray Charles." Ray was playing at a club in town. We took a cab to the club. When we arrived, Ray was starting his last show. All the numerous times I saw Ray Charles, he was great. On this particular night, he must have known that Cosby was in the audience, because that night, Ray lit up that stage; I mean he was cooking, smoking, and boiling water with the music. It was a fantastic show. After the show Ray invited us to drop by his hotel for a while. I wanted to go, Marcus wanted to go, but Cosby told Ray he'd catch him another time. We were walking out of the club and I asked Cos why not hang with Ray for a minute before going back to the hotel. Bill said we're going to our hotel, and I'm going to call my wife. That's the way he speaks most of the time. You will rarely hear him say: "I'm gonna do this, or I'm gonna do that." He will likely say: "I'm going to do, thus and so." He's not "putting on airs"; Bill is like a singer who has good diction, like a Nat Cole, Sinatra, Sarah Vaughn, Ella, or LL Cool J.

Cosby is in no way "stuck up" or other such nonsense; he is an educated individual who carries himself like an educated person. He believes in education. Meanwhile back at the club after enjoying Ray Charles, Bill, Marcus and I walked outside to get a cab back to the hotel where we were staying. We crossed the street to hail a cab. There was a taxi parked, obviously waiting for a fare. We approached the taxi and opened the rear door, and the cab driver started to pull away before either of us could get into the cab. He pulled up about ten feet and stopped. We tried to get into the cab, the driver started to pull off again before we could get in, so I called out to the driver: "Hey man, let us get in before you take off, ok?" This fool yells back: "I don't pick up your kind." This pissed Cosby off. Bill rushed and stood in front of the taxi, and said: "You're going to pick up our kind tonight!" As Bill stood in front of the taxi, the driver started to race his motor as if he were going to run Bill over. Cosby stood his ground. I made my way to the driver's side so I could reach in his window and grab him by the throat if he tried to run Cosby over. Marcus, being concerned, called out to Cos: "Hey Bill, come on before we have to mess this fool up."

Some people started coming out of the club, not knowing what was going on. One of the ladies recognized Cosby. The women said to the guy she was with, "That's him, that's Bill Cosby—baby, I told you I saw him in the club." When the cab driver heard this, he peered through the windshield and recognized who he was threatening. I said to Cosby: "Come on, man, let's take another cab." Bill's voice was chilling, as he stared through the windshield at the stupefied cab driver. I never heard that icy tone in his voice, nor seen that kind of fire in Cosby's eyes until he replied, "We're going to take this cab." We got into the taxi. The ignorant racist cab driver was too embarrassed and frightened to speak as he drove nervously to the hotel. Upon arriving, I looked at the meter and paid the idiot exactly the fare and no tip. Ordinarily, I probably would've given him a twenty dollar tip.

Unlike Flip Wilson (with whom we also toured after Cosby enrolled in U Mass, may he rest in peace), who always had four or five thousand dollars on him in cash, Bill carries hardly any cash on him. He would always reimburse us when we laid out cash for taxis, etc. Cosby was the last one to get out of the taxi. Marcus and I stayed close by. When he got out he crossed in front of the taxi, walked to the driver's side, stared at the fool cab driver for about thirty seconds, and said with that ice cold voice: "You-are-Pi-ti-ful."

The thing that shook us the most, what was so utterly disgusting, was that the racist cab driver was black. That's one of the few times I saw Bill Cosby really pissed off. No doubt, being human, there are other times, but based on the three plus years that we worked together, in my humble opinion, Bill Cosby is an unflappable king of cool.

Once when I was doing a solo act, Bill called and asked if I wanted to do some shows with him in Houston. I agreed to do it. When I arrived in Houston, that whole first day was a comedy of errors. First of all, the personal assistant that got too big for her britches had booked me into the wrong hotel. I finally arrived at the concert hall about ninety minutes before the show. Naturally I had missed the sound check and rehearsal which was mainly for my benefit. Bill does not need sound checks. All he requires is a proper mike level, which he gets when he starts to do his act.

I had purchased a new guitar and was anxious to test it at the sound check that was scheduled from 3:00- 4:00 PM. I arrived at about 6:30 and the show was at 8:00 o'clock. I barely had time to get to the hotel and get ready. Bill was totally cool. When I told him that I had been booked into the wrong hotel, he sort of chuckled and said: "Your musicians were concerned that you would not make it, but I told them not to worry, because I knew you'd be here." It made me feel good that someone had that kind of confidence in my professionalism. It felt even better to know that I had earned that respect. In all those years, I had never ever been late or missed a show.

Mrs. Bailey used to tell us that "punctuality is the courtesy of kings." This lesson was reinforced during the years we played Vegas. To any young performer with hopes of appearing on a Las Vegas stage, the first lesson you must learn is, when you are to be off stage at let's say 9:30, that does not mean 9:30 and 20 seconds, that does not mean 9:28, it means 9:30 period. What I learned from being around Cos is in many ways priceless, but I have also been able to learn from mistakes I have seen other people make. For an example, once the "The Pair Extraordinaire" had a prior commitment that was not with Bill Cosby, and Cos had an added-on date come up unexpectedly at Carnegie Hall. Because of our prior commitment we were unable to make the Carnegie Hall show with him. He hired the late great singer, Nina Simone, to fill in for us. Nina showed up about ten minutes late. Bill always starts his shows on time, and when Nina arrived he was on stage. He did the whole show by himself, and to my knowledge, Nina—God rest her soul—was never hired to work with him again. She was an incredible artist, and a free spirit. Bill Cosby is a consummate professional, and no matter how hard he has to work, he will never shortchange his fans, nor will he let anyone compromise his principles of professionalism.

Meanwhile, backstage before the show in Houston, I tuned my new guitar, and warmed up my vocal chords. As was his custom, Bill would open the show; he started doing that after the second week we worked with him. The reason he did this was that one night he noticed that when we opened the show, the people who came late would sort of distract the audience when going to their seats. After that show, he told us that tomorrow night he wanted to try something. He said that he would do twenty or thirty minutes while the audience straggled in, because he said we deserved to have the audience's full attention when we performed. We could not believe that a headliner would do that for an opening act. That's why opening acts are hired to warm up the audience and play through the distractions of late-comers, and technical mishaps, etc. before the headliner takes the stage. Because it worked so well the first night he opened, we continued on that way.

His generosity turned out to be a win-win situation, in that he started to ad lib with the audience—he messed with everybody that came in a few minutes late. If they had seats in the back, sometimes he would call them down to the front, maybe make them come on stage, and he would have fun with them. The audiences loved it, and the late-comers would have the experience of a lifetime, being on stage with Bill Cosby. This more than endeared him with the audience. Plus, when he would ad lib, he got wonderful ideas for new material which he developed into some of his most memorable stories, such as, "Turtle Heads," "The Dentist," "Urped," and tons of other sketches that ended up on his many albums that became fan favorites. I soon realized that his genuine desire to make us look good paid super dividends to his own creativity.

After twenty minutes or so, he introduced me. I came on stage and as usual Bill and I clowned around for a few minutes, and he left the stage to huge applause. I would do fifty minutes and there would be an intermission, after which Cosby would return and do the final hour.

For my first song in Houston that night I accompanied myself on guitar. I started to strum my new guitar but not a sound came out. It was an acoustic guitar so I knew it was not an electrical problem. After about thirty seconds, I could feel the audience getting nervous for me. I remember saying: "Next time I get a new guitar, maybe I should send in two box tops." The audience laughed. I drew on my comic timing that I had learned from working with this comedic genius. I tried in vain to fix my guitar because, unbeknownst to me, the bridge on my guitar had collapsed. I pulled it off by doing the rest of the show to piano accompaniment. That night after the show, we were having dinner at a wonderful restaurant, and Cosby was his same old cool self. He never said a word. He acted as if it had never happened, although he teased me about it a year or so later just to let me know he remembered.

I have known Bill and Camille since 1966. The Pair Extraordinaire was appearing at the "Hungry I," an internationally famous nightclub in San Francisco. We were appearing with a comedian named Bill Dana. He was a very successful comedian whose act was built around a Mexican character he created that he called "Jose Jimenez." Although Bill Dana was not a Latino, in those days, people could poke fun at themselves and others as well, as long as it was not mean-spirited, vicious, or degrading. Dana would begin his show with the line that he spoke with a mock Mexican accent. He started his act by saying, "Hello, my name is Jose Jimenez." Then he proceeded to do an hour show as this lovable but somewhat misguided character. He was a fairly big star until it was no longer politically correct to "poke fun" at an ethnic group of which you were not a member.

On opening night, after the last show, my partner, Marcus Hemphill, and I sat in the dressing room talking with Bill Dana. We were a good match and the audience loved the show. I learned some interesting things about comedy from Mr. Dana, too. During the week, he explained some of the different genres of comedy (i.e., he demonstrated the difference between a spoonerism and a pun, the difference between a comic and comedian etc.).

An example of a spoonerism would be instead of saying, "opportunity knocks but once, a spoonerism would be: "oppor-knock-ity tunes but once". An example of a pun is: if you asked me, "Do you like mushrooms?" And I replied, yes I live in a mushroom. Dana told us that the difference between a comic and a comedian is that, a comic wears funny clothes- baggy pants, does prat falls, uses props etc. to get laughs. A comedian tells funny stories, and interprets real life situations in a humorous way. It was fascinating information and I soaked it up like a sponge.

Bill Dana alerted us that on the following weekend, he would not be with us because he had a prior commitment and someone else would replace him for the Saturday night show. He added: "Not to worry, Enrico (Banducci, the owner of the club) will get somebody good to fill in." And did he ever get someone good. I shall never forget.

It was my birthday, April 9, 1966. At the end of the first show, we had just finished our second encore. I was not aware that my partner had told one of the waitresses that it was my birthday. We were about to leave the stage when I noticed a man walking towards it. When the spotlight is on you, it is difficult to recognize faces much beyond the first few rows. The person was carrying a hostess cup cake with one candle on it. When he came closer to the stage, Marcus said, "Bill Cosby, is that you?"

Cosby came up on stage and, extending the chocolate cup cake towards me, began to sing "Happy birthday to you." I could not believe it; Enrico Banducci had asked Bill Cosby to fill in for Bill Dana that night. What a fateful night it turned out to be. Cosby stayed on stage with us for about fifteen minutes. The three of us clowned around, Cosby played Marcus' bass fiddle, and we had a really good time. At the end of the evening, Bill came into the dressing room and told us that in two weeks he was going to appear over the weekend at the Circle Star, a top class venue located in San Mateo, a suburb of San Francisco. "How would you guys like to open for me?" he asked. I said: "For real?" He was serious.

Two weeks later, Bill Cosby and the Pair Extraordinaire opened at the Circle Star Theatre, two shows a night for three consecutive nights. The shows left audience after audience on their feet. Thus began more than three wonderful years of working with one of the greatest entertainers and funniest people to set foot on a stage.

Most people will never know what a gifted and multi-talented individual Bill Cosby is. He's a true to the bone intelligent black man who is a gentleman and a scholar in the truest sense. It is his right as an American to express his opinion. I do not suggest that he is some kind of saint, but the way he has conducted his very successful life affords him the added privilege to speak his truth.

The black people who now see, and have quietly watched for so long, the rising tide of destruction emanating from within as well as outside of our community need to recognize the importance of looking into our own misguided direction. Constructive criticism is a forerunner to positive change. Dr. Cosby's courage and wisdom will one day be a cornerstone of our twenty-first century emancipation from the enemy within. That enemy has wrapped us in a cloak of denial for far too long. Just as the children of those who hated and vilified Malcolm X recognize him today as a courageous and forthright individual who withstood the bitter criticism of white, and black Americans alike. In his own way, Mr. Cosby is likewise a courageous and perceptive purveyor of truth.

In addition to the previously mentioned gifts, skills, and enormous talent, this man's well-earned success is also based on the fact that he is a person who shows respect for all deserving people. Case in point: what Bill said about the last "Cosby Show" (not the one with Malcolm Jamal Warner, Keshia Knight Pulliam, Raven Symone, et al, but the one that followed on CBS). According to Cosby himself the first couple of seasons were not quite as tight as he knew they could be. When that show was first announced I recalled that he thanked among others, Les Moonves, the Chairman of CBS, for his commitment to the show and giving it time to develop. For a person of Cosby's stature, that type of a public gesture usually comes only from those whose self-awareness, self-respect, and self-confidence gives way to a genuine humility that has not been thwarted by ego.

His ability to show respect for people has been an important part of his success and was unbeknownst to him, an important lesson to me. The experience that I am about to share, goes back more than thirty years when Cosby was doing The Bill Cosby Show—a weekly TV variety show at NBC. The show was only on the air one season. It was the show that preceded the sitcom in which he played a schoolteacher named Chet Kincaid.

One afternoon, I decided to drop in on Bill at the studio. It was camera-blocking day. I went to the artist entrance, the guard called the sound stage and Cosby cleared me and the guard let me through. When I got to the stage, the AD (Assistant Director) had just announced the lunch break. Bill was talking to one of the production assistants. I approached, and stopped an appropriate distance away so as not to interrupt their conversation. Quincy Jones was the musical director of the show and he was standing a few feet away, so I started to walk over to Q, whom I had never met, and introduced myself. Just as I approached Quincy, one of his arrangers walked up and started to conference with him. Again, I was not going to interfere with Quincy's conversation with his musicians, so I just walked past him and gave him a wave, which he acknowledged with a nod. Cosby saw me and beckoned to me. I walked over as he was finishing his conversation with the production guy. Bill said, "Let's get some lunch, but first I need to talk to George." George Schlatter was the producer of "The Bill Cosby Variety Show". Cosby asked one of the production assistants, "Where's George?" and a female voice to the rear of us answered, "He's in the control booth." When we entered the booth, George Schlatter, the producer and a guy in a suit were discussing the show. Bill walked over and joined them. I heard Cosby's voice saying, "George, let's do a couple of shows using my guys (meaning The Pair Extraordinaire)." Slaughter replied, "I don't think that's the answer." Bill: "I think it could be. Let's do a couple and find out." George Slaughter looked at the man in the suit and tie, paused, and said again, "I really don't think that would be the answer." The room fell silent for a moment, and then Cosby said,-almost matter of fact, "George, I'll bet you $10,000 that if we do three shows with my guys, we'll turn things around." George Slaughter mused over the idea briefly, and said "I don't know." Cosby said "Let's talk later," then we left.

It might not seem like a big deal to some, but it left a strong impression on me. The way Bill challenged George Slaughter was in a completely non-threatening way. Cosby let it be known that he believed—based on the consistently great reviews we were getting, and the overwhelming response we received from audiences in our live concerts—that we could turn those TV ratings around as well. And we could have, had we been given the opportunity.

I don't think it bothered Cosby too much, if at all, that the following season the show was not picked up. Bill Cosby didn't miss a beat. He continued to sell out stadiums, concert halls, Las Vegas showrooms, and college campuses. He was, as he is today, one of the most sought after guests (and guest hosts) on late night talk shows. It was good for me to see the class and total masculine (but not macho) aplomb with which Bill Cosby carries himself, in public and in private.

Before working with him, I had a different view of stardom. Many of the celebrities I had worked with before and after meeting Cosby were cocky. Some were prima donnas who were generally full of themselves. I observed that more often than not, the bigger the star, the nicer the person. Although my professional attitude and work ethic (i.e. punctuality, hard work, respect for my audience, and for most of my employers) was molded long before I met Bill Cosby, I appreciate the influence that he had on my personal and professional life. I don't believe he set out to "teach" anybody. I'm sure he has no idea of the vast amount of respect he has earned from those who know him well.

Dr. Camille Cosby Ed. D, is intelligent, bright, elegant, unpretentious, and a dedicated wife and mother. About a month after we started to tour regularly with Bill we did our first East Coast tour. When we got to New York, he said: "Tonight you guys get to meet the Mrs."

I had heard him mention Camille's name on various occasions, but I had never seen a picture of her, to my knowledge. When Camille walked into the dressing room about an hour before we went on stage at Philharmonic Auditorium, I thought to myself, "She is as pretty as Lena Horne," —who was to me the quintessential beauty of our time. My childhood beauty queens had been Lena, Elizabeth Taylor, Dorothy Dandridge, Jane Russell, and Audrey Hepburn. Mrs. Cosby was striking. I do not intend to flatter when I say that Camille is still an extremely beautiful woman, and this statement absolutely defies dispute.

The most indelible memory I have of that first meeting is this: Bill introduced Marcus and me to his wife, and thirty minutes later it was as though Camille had known us for years. Back at the hotel, after the show that night, I went to Marcus' room. We ordered room service and talked about how surprised we were that a woman that beautiful and married to the boss, would be down to earth, and funny as hell. Camille and Bill kidded around with each other from the time she showed up until we were ready to go onstage. At one point, when Bill or Camille said something funny about the other, somebody commented that "this goes on all the time." From that evening on, Camille treated us as welcomed friends.

This was shortly after their first child, Erika Cosby, was born. When Camille was carrying their second child, Erinn, Bill created some of his most memorable routines based on his wife's pregnancy. I'll never forget the first time I heard him do the bit about Camille going into labor. I was in the dressing room getting ready to go on. We were midway through a long stretch of one-night stands, and I had a bad case of the flu. Every night before going on I had to gargle with warm salt water and sip a lemon and honey mixture in order to get through the show. I was dressed but, thankfully, had not put on my coat yet. Bill was opening the show and doing his ad lib with the audience. As usual we listened to Bill's portion of the show over the intercom in the dressing room. A young couple came in a few minutes late. As they walked down the isle to their seats near the front, Bill, in the character of an old fashioned, strict schoolteacher said something like, "Wait just a minute, why are you coming late to my class?" The audience roared with laughter. He noticed that the lady was pregnant and continued his ad lib, and said to the husband, "You were fooling around outside. Now you come in here almost three minutes late and you've gotten her pregnant."

He then started to make up a story of Camille's pregnancy with their first child. When he got to the punch line, he said: "Camille woke me in the middle of the night and said, 'Honey wake up, my water bag just broke'"; Cosby said, "I told Camille to "Go back to sleep, I'll get you a new one in the morning." I nearly fell over from laughing. I spit the gargle water halfway across the room. It struck me so funny because I recalled when my first child had been born—a few months prior, and my girlfriend, who later became my wife, had awakened me to tell me that her water had broken. The punch line to Bill's story was so funny to me that when I later told her the story, both of us must've laughed five minutes straight. Many comedians have told that joke over the years, but they stole it from Bill.

By the time the tour was over, he had developed that brief moment of ad-lib with the young couple into one of his most memorable pieces. Such is his spontaneity and creative genius. Camille was always good-natured about the jokes Bill told based on their marriage and family life. I recall another time when we were on tour and Camille joined him, as she occasionally did. It was towards the end of the tour, and I guess they had plans to return home right after the tour ended, but they changed their plans and decided to do something else.

The following morning, Mrs. Cosby called and asked if we would stop by their suite before checking out. Marcus and I packed, and sent our bags downstairs. Marcus came to my room, and together we proceeded to the Cosby's suite as requested. We knocked and Camille came to the door. She greeted us in her usual friendly manner and Bill stood behind her. She informed us that she and Bill had a change of plans, and asked if we would mind taking her bags back to L.A. and dropping them off at their house. Of course we were glad to help. Bill was rolling his eyes upwards, the way he is famous for doing—he was slowly shaking his head indicating "no." I thought he was just fooling around as he often did with his wife. We said: "No problem, we'd be happy to drop your bags off. This was when they lived in Beverly Hills on Linden Dr. before they moved to Tower Rd. This house was near Lucille Ball's home. Bill continued to slowly shake his head "no" as we agreed to drop off her bags on Linden Dr.

Mrs. Cosby said, "Thanks guys—I'll have the bellman place them in the lobby near the door so the driver can load them into the limo just before taking you to the airport."

When Marcus and I got to the lobby, the limo driver was standing near the entrance waiting for us. He greeted us in a jovial tone, "Good morning gentlemen. These are Mrs. Cosby's bags. She said you'd be dropping them off at their house when you get to LAX." Marcus and I were stunned! There were about sixteen pieces of large to medium size luggage. Marcus looked at me and said: "Naw, she didn't." I said: "That's what Cos was shaking his head about."

On the flight back to L.A. we laughed and joked about it, saying things like: "Man, where were they going before the change of plans, to the moon?" This was extremely funny to us because man had not gone to the moon yet—in fact, a few years later, we were appearing in concert with

Bill Cosby in Hawaii, when Neil Armstrong and Buzz Aldrin first landed on the moon. Months later, we kidded with Camille about the luggage thing. I said something like, "Camille, you need someone to drop off your luggage?" Before she could answer, Marcus chimed in "Well, we're not going that way." She chuckled and said something like "You guys better shut up." She was ever the good sport.

The night I saw Bill Cosby almost kill Jack Lemmon

One evening after Marcus and I had finished rehearsing, Marcus said he had spoken to Bill and asked if he was going to be home later. Bill had said yes he would be home, and Marcus said he'd come up to the house and Bill said, yeah, come on up. Marcus asked me if I wanted to ride up to Bill's with him. I had no plans so I agreed to go. We were sitting around listening to music, talking and just kickin' it. Bill's good friend and next door neighbor on Tower Road, the late Jack Lemmon, came over and joined us. It was the first time I met Jack,--may he rest in peace. Cosby brought up a couple of bottles of wines that he wanted us to try. Although Cos does not drink, he has one of the best wine cellars I'd ever seen. Bill and Jack started swapping funny stories. At one point I asked Bill what was his first paying gig as a comedian and he said that his first gig was on the bill with Lola Falana and a male singer named Billy Paul (whose big hit song was "Me and Mrs. Jones." Then he remembered that he got hired at one other club before the gig with Billy Paul and Lola Falana, but he didn't get paid because he got fired. Jack Lemmon asked, "What'd you get fired for?" Bill said, "Jack it was Pi-ti-ful". He said, "It was my very first gig, and not knowing how to pace myself, I sort of ran out of material, so I started to tell stories that I had told to my friends in the neighborhood. They thought the stories were hilarious."

Bill started to tell how the club owner was trying to get him offstage. Obviously I could never tell the story the way Cosby did so I won't even try. He said when he ran out of material, he started to tell a story about a guy who was crippled; He had a medical condition named "Saint Vitus Dance" and the club owner was doing everything he could think of to get Bill off the stage. It was mad funny. Marcus and I were laughing also but by the time Cos was midway through the story Jack Lemmon was literally rolling around on the floor. The harder Jack laughed, the more Bill poured it on. At one point Jack was begging him to stop; tears were coming down Jack's face in sheets, and his face was beet red. Cosby would stop and let Jack recover, and when Jack would finally stop laughing, Cosby would start to embellish again. After a while, I was getting concerned for Jack; his sides were cramping, he was doubled over in the fetal position, and he was howling with laughter. I think at that point Cosby must've realized that Jack might really be in trouble and that's when he finally stopped adding to the story.

It was one of those situations when, fifteen minutes later, and we had been talking about something altogether different, Jack would remember something Cosby had said about that first gig, and out of the blue, Jack would start laughing all over again. To Bill's credit, he let Jack laugh, but he didn't embellish the story anymore. When Jack left a couple of hours later, he told Bill that was probably the funniest story he'd ever heard.

I can see why Bill Cosby and Jack Lemmon were good friends; in my mind they had a lot of the same qualities. They were both musicians, they were both natural actors, they were both completely genuine, they both were funny as hell, and they both lived next door to one of their favorite people—each other. I met so many fascinating people at Bill and Camille's home on Tower Road, but Marcus and I agreed that Jack Lemmon was special for a number of reasons. One reason was the way he loved being around Cosby and Cosby's musician friends.

In 1968 before the Cosbys moved to Tower Road, my mother brought two of my nieces and a nephew to California to visit me at my Hollywood Hills home for two weeks. They had been here a few days when I mentioned to Cos that they were in town. His immediate reply was, "Bring them over for dinner". He set it up with Camille, and the five of us went to dinner at their home on Linden.

The Cosbys were wonderful to my family. Recently I was in Dallas, and my niece Debbie Durham, who was thirteen when we went to the Cosby's home for dinner, came by my house in Dallas. When she stopped by I was working on this book. I told her what the book would be about, and she started to recall things about our visit with Bill and Camille that I had forgotten. She reminded me of how gracious the Cosbys were, and how Camille made them feel so welcome. My niece told me how nervous she had been, sitting at their dining room table with all of those forks in front of her, and not knowing which one to use. Debbie asked me if I remembered (I did not) that at one point she picked up a fork and it dropped to the floor. She said: "I was so embarrassed I could've crawled under the table." Mrs. Cosby must've sensed my embarrassment because she picked up the fork for me and said, "Don't worry, I'll get you another one, and she did. She made us all feel so comfortable."

My nephew, Kerry Bell, who was fifteen, said the thing that impressed him most was the way Bill and Camille kept the conversation going by talking about things that they could all relate to. My niece Toni Nichols was sixteen she recalled, "After dinner when we went into the den, I was feeling like a movie star myself, sitting on that big beautiful couch, and knowing I was right up the street from Lucille Ball's house".

My dear mother—may God rest her beautiful soul—told me that she was so moved by and proud of all the nice things that Mr. Cosby said about Marcus and me, like how intelligent Marcus was, and what a really good singer I was. I took them many places during their stay, and when I took them to the airport for their return trip to Dallas, I asked my mother if she enjoyed the two weeks in Hollywood. She said they all enjoyed everything immensely, but that she would always appreciate most how Bill and Camille treated them with such genuine warmth. She said: "If I should meet a thousand movie stars, I can't imagine that anybody could ever be as sophisticated, yet so very down to earth as the Cosbys are." She added: "If I live a hundred years, and never meet another celebrity, that would be perfectly alright with me, because they have forever changed my opinion about people who are that rich and that famous, and I know God will bless Bill and his family for the rest of their lives." I can say, without a doubt, that my mother prayed for them and their family every day and every night until the day she died.

In 1986 Bill and Camille invited my then wife and me to spend our twentieth anniversary in Lake Tahoe with them while Cosby was appearing at Harrah's. We took a flight into Reno where Bill had sent a Limo for us.

The chauffeur picked us up at the Reno Airport and drove us to Lake Tahoe. It was late afternoon when we checked into our suite at Harrah's. We got settled in and I called Cos to let him know that we had arrived. He had stopped by his dressing room to get a book he was reading, and told us to come by for a minute.

When we walked into the dressing room he was seated with his bare feet propped up on an ottoman, wearing one of the sweat suits that he made popular. He was glad to see us, and said Camille was out shopping and we would all get together later. We spoke briefly about the shuttle disaster that had occurred less than a month prior. My wife had been really stricken by the Challenger disaster because she was a teacher. Christa McAuliffe was to have been the first teacher in space and Ronald McNair was the second African-American Astronaut. Shuttle Commander, Francis R. (Dick) Scobee, Michael J. Smith, Judith A. Resnik, Ellison S, Onizuka, and Gregory B. Jarvis were also members of the Challenger's team. Our hearts went out to the families of those heroic Americans on board that fatal mission.

We hung out with Cos for about twenty minutes then Bill told us what time we should meet. We left him in his dressing room with his book. While I do not consider myself extremely well read, I have always read a lot—but Bill Cosby reads as much as just about anybody I know, with the exception of a few friends whose profession or job requires it, i.e. lawyers, proof readers, literary editors, etc. No matter where he is, on the plane, in his hotel or around the pool there will usually be a book that Bill is reading nearby. I emphasize this in order to point out that he understands the importance and necessity of teaching and encouraging our youth to read. I have constantly tried to explain this to my own children. I have seen their eyes glaze over when I mention it. I'm sure they were bored to pieces when I talked to them about it, but I know that two of my three sons read a lot more now. The truly educated and most of the successful people I know are readers. Billionaires, Warren Buffet and Dallas Maverick's owner, Mark Cuban have stated in interviews, that they read on average eight hours a day.

The Cosbys are not the kind of folks who are show offs who use unnecessary "big words" in conversation. They are highly intelligent people who believe in education; they understand what it takes, especially for black people, to have a chance at a decent life in America. Let's not criticize-or hate on the Cosbys for trying to wake black parents up to the need to reorder our priorities. Until we do, our young people will continue to be grist for the mill that helps sustain the prison industrial complex, and our lack of awareness unwillingly assigns young African-American men to a destiny of the new slavery via systematic incarceration that all too often traps them into servitude.

It was about 4:00 PM when we left Cosby's dressing room and headed back to our suite. We wanted to decide what to do between now and the time we were to meet up with him and Camille just before the dinner show.

Getting to the performers' dressing rooms at Harrah's is like going through a maze, but having appeared there so many times with Cosby, I had no problem getting back. However, when we got to the lobby, the electricity in the entire city of Lake Tahoe went out due to a storm. It was still daylight, and when we reached the lobby, I spotted John Denver—may he rest in peace—standing in front of the elevator bank. None of the elevators were running until the back up generators at Harrah's kicked in, which took about ten minutes or more in those days (although it seemed like hours). John Denver (who I used to call Johnny D,) was hosting his annual Celebrity Ski Classic at Heavenly Valley, in Tahoe that weekend.

Johnny D. and I had met years before I started working with Cosby. From time to time our paths would cross while doing college concerts. We were cordial and always got along well. We became friends one evening while touring on the college circuit for Variety Theater, which was a mid-west entertainment company, owned by a gentleman named Lenny Namark. Lenny booked a lot of the college concerts in Illinois, Michigan, Wisconsin, North and South Dakota, Minnesota, Idaho, etc. It was a winter tour and John Denver and I often performed at the same venues, but mostly at different times. Such was the case one winter evening in Fargo,

North Dakota. We were checked into the same hotel, and after finishing our respective gigs, we were hanging out in the hotel lounge. I remember that it had been a challenging week for Johnny D, because in the middle of his tour, his band quit on him and went back to Colorado.

That night he was in the hotel alone and feeling let down. He said he was not going to hire any pick up musicians, and that he would play the remainder of the dates solo, which he did. It was not the first time a performer that we were on tour with had his band quit during the tour. John Denver took it in stride; he told me that he had to work a little harder without the band, but that the audiences seemed to enjoy his show just as much.

We knocked off several beers, and stayed until the bar closed. There were no more than five or six people in the bar, and since we were not celebrities at that time, no one seemed to notice either one of us. So few people in the hotel lounge made it feel like the loneliest place in the world. At one point, John commented that this place was lonely enough to write a song about. I said, "Let's do it." I started by saying: "I'll never go back to Fargo," Johnny D added: "cause it's cold and lonely there;" I continued, "Where's everybody in Fargo?" John replied: "They're hiding from the cold night air." We made a few more rhymes about it, but neither of us wrote anything down. When we would run across each other from time to time, we'd promise to finish that Fargo song. We never did.

By 1986 John Denver had become a superstar. His Lake Tahoe Ski Classic had concluded for the day and he had just returned from the slopes. There were five or six people in his entourage also waiting for the generators at Harrah's to kick in. A shuttle stopped in front of the lobby doors and dropped off a group of skiers who were coming in from the slopes. Once inside the lobby they headed towards the elevators and spotted John Denver, and gathered around him for autographs.

Five minutes later another shuttle unloaded thirty or forty skiers who entered the lobby, noticed JD and moved in on him, asking for his autograph. He was signing, and being jovial when a third shuttle arrived and dropped off more people. The crowd was growing, and starting to press in on John.

From across the room I could see that John was beginning to get a bit uncomfortable with the growing crowd. So I yelled out: "I'll Never Go Back to Fargo," Johnny D. answered: "Cause it's cold and lonely there." With that he started to push through the crowd, saying "Excuse me I have to talk to a friend." My wife and I moved toward him. We reached out and shook hands, I introduced him to my wife, and at that moment the generators kicked in and the elevators lit up. John said: "Let's get together later." I told him that we were meeting Bill and Camille Cosby later. We agreed to hook up the next day on the slopes which we did. On the slopes, he thanked me for "rescuing" him from that crowd. It was February 22,-- the last day of his Ski Classic. We hung out for a few minutes and once again we promised to finish the Fargo song. That was the last time I saw him.

That night before the dinner show at Harrah's, we went to Cosby's dressing room. Camille was at the casino. A few minutes later she came to the dressing room. As usual, she was elegant and gracious. My wife was quite taken by the outfit Camille was wearing. I made a mental note to try to find her a similar outfit for Mother's Day.

FYI to the ladies reading this: Camille was wearing a powder-blue, soft suede, below-the-knee length dress, with Native American fringes on the shoulder and at the hem. She was wearing knee length boots of the same material and color; she looked exquisite. Cosby usually wore one of his patented original design patterned sweaters on stage, but tonight he was dressed in an off-white suit, a silk shirt and a tie that complemented perfectly. I thought to myself, "Wow! Bill dressed up for our anniversary."

We have always thought that Camille and Bill made a wonderful couple and that night they reaffirmed it. As usual, he did a fabulous show. It was a wonderful evening and a very special way to spend our twentieth anniversary. I shall remember it with fondness and gratitude.

Bill and Camille Cosby are enlightened individuals, top of the line human beings, and as a couple seem perfectly matched. They have earned, and deserve the respect of this entire nation. Bill Cosby has been a mega-star longer than any other entertainer living today, including Michael Jackson, Paul McCartney, Mick Jagger, or any other celebrity I can think of.

Most people cannot imagine the pressures, envy, jealously and hidden resentment that can accompany even the smallest success. In spite of it all, (even in today's irreverent and often mean-spirited society) there are many, many more people who love and respect Cosby and what he stands for than those who decry his place of eminence. He has been a quiet ambassador of human equality, of racial harmony, and is an example of tolerance and goodwill that is second only to Dr. Martin Luther King, Jr. There should be a thesis based on his life, titled: "How to succeed in a Racist Society without Blaming Everyone but Yourself."

Every man, woman, and child in America needs to recognize the contribution this man has made to the cause of human dignity. All black children should be given Bill and Camille Cosby dolls upon which to fashion hopes, dreams, and aspirations. Every African-American parent should constantly remind their children that racism is not nearly as prevalent today as it was when Bill Cosby, Muhammad Ali, Marian Anderson, Jackie Robinson and the like grew up. Yet bigotry is still bigotry—it is an evil that resides in the hearts and minds of those who practice it. It will stop those who give to it added power by believing that it alone is the cause of our individual wretchedness and our collective immobility.

Racial bigotry is a malignant mindset, designed to paralyze those who are not taught, and those who do not learn the importance of self-worth. Life on earth can be much more unfair to some than it is to others. Still, that must not be a reason to squander initiative and surrender to the poverty that misplaced blame and unfettered anger has deposited in the collective psyche of a subjugated people.

Let's not forget that Bill Cosby paved the way and created the matrix by which American society built its acceptance of black men as human beings that are worthy of equality. Bill Cosby's respectability established a pattern of wide ranging acceptance, and his longevity helps to fuel the hope and sustain the promise of true and lasting equity. If that promise is diminished, it is us, with our reckless disregard for life in our own community, and the wanton disrespect for each other that invites intrusion, and fashions the demise of our heroic capacity. It leaves us defenseless against the propaganda that our own commercialized actions solicit and perpetuate.

Unfortunately, year after year, some of our people float along in homegrown degradation like dead fish in a polluted tide, drifting aimlessly in search of what: The status quo or the Rip Van Winkle award? We seem not to realize that even those who do manage to prosper also suffer misfortune. Many of us have heard the old saying, "into each life some rain must fall." Most mature folk believe that no one completely escapes the truth of that adage.

The first time I saw pain and sadness in Cosby's eyes was in 1968; we were on stage appearing in concert at the University of Kansas (KU) in Lawrence, Kansas. Bill had just finished his ad lib opening bit where he joked with a few late comers in the audience. He had introduced The Pair Extraordinaire. Marcus and I were on stage and as usual the three of us were starting to clown around before Bill would leave the stage and The Pair did our fifty minute show. As Cos prepared to exit the stage, one of the faculty members who was involved with promoting the concert, walked onto the stage and politely interrupted the three of us. She whispered something to Cosby who turned to Marcus and me. He had a completely vacant expression in his eyes as he stood speechless, staring blankly at us. The faculty member gently took the mike from Cosby's hand and spoke quietly to the audience, "Ladies and Gentlemen, I have an unfortunate and sad announcement to make. Dr. Martin Luther King, Jr. has been assassinated in Memphis, Tennessee." The audience gasped loudly, and in stunned silence Bill turned and walked offstage. Marcus and I followed bewildered, shocked and confused.

Backstage in the dressing area, Bill, Marcus and I were sitting quietly when the faculty member approached us. Bill asked her how it had happened. She explained the news report in detail. She wanted to know what to do about the remainder of the show. Cos looked at Marcus and me and asked us what we thought. We told him that it was his call. He lowered his head for a moment or two. We could hear the eerie sounds of an extremely shaken audience from where we sat. It sounded dark, a drone that hung like an imaginary cloud hovering over the heads of the people in the auditorium. After a couple of minutes Cosby raised his head and said, "Let's give these people a great show." We could see that he was grief-stricken, but for the moment he was concerned about giving the people who had come to see our show some temporary relief from the terrible news we had all just heard.

Marcus and I changed our song list slightly before we took the stage and did our funniest material. Fifty minutes later Bill Cosby did the best show I had ever seen him do. That show was to have been the first stop on a two-week tour through the South. After the show, Bill canceled the tour out of respect for our fallen leader. We flew back to L.A. that same night. When we parted, Cosby was stoic and poised but his eyes and his somber mood revealed that the depth of his pain was tantamount to what Marcus and I felt. We were numb and angry.

In my own life, 1997 was the most devastating year I have experienced to date. I lost two sisters, a brother, and a close friend in a twelve month span. Plus that was also the year that we lost John Denver "Johnny D". In spite of the overload of misfortune I endured throughout the year, the pain I felt on January 16th of that year seemed chronic. The anguish I felt was acute and lingering, but in my mind it did not match what I felt Bill and Camille must have had to endure with the tragic loss of their beloved son Ennis, whom I had met when he was a child. Naturally, like millions of other people, I sent my condolences, and I prayed, prayed, prayed.

Father's Day of that year I went to the Playboy Jazz Festival at the Hollywood Bowl where Bill had been the host and MC since its inception. I had attended the festival before, but I usually left afterwards without going backstage to say hi to Bill and other musicians on the show.

In 1997 my friend Cedar Walton, the great jazz pianist was appearing at the festival. I went backstage to see him. However, my main reason for attending that day was to see Bill. He came offstage after having introduced the late great Tito Puente, and I approached him. There were no words available to me that could do justice to what I was feeling at that moment. We spoke not a word. We embraced and I tried to send the peace of God through me to him. Perhaps I was able to do so in some small degree because we embraced for what seemed to be at least minutes. No words, but when I looked into Bill's eyes, somehow I felt that he understood what was in my heart.

For weeks and months I thought of dear Camille and the entire family, and truly understood the meaning of one of the final pages in a book I had read in high school. I identified with Holden Caulfield, in the J.D. Salinger, novel, "Catcher in the Rye." Like the character in Salinger's book, I was confused, angry, and I wished I could stop people from dying. My only solace that year could be found in prayer and meditation, for which I am thankful to God.

I thought about Bill's dear mother and father, Mrs. Anna and Mr. William H. Cosby Sr. and the first time we went to Philadelphia. Bill took his brother, Russell's car and drove Marcus and me around the neighborhood where he grew up. He pointed out where his boyhood friends whose names he had made household words had lived. From that first meeting on, Mrs. Anna called Marcus and me her boys. Whenever we would see her, she would say, "How are my boys today?" What a dear lady. We saw Camille's father on occasion at Warner Bros. Studios where Bill had offices. Camille's father was a quiet man, cordial but usually absorbed in the newspaper, or reading a book. The stories Bill tells on stage about his parents and in-laws are funny and endearing, and underneath the humor you can feel his love for them.

My heart goes out to the entire Cosby family for their devastating loss, and I am so proud of Camille and Bill for the way they have endured what must be the most painful experience a parent can suffer—the loss of a child. That alone should make them heroes to us all. I am grateful that they are a strong and courageous couple, and that they have each other.

Bill Cosby is the town crier, traveling purposefully through the darkness, desperately trying to warn us of what lies ahead, and some of us angrily retort: "WE DON'T WANT TO HEAR IT!" while others weakly moan, "It's not our fault."

Dr. William H. "Bill" Cosby, Jr.: for your legacy, courage, and your wisdom, it is with sentiments of esteem that I acknowledge your great worth. We salute you for your profound contribution which has fashioned an image of the best of what and who we are as African-Americans. Please allow us to honor you with **A Simple but resounding Thank You,** for the road of respectability you have forged, that others now follow towards the fulfillment of their own dreams. (See Cosby photo pages)

Mable M. Chandler

Personal Hero

Mable M. Chandler, "Mama" Chandler, as she was known by her students, was the school counselor. As such, she touched the life of every student that attended Lincoln High School during the more than thirty years of her tenure there. If there was a teacher, male or female, that was as revered by her students the way Maurine F. Bailey and Col. Carrington were, Mable M. Chandler would be without question the one.

The two women were in many ways complete opposites: "Ma" Bailey, a member of Delta Sigma Theta sorority was mellifluous, soft-spoken and single minded about her purpose. She was a fashion plate and an elegant and refined patron of the arts. "Mama" Chandler belonged to Alpha Kappa Alpha sorority and she was earthy and raw, full of wisdom. There was no way a student could BS either of these women, but Mama Chandler could listen to your story and know if you were telling the truth before you finished. As we used to say about Mrs. Chandler, "she could peep through muddy water and spot dry land". If a student had a serious issue that was about to get him or her expelled, or was going to flunk a subject, she would work through her break if necessary to get that student on track.

Once when I was full of myself and about to do something stupid, Mama Chandler heard about my scheme and sent for me. I was in class and she told my teacher to send me to the teacher's lounge where she was on her break. I walked into the lounge; Mrs. Chandler had kicked off her shoes, and lit a cigarette (smoking was fully accepted in the Fifties and Sixties). She told me to sit down; then she got head to head with me and when she finished dialoguing, and dealing with me, it was as though she had looked into my mind and soul. She knew exactly what to say to make me realize how much I had to lose if I did not get on track. She did not threaten, scold, or talk down to me. She appealed to my interest and my goals in life, and when I left the teacher's lounge that day, not only was I ready but I was committed to toeing the line, and I did. If I had followed through with my plan, I most assuredly would have ended up in jail for doing harm to someone whom I felt had done me wrong. Mama Chandler was a street- wise, highly educated woman who finished first in everything she undertook. She was a purely Christian woman who could not be fooled. Mr. John Chandler, her devoted husband, was the love of her life. They were married more than forty years before he preceded her in death.

A real gift to me for writing this book is that I get to look deep into the hearts and minds of the people who directly touch my life. Since hind-sight is 20/20, I can see the truth of their being. I am sometimes overwhelmed with love for many of these really important individuals who helped engineer my survival, and fashion my life. It amazes me how these two great ladies could be so absolutely different and at the same time have so much in common.

They each had an appreciation and love for life, as well as a profound understanding about what it takes to become healthy, wealthy, and wise. They respected and adored each other. Because they both were loyal and dedicated members of their respective sororities—as I said, Ma Bailey belonged to Delta Sigma Theta, and Mama Chandler, Alpha Kappa Alpha. I once wrote a song about them. I called it "My godmother was a Delta, My favorite Aunt was an AKA." I regret that they never heard it, for I know they both would have gotten a huge kick out of it. No doubt I would've had to sing it for them every time we all got together, but I would have loved singing it for them. The thing they mostly had in common was a heart full of love for the children that they were responsible for guiding. They never faltered, they never failed. Neither of them had children of her own; they put the well being of the children that came to them above all else.

Mable M. Chandler was unique and special in her own right. Even when she fell ill, she remained upbeat and positive; the light in her eyes was as clear as an infant's until the day she left this world to meet her dear and beloved husband John in Heaven. For the kindness of a kitten, the strength of a lioness, the insight of a wise one, a heart of pure gold, and for sharing it all with so many others like me. I send you with deepest love and fondest memories… **a Simple Thank You.** (See chandler photo pages)

Colonel Reginald W. Carrington
Personal Hero

Colonel Reginald W. Carrington, US Army (Retired), is a man for whom I have utmost respect. This is mainly because the colonel's influence on my life is profound. As a rule, one's high school years are the years when one begins to decide what direction one's life should take. In many cases, young people might change their minds about decisions they made in high school for whatever reasons they might have. Even so, by the time we reach high school age, our character and personality have begun to take shape. There are exceptions to every rule, but generally speaking I believe most people will agree.

Colonel Carrington, like Mrs. Bailey, Mrs. Chandler, and Dr. H. I. Holland (the principal at Lincoln when I graduated) came into my life during this crucial period of my development. You have read about some of the ways I benefited from Mrs. Bailey and Mrs. Chandler taking an interest in me. The Maurine F. Bailey Cultural Foundation presented Col. Carrington with the 2004 Community Service Award. Since then he has become President of the Bailey Foundation.

The colonel was Lieutenant Carrington when I first met him. When I first saw him I thought he was a student. He looked younger than some of the eleventh and twelfth graders and in fact, I thought he was a freshman. One of my friends from the projects where we lived walked by and I stopped him and said, "Hey, Blood (Medlin) let's dribble that boy over there wearing the Army suit." Blood said, "Dribble him? You can't dribble him; he's a teacher." He was dressed in his army khakis and even with that gold bar on his shoulders and collar, he still looked like a high school ROTC cadet instead of the ROTC teacher. He was the US Army second lieutenant assigned to install the first ROTC Unit (55 C) in a black Dallas school.

Dribbling was a form of initiation at Lincoln for freshmen whereby a group of guys would lift the new student off the ground, turn him upside down and shake the coins out of his pocket. If you were a freshman on the first day of school, you would be smart to place some change in your pocket (perhaps a nickel and two or three pennies) and when the coins fell out, you would be left alone. If no change fell out, the guy would get "dribbled," according to his size. If he was of small stature, he would be dribbled (thrown to the ground) without much force. The bigger the student, the harder would be the dribble. It was never done with the intent of hurting anybody and, to my knowledge, not one student was ever hurt because of it. Otherwise, it would not have been allowed to continue. Most of us took it in stride and were proud that we had been dribbled, or that we had not been dribbled. The original idea of dribbling was started in "The Bottom" (the section of Oak Cliff, in Dallas, Texas, where I grew up). It was a method of roughhouse tackling in sandlot hard tackle football.

Mrs. Bailey was instrumental in getting me to join the ROTC; she told me it could be a fun way to learn to take discipline and she was right— Lieutenant Carrington's LHS ROTC Drill Team was second to none. A fellow named Charlie George was the Lieutenant's assistant and had been an Army drill team captain. He knew all the moves and he taught them to us, and we worked them like the champions we became. I was promoted to the rank of lieutenant colonel before I graduated. Ma Bailey was right; the discipline–which I admittedly needed—gave me a focus and a sense that someone else believed in me, and I did not want to let them down. I loved every day of it from the day I started until the day that I graduated.

Lieutenant Carrington was also the first person to turn me on to jazz. I had listened to a couple of jazz tunes up on the show hill, coming from the juke box in the pool hall. I liked King Pleasure's song, "Moody's Mood for Love," and Billie Holiday's recording of "Gloomy Sunday," a song about the almost "social" lynching of innocent black men in the south. In many instances, the random hangings were carried out as a white man's sport. I had heard of Charlie Parker and Dizzy Gillespie but there were no "jazz" radio stations, and in our house we listened to gospel, blues, rhythm and blues, country, and pop.

The lieutenant formed a jazz club; he played trumpet with the local professional bands and that gave him credibility, which is a prerequisite when dealing with teen-agers. Plus, he had an easy manner, but was always, without question, in control of his class. I believe that every one of his former students feels special about him. So many of them have gone on to become outstanding citizens, such as Joe Bagby, Police Constable in

Dallas County; Dr. Beverly Mitchell Brooks; Councilman, Leo V. Chaney, Dallas City Council 7th district; Judge Prince Cartwright; Major Wayne Crudupt; US Army, Rev. Joe Patterson, Pastor of Greater New Zion Baptist Church; Major Hudson Griffin, US Air Force; Abner "Butch" Haynes, NFL running back with the Kansas City Chiefs; Samuel Hudson Jr., Texas State Legislature; William Jacobs; Thomas Jones, Attorney; Leon King, Principal, DISD, Lt. Colonel Nolan Stone, Texas Air National Guard, W. Maurice Lacy, Artist/poet/musician, and yours truly, Carl E. Mathis Craig A.K.A. Kingston DuCoeur: Singer, Actor, Musician, Writer, and others.

I remember the first meeting of the jazz club, Lt. Carrington showed us different styles of jazz; he demonstrated various things on his trumpet, and it was great. At the end of the week he told us to pick out our favorite jazz recording and bring it to class next week. He wanted us to pick an instrumental version of a song. I was listening to the radio one night and heard the Stan Kenton Band featuring alto saxophonist, Lee Konitz playing "Pennies from Heaven." I dug it, and that's the first jazz record I ever owned.

The three most important things in high school to me were Music, ROTC, and Creative Writing and this gentleman had a direct hand in two of the three. To this day I defer to his judgment more than anyone since my dear godmother, Maurine F. Bailey, passed away. To know that Col. Carrington, thanks to God, is in this world, assures me of my own humility.

I have always appreciated, in my adult life, having some one that I can look up to. There have been a few such people in my life and there are some today. They are people whom I believe know more about life than I do and who are loved and respected the way Col. Carrington is. He is admired by everyone I've ever spoken to that worked with, or studied under him. The bonus for all this belongs to me, because on top of all of the perks (i.e. we can play music together, I can seek counsel from his wisdom, I can laugh at the funny stories he tells, I can tell him funny stories), I trust him, and he is someone who believes in me, and is willing to trust me. That alone qualifies him as my friend. To be friends with those you really respect, admire, and to whom you are willing to defer is, in my opinion, keeping very good company.

The main reason he came almost immediately to mind when I was deciding who to choose for chapter C of this book, is because of something he wrote in my high school yearbook. I have never written it down and I've never had to memorize it; it has been alive and a conscious part of my life since the day the colonel wrote it and signed his name to it. His words have coaxed me back onto the right path at times when I might have made a wrong choice. It has taught me that an honest word sincerely spoken has power and can last a lifetime. That power can uplift, inspire, motivate, encourage, and instruct, especially today, when bad choices and wrong decisions are so available, and relentlessly attempt to override our reasoning.

Col. Carrington, here are those simple but powerful words, written by your own hand: (See Carrington photo page)

To Colonel Reginald W. Carrington, your untarnished words have carried me away from places where I did not belong on more than one occasion. The way you have lived your life, rewards me with someone to look up to. I am all smiles and gratitude when I offer you, your lovely wife of more than fifty years, Betty, and family…**a Simple Thank You.**

(See Carrington photo pages)

Chapter

D

Miles Davis
American Icon

Miles Dewy Davis is arguably the greatest jazz trumpet player since Louis Armstrong. Miles was known as much for his eccentricities as he was for his great musicianship. Even his detractors concede that his genius as an artist is unquestioned. Along with technical dexterity, the unique and soulful sounds that flow from his horn are like rivers of silk. The depth of imagination that his compositions reveal is equally germane to his lasting legacy.

Unpredictability, both on and off stage, became his hallmark and is worthy of a place in the Standard English dictionary under: "Miles-isms". The child of a successful professional (his father was a prominent dentist). Miles' self-sufficient personality developed early, and he remained his own man throughout his life. Since this book is not meant to be an in-depth report on anyone, some of the chapters will be longer or shorter than others. My original intent was to write about people who are still with us, however, I discovered early on that there are some people who have made significant contributions to my life that have passed away; Miles is one of them. Unfortunately, a few have passed away while I was writing this book. I did not spend a lot of time with Miles; I probably saw him a half dozen times, but each time was usually memorable in some way.

My first encounter with Miles Davis was in New York in1969, at the Philharmonic Auditorium. He had come to see Bill Cosby in concert at Lincoln Center, and The Pair Extraordinaire was on the bill. From the very first conversation, brief though it was, Miles lived up to his legendary reputation of being genuine and candid. He came backstage after the show to see Bill. There were hoards of people —mostly big name celebrities trying to get back to see "Cos", as most folks called him back then. I was standing in a mob of people who were congratulating us on our portion of the show.

I had never seen Miles in person before, but I was (as were all of the cats that I hung with) a huge Miles Davis fan since high school. I used to try to dress like him, because he was **the** trendsetter among young musicians.

I noticed Miles making his way towards us. Even though there were wall to wall and elbow to elbow people backstage it seemed like Miles was gliding through the crowd with the ease of a figure skater. When I realized that it was really him, I tried to politely end my conversation with the person I was talking with. Before I could get free, Miles walked up, extended his hand and said (in his raspy voice): "Miles Davis." I replied excitedly: "I know who you are." I shook his hand, and the next five words he spoke sounded like they were wrapped in gold. He looked directly in my eyes and said: "Cooking, cooking, ya'll was cooking." At that moment, I could have departed for the Pearly Gates and life would've seemed complete.

I had never heard Miles speak before, and I thought he had a cold, but later learned that it was his natural voice. I said: "You really dug it?" He looked at me with an almost puzzled expression and said: "I said I did, didn't I?" I was embarrassed, and he must have picked up on it because he led the conversation by telling me: "Man, some of these people are wiggin' (confused); on my way backstage some people thought I was you, and asked me for an autograph. I asked him (jokingly), "What did you do, did you sign it?" He said: "Yea, I signed it; I signed it Miles Davis." I laughed; he didn't. Then he asked: "Where's the man?" I pointed to Cosby's dressing room and said: "He's in there getting mobbed." Miles replied: "I'm gon' mob him some more." He proceeded to move through the crowded hallway towards Bill's dressing room. As he left he gave me a slight squeeze on my upper arm and I watched him disappear into the crowd. He was shorter in stature than I'd imagined, but at that moment he was a giant in my eyes.

At the hotel that night, I went to Marcus' room and told him that I met Miles backstage, Marcus said: "Yeah, me too, I was in Bill's dressing room when he came in"; "he said we were cooking, and asked me what kind of bass I was playing." I said to Marcus, "Did you know Miles was that short?" Marcus said: "Yea he's short but when he's got that trumpet in his hands, he looks ten feet tall." The fact that Miles dug us had made **me** feel ten feet tall, and the next day I would have to draw on the previous night's elation.

The day after meeting Miles Davis was another first for me. That afternoon I stopped by Cosby's suite. We were sitting around, and out of the blue Bill says to me: "Now don't take to heart any reviews you get here in New York." I didn't respond because we had literally never had a bad review, not even when we had previously played New York.

Later on, someone in the entourage brought the newspaper to the room. The show had gotten very good reviews, however, the reviewer wrote: "The only soft spot of the evening was that the singer, who has a good voice, needs to do more singing and less chatter." We had a tight show; all over the country audiences loved the bits of humor we injected into our shows. Bill himself enjoyed it, and would sometimes ask if we would do our version of "Hang on Sloopy Hang On" because we did a completely humorous version of the popular song. Everywhere we performed that song the audience loved it and enjoyed the brief patter we included in the show-but not this reviewer. I asked Bill If he knew about the review before Ron brought in the paper. Cosby just did that lifting of his eyebrows thing, you know, with that patented smile of his. To my knowledge, that is the closest I ever came to getting a bad review while touring with Bill Cosby. I kept it in mind when we played New York again later that year and all was well. I probably would not have felt bad anyway, because every time it would try to enter my mind, I'd recall the moment when Miles Davis said to me, "Cooking, cooking, ya'll was cooking." I learned from it and from then on, whenever we played New York, almost no chatter, just singing. It was a good lesson.

One evening Marcus and I were having dinner with Bill and Camille; they had recently moved into the house on Tower Road. Bill had just completed an album with his Bunions Bradford big band or maybe it was his "Hooray for the Salvation Army Band" album; I'm not sure. While we were having dinner, Miles sent Cosby a five page telegram which Bill read to us. He laughed as he read every page of it aloud. The entire message in the telegram was: "A one, a two, a three, a four, a one, a two, a three, a four, a one, a two, a three, a four." It was no doubt an inside joke between Bill and Miles having to do with music.

One of the greatest lessons I ever learned as a performer, came from Miles Davis.

In the summer of 1970, The Pair Extraordinaire was appearing at another nightclub in San Francisco's North Beach. The name of the club was "El Matador." We had appeared at this nightspot a number of times, and we had the nightclub routine down pat.

Other than logistical things, for an entertainer, the primary difference between a nightclub and a concert hall is the fact that a concert facility is obviously larger, and usually consists of one performance per evening-sometimes two. The exception being, theatres in the round, or smaller concert venues where two shows per night were common. Most nightclubs, if not all, will sometimes have one or two shows during the week and three shows per night on the weekend.

We opened at El Matador on a Friday night and as usual breezed through all three sets with ease, receiving two standing ovations for the last two shows. My partner and I, as was our custom when appearing in San Francisco, had rented a houseboat just across the bridge at gate six in Sausalito. During the day we usually had lunch at "The Trident," a popular restaurant on the Bay that entertainers, musicians, and the like frequented. Saturday afternoon, Marcus and I went to the Trident for lunch. We walked in, spotted a table, and on our way to be seated, we heard this raspy voice say: "Pair Extraordinaire." It was Miles Davis; we walked over to his table where he was seated with two guys and a lady. He introduced them and said if we wanted to we could take his table because they were about to leave to pick up his wife. I asked Miles how long he'd be in Sausalito, and if he was playing in the city. He said that he and his wife were going to New York on Tuesday. We told him that we were at El Matador and asked him to come by. He said he had plans for tonight, and asked how many sets we would do on Sunday. I told him three. The waitress brought the guy who had paid the tab his change and as they were leaving, Miles asked: "What time do y'all hit tomorrow night?" Marcus said, "Dinner show is at 8:00, second show 10:00, and last show at midnight." Miles: "I'll catch you at El Matador." They left and we took their booth.

Over lunch Marcus and I started to plan what tunes we would do tomorrow night that would knock Miles out. At the club that Saturday night we included the special songs in our sets in order to brush up and really be ready, and we had a great show.

The next night we were ready. As usual the dinner show was the show we sort of coasted through our set. People were eating, being served, the sound of silverware clicking on plates etc. The audience laughed and talked, not being rude, but that's what dinner shows are about. Waiters and waitresses moved about the room as quietly as they could. Because we were a headlining act the people came to see our show, and considering that it was a dinner show, the audience paid an unusual amount of respect to our act. Sometimes entertainers might try out new material and tighten up songs that need more work and so forth, during the dinner show. As long as you do a fairly good show, the audience will enjoy it, because they're usually preoccupied with eating, and enjoying the company of those with whom they are having dinner.

We were saving our dynamite material for Miles, because we knew (like all other musicians) he would most likely come to the second show, and maybe hang out during intermission the way Sidney and Belafonte had done that night when they caught our act at the Bitter End. We finished the second show, all the time looking for Miles to come through the door. We did a hot show but held back our killer tunes, and the second show ended, but no Miles. For the third show we came out cooking and didn't let up. We did three encores, and when we finally left the stage, the crowd was still on their feet asking for more, more, more. We lit up that stage, and to our utter disappointment, Miles didn't show up.

The next day we went back to the Trident for lunch, and lo and behold we entered the restaurant and there was Miles at his same table; he was alone. We walked in; he waited as we approached his table. He said "Pair Extraordinaire, have a seat." We sat down and right away the waitress came to the table, took our order and soon as she left, I said to Miles: "Man you told the biggest fib I've heard this year." Miles said: "I didn't tell no lie." Marcus said: "You told us that you were coming to El Matador Sunday night." I added: "Not only did you fib, but you did it in front of your friends." Marcus said, "Miles, the last thing you said was I'll catch you at El Matador." Miles seemed a bit irritated when he said, "Miles don't lie to no M----- F-----. Miles came to check y'all out." He continued, "I came to the first show, came through the kitchen and stayed halfway through the set, but y'all wasn't cookin, so fuck it, Miles left." He named a couple of the songs we did, so we knew he had been there.

Sometimes, during the dinner show, we would clown around. I did some country western impersonations of Johnny Cash, Hank Williams and others. The dinner crowd loved it because it took them by surprise that I could sound so much like the country singers I impersonated. I have always loved all kinds of music-including some country tunes. Miles said, "Y'all wasn't cookin, so what'd you expect?" That night was the first time I'd ever heard him speak of himself in the third person, but it wouldn't be the last time, but that was definitely the last time I ever held back on a show, dinner show or whatever. I appreciate Miles for being honest about the show he saw us do that night, but I am most grateful that he cared enough to return to the Trident restaurant the next day to set us straight. If he had not liked us he could have easily gone back to New York without letting us know how he felt. That would have been unfortunate because we would've never learned that important lesson.

About a year later I ran into Miles one day at Fred Segal's, a hip men's clothing store in Hollywood; he was cool. I asked him what he was up to these days; he replied, "Gittin' high and painting." I asked, "You remodeling your house?" Miles: "Hell naw, I'm painting art, you know Picasso kind of painting except I ain't stealing nobody's shit the way he did." I said; "I didn't know you could paint". Miles replied: "There's enough shit you don't know about Miles to fill a cash register."

We talked for about ten minutes. He asked if we were doing anything in town, but we weren't appearing anywhere in the L.A area at the time. When he was leaving the store, he did say: "If I see y'all playing anywhere I might check you out." I said: "Yeah Miles, give us a chance to clean up that El Matador thang." Miles chuckled and replied: "Y'all need to clean that shit up, but I'm hip to it; y'all was just fucking around that night, cause you thought Miles was coming in later." I said, "Come on Miles, you do all kind of stuff on stage; you be playing two or three tunes with your back to the audience." Miles looked at me and he was dead serious when he replied in that raspy voice: "Miles Davis can get away with it, but you can't, cause that ain't your rep (reputation)." I asked, "You really gon let us clean it up the next time we're appearing in town?" He said, "Yeah I will, 'cause I know next time you'll be cooking." I said, "I promise!" He nodded, and split.

Because the encounter with Miles in Sausalito was a life lesson well learned, and because I cherish it to this day, I teach it to young entertainers, musicians, and young people in general, every chance I get. I drove home reflecting on our previous meeting at the Trident in Sausalito. In my mind I could hear Miles saying to Marcus and me: "Y'all wasn't cooking so fuck it, Miles left." I still felt a tinge of embarrassment that we had disappointed him that night in San Francisco. Then I thought back to when I was four years old attending Miss Billie's Kindergarten School, and I remembered us kids shouting in unison Miss Billie's motto: "If a job is great or small, do it well or not at all." I wish with all my heart that the late Miles Davis were still with us for a number of reasons, and among those reasons is my wish that he could be here to read this book and know that his words were well taken, and as a token of my gratitude, I offer **Miles Davis**... a **Soulful Thank You.**

Polly Draper

Personal Hero

Polly Draper is one of Hollywood's most talented actresses. Aside from her obvious beauty, and her skills as a performer, she is a gifted writer who has written movie scripts such as "Lessons in the Tick Code," a moving story about an eight year old boy who is a musical genius, but suffers from Tourette's Syndrome. This is a wonderful film in which Polly starred with the late, talented and lovable Gregory Hines. She has also written plays for the theatre; one of which will no doubt appear on Broadway in the not too distant future.

Polly has written and produced what many people-including me, believe to be one of the best sit coms since "Happy Days". The show is completely fresh, wildly imaginative, and is saturated with 21 Century innovation that is second to none. The name of this TV show is: "The Naked Brothers Band" and airs on Nickelodeon, Saturday nights at 8:30 PM. Although the show is designed for preteens, adults absolutely love this show as well. This is not intended to be a commercial, but the writing is superb. It stars Nat and Alex Wolff (Polly Draper and Michael Wolff' two gifted sons about whom you will hear more in this chapter. "The Naked Brothers Band also features Michael Wolff and the zany dad, and Polly appears in some episodes as the mother. It's funny, funny, funny with a message for young people that they will definitely relate to. This show will be around for a long time. The copy cat shows are obviously already in the making. The problem that the copy cat shows will have is that they don't star Nat and Alex Wolff.

A graduate of Yale University, her multi-layered intelligence is evident but not showy. I have enjoyed many stimulating conversations with her and her equally talented husband of fourteen years, Michael Wolff, a world class jazz musician."

Polly is remembered by many of her fans for her role in the 90's hit television series "Thirty Something," in which she played the role of Ellen Warren. Her work in the Danielle Steel, made for TV movie, "Heartbeat" is timeless and continues to be fun to watch. Michael appears regularly in night clubs, concert halls, on college campuses, and music festivals across America, Canada, and Europe with his band "Impure Thoughts."

Michael Wolff was first discovered when he was attending UC Berkley. His music teacher introduced him to the late great saxophonist, Julian "Cannonball" Adderley. A few years later, Michael had left Berkley, and was playing piano with the great Cal Tjader. Cannonball heard him again, and hired him as his piano player, and as they say, the rest is history. He cultivated a close relationship with the talented Nancy Wilson, and funny man, Arsenio Hall, both of whom were also part of Cannonball's show.

Polly Draper and Michael Wolff's two wonder kids, Nat, and Alex, are also talented in sports, music, art, comedy. They both have IQs that must be off the charts.

On the social side, Michael and Polly are known for giving some of the best parties in Hollywood. The interesting and well-known people who are fortunate enough to get an invite will always intrigue you. As wonderful as all these things are, the reason I included them in this book is for their heart, their caring about young people, and their willingness to put their time, energy and money where some people only put their mouths.

I met Polly Draper in 1991; she was one of the Hollywood celebrities that came to Jordan High School in Watts, CA to work with the under-privileged youth in that community. From the first day, Polly was committed, and after a few weeks, she brought Michael (they were dating at the time) to one of the Saturday classes. The kids adored Polly from the beginning because of her down-to-earth, open and honest attitude. Shortly thereafter a young man was shot in Hollywood and died on their front yard. They decided to try to do something to help stop the violence that was a daily occurrence in Los Angeles. This tragedy happened before they got married and moved into their lovely home, in the hills above Studio City. As one might imagine, they were so shaken by the killing on their front lawn that Michael wrote a poignant and moving song and shot a video based on the incident.

The name of the video was "No Happy Ending" and they used the young people from Watts, Compton, Venice, and East L.A. that were in our after-school program in the video. The day of the video shoot, Polly and Michael introduced us to a number of celebs like David Keith, Mary Steenburgen, the Rappers, Dr. Dre, the late Easy E, and others. The video featured two of our high school students, Belinda Sadberry, an African American, and Domingo Maldanado, a Latino student. They played the lead roles in the video of a mixed race teenage couple that got married after graduation. Near the end, one of them is killed because of racial hatred.

Having met David Keith on the set of Michael's video "No Happy Ending", David became a good friend. He is another actor whose work I enjoy and would like to do a project with. Since he and his family now live in his hometown, Knoxville, Tennessee I don't see him too often. To be perfectly honest, what I miss most are his great Super Bowl parties each year at his Hollywood home. David is now married and the father of a beautiful little girl named Presley Jane. His lovely wife Nancy, was a friend who took a real interest in the kids in our program. We met Nancy when she was the manager of "The Laugh Factory," a comedy club on the Sunset Strip in Hollywood.

The owner of the club, Jamie Masada, ran a Comedy Camp in which the students in the group participated. The kids absolutely loved Nancy. She had a way of making things turn out well when a kid had a problem while attending Comedy Camp. I hope David and Nancy won't mind my telling the following story. I'll tell it because I still have to chuckle whenever I think about it. Before David and Nancy started dating they met at a Swing Dance club to which they both belonged. David Keith's good friends Polly Draper and Michael Wolff used to sort of tease David because when he would stop by Michael and Polly's place he would usually be with some beautiful lady. Polly would ask David when he was going to settle down. He would reply something to the effect of, "I'm looking for the right one; still looking for the right one." This went on for quite some time.

One evening my phone rang. It was David on the line. He cut straight to the chase as we say. The conversation went something like this: The phone rings. I pick up. ME: "Hello". David's voice: "Hey Kingston, David Keith here. I got a question that only you can answer." ME: "What's that David?" DK: "Kingston, I met a lady at my swing dance club last night. She is a very beautiful young lady and I'd like to ask her out. I know she's a friend of yours and I want to know what kind of young lady she is." ME: "What's her name?" DK: "Her name is Nancy Clark. What's she like?" ME: "You're going to marry her." DK: "Naw, I'm not thinking bout nothing like that, I just want to know bout her character and reputation, you know. ME: "She is a high class lady; her character and reputation are impeccable." DK: "Is that right?"

ME: "Like I said, you are going to marry her." DK: "Hold on Kingston you're getting way ahead of me, I just want to know what she's like. I don't want to ask a woman out if she's a typical, run-of-the mill Hollywood type. No matter how beautiful she might be. You know what I mean? I'd rather not be bothered." ME: "I know just what you mean. Nancy Clark is no-run-of the mill typical female. She's special and I think you're gonna marry her. David and I chatted a few minutes longer and he hung up.

The following morning my phone rings. I answer: "Hello." The voice on the other end said: "Hi Kingston, this is Nancy Clark. I've got a question for you."

ME: "And what might that be?" Nancy: "I met a guy at my swing dance class the other night. He seems like a real nice guy and he asked me out. His name is David Keith and I know he's a friend of yours because you guys were hanging out at the premiere of the documentary film about you, your partner, and some of the kids in our Comedy Camp." Me: "David is a great guy and a star." Nancy: "I don't care how big a star he is, if he's not a nice person I'm not going out with him." She continued, "Kingston, I know you'll tell me the truth. Is he a nice guy?" ME: "David Keith is a great guy with his head on straight. You'll have nothing to worry about if you go out with him." You got my word on it." Nancy: "OK Kingston. If you say he's alright, I'll think about it." She hung up.

It was true, David is a cool guy. Like Michael Wolff, he's got his head on straight and is not full of himself like a lot of actors with the kind of success he has enjoyed. And every guy who came to the Laugh Factory, big-named comedians or a struggling "wanna be," knew that Nancy Clark was like a breath of fresh air around Hollywood.

One afternoon about a year later, my cell phone rings. I hear this voice saying, "Hey Kingston, David Keith. Guess where I am." ME: "David, where are ya, man?" DK: I'm at the Orange Bowl, me and my sweetheart Nancy are watching my Tennessee Vols play for the championship. ME: "Yeah, I can hear the crowd." DK: "Nancy and I want you to be one of the first to know that we're getting married." I yelled with delight, "Congratulations! That's wonderful! Didn't I tell you?" DK: "You sure did". You'll get an invitation as soon as details are finalized." ME: "Great! I'm looking forward to it. Give my regards to Nancy." We hung up.

My friendship with David continued after meeting him on the set of Michael's video. Michael's and Polly's involvement with Colors United also did not stop after the video was finished. They showed up often at Jordan High School to work with the young people. Michael did an abbreviated score of the music to our flagship performance, titled "Watts Side Story," a hip-hop musical based on Romeo and Juliet. He also worked with the student piano accompanist in the class.

The first time Polly brought Michael to the group he was a huge celebrity and very popular with the students, because the kids in our class used to watch The Arsenio Hall TV Talk Show, every single night and Michael was the bandleader for that show. Most of the young people in the class had already met so many celebrities that they were not intimidated. They had been taught to be respectful and to not make a nuisance of themselves. One young man named Robert had recently joined the group as the piano accompanist for the choir. Michael Wolff sat down at the piano to give Robert some pointers, but Robert was so excited, having seen Michael Wolff on TV every night, that he froze up completely. When Michael asked him a question, the young man literally could not speak. He could not even lift his hands to the piano keys; we all felt very uncomfortable for Robert.

Michael understood the young man's predicament and handled it perfectly. He remained seated on the piano bench beside the terrified student, and spoke to him casually and patiently until the young man relaxed. It was masterful the way Michael was able to help him become open and able to learn all the professional techniques that a musician of Michael Wolff's caliber was able to teach him. By the time class ended, Robert was as comfortable as the rest of the kids in the class had been from the beginning. In fact, he became the main accompanist and traveled to Washington D.C., when President Clinton invited us to be part of the "Bells of Hope" march and ceremony during the 1993 Presidential Inauguration.

Polly and Michael were there for them year after year. Their very presence gave these students hope, and a belief in themselves that was without a doubt a big reason that many of these "at risk" kids graduated from high school. Everyone in the class really looked forward to Polly and/or Michael's visits to the campus. Polly helped the young ladies with whatever issues they were dealing with. She would be onstage singing, dancing hip-hop, giving acting tips, or whatever the situation called for. When Polly first became involved with the kids, she noticed that many of them did not have adequate shoes. So that no child in the program would feel left out, she purchased about fifty pairs of shoes. Both Polly and Michael were big favorites with the kids and deservedly so.

When Polly shot the Danielle Steel movie, she had the studio hire some of our students as extras. It was a good opportunity for the kids to be on a set, watching real pros at work in front of and behind the camera.

Michael helped arrange a weekend-long youth congress at USC that brought young people together from high schools from almost every part of the city. The work that the students carried out after the conference concluded helped to keep the dialogue going, which would sustain the effort to slow the incidents of youth violence throughout greater Los Angeles, and it worked. Because of their contribution to the young people of Los Angeles, on behalf of all of the students, staff, volunteers, parents and directors of the program, I hereby extend to **Polly Draper and Michael Wolff,** and their good friends, **Nancy and David Keith** as talented and caring individuals, **A Combined and sincere Thank You.**

(See Draper photo pages)

Patricia Duff
Personal Hero

Patricia Duff, one of the real movers and shakers in Hollywood, got involved with our youth program and things really started to hum. A young woman named Chris Svoboda was on the Board of Directors of "Living Literature Colors United"-the youth organization that I co-founded. At that time, Chris was Ms. Duff's personal Assistant, and she introduced us.

Patricia became a board member, and her good name was like a magnet. She brought more to the table than fifteen of the other twenty board members combined. The supporters that came as a result of Patricia's involvement were quality people, as were some of our original board members. She used her enormous influence to help grow, what was at the time, a fledgling organization. She spent time in the inner city, helping and encouraging young people, some of whom had been written off as gang-banging losers.

In three short days, this remarkable woman along with the help of Gail Simms, the sister of Phil Simms, my former partner, who was the founder of the organization, arranged the trip to Washington D.C., complete with new outfits that were suitable for the weather and fashionably up to date. Once Patricia met the students, and saw first hand how much these young people really wanted to do well, she became committed to helping them.

Getting invited to the nation's capitol was a magnificent experience for all of us. The kids were fascinated by everything that happened the entire week, but the highlight for many of the students was when it snowed. Most of these young people had never been out of L.A.; they had never been on a plane before, and as you might imagine they loved every minute. The first night we were in Washington, DC, it snowed, and when the instructors did the second bed check around 2:00 AM, we found the entire group of kids outside standing on the lawn of the hotel watching it snow. It was the first time they had ever seen real snow, and they could have stayed out there for hours just looking in absolute silence as the snow fell.

These former street gang kids, from the inner-cities of L.A., Venice, Compton, and East L.A., were so well behaved that President Clinton's Chief-of-Staff, in charge of the inauguration, was so impressed that he placed our kids in the very front row, immediately behind the President and the First Lady. I told them the same thing that Mrs. Maurine F. Bailey had told us when we were in high school; "You are not here just to perform, you are here to be remembered and respected." Patricia was so proud of them for the way they conducted themselves throughout the entire trip.

It would take some time to list all of the benefits for which Patricia Duff was directly or indirectly responsible.

Patricia and her husband at that time, Mike Medavoy, to whom we owe a huge debt of gratitude, traveled to Salinas, California to support the students on their opening night at The John Steinbeck Literary Festival. The festival takes place in Salinas every year. Patricia acted as chaperone for the young ladies.

Tom Steinbeck, John Steinbeck's son is the head of the Foundation that created and runs the festival. He was deeply moved and expressed his surprise and obvious delight when he realized that his father's writing impacted these under-privileged students so profoundly that his works became a center-piece of their artistic endeavors, and more importantly a catalyst for effective change in Los Angeles' inner-city. Tom Steinbeck shook his head with gratified amazement as he revealed these feelings to Patricia and Mike.

Each year the group performed at a different festival and each year they were successful at making the young people in the various cities and towns more aware of the common problems that kids face. The proven solutions that our students from LA had created, designed and distributed to their counterparts, were absorbed to varying degrees and implemented as far away as Copenhagen, Denmark.

In 1991, the year that Patricia Duff first got involved, my partner and I were running the organization out of his house. The only office we had was my briefcase and his dining room table. Within a few weeks, Patricia, through her contacts with The Show Coalition, had arranged for our first office space. It was in a building that was owned by "Children Now," a non-profit advocacy organization that is well known for the great work it does dealing with a wide range of children's issues. A year or so later-thanks to Patricia, we moved into a suite of offices that were located at one of the major independent motion picture companies on the west side.

Patricia accompanied us to meetings with important people that we would not have had access to without her influence. We forged a very good relationship with Sony, TriStar and Columbia Pictures. Patricia introduced us to wonderful people like Sue Jameson and her staff, which included Janice Pober, Isisara Bey, and others whose help was a primary factor in the program's success. Again, we owe a special debt of gratitude to Mr. Mike Medavoy without whom it could not have happened. Jordan and Helen Levin were also instrumental in the growth and development of the program. These are people that I admire and will always respect for their energy and commitment to the youth of inner-city Los Angeles and ultimately to the nation's youth.

The thing that is the most telling about Patricia's concern for young people is the fact that she personally mentored a troubled young lady who later graduated high school, entered college and today is gainfully employed and doing quite well. Because of the positive turnaround she made, LaToya Howlett, became one of the poster children for the success of our after- school program. Ms. Duff was forthright and unassuming. I can not count the many times she climbed into her little white Jeep and spent some time in South L.A. helping kids who needed encouragement, and someone to believe in them. Her attitude was never sour or self-indulgent. Everyone agrees that she was like a light whenever she came around. I think she looked forward to reaching out to these sometimes desperate and disenfranchised kids. How could this dear lady ever know the extent of the hope and self esteem she inspired in those young people?

Patricia Duff is bright, and highly intelligent; her wit is quick, her personality low key, charming and engaging; she is strong and resilient, and the students often rated her as one of the ten most beautiful women in the world. Knowing Patricia, this is a fact that she will probably eschew, but the truth must be told. She has a darling young daughter whose IQ is no doubt over the rainbow, and who absolutely adores her, and dear Caleigh is the apple of Patricia's eye.

There are so many wonderful things that could be said about this lady, but I still could not begin to express my gratitude for having had the opportunity to see her altruism in action. It is my hope that she will accept from all of the students that she uplifted, all the good she has done, all the light that she still bears, and for everyone from whom I have permission to send **Ms. Patricia Duff... a Simple and Lingering Thank You.**

(See Duff photo pages)

Chapter

E

Clint Eastwood

American Icon

Clint Eastwood is a person that I do not know personally. In fact I have only met and talked with him briefly on two occasions. The first was at the Beverly Wilshire Hotel. We were attending an affair for the benefit of the Fulfillment Fund, a non-profit organization founded by Dr. Gary Gitnick. Its mission is "to help promising, yet educationally under-served and economically-disadvantaged, students achieve high school graduation".

It was a star-studded affair that included Frank Sinatra, Warren Beatty and Anette Benning. Also present at the Beverly Wilshire Hotel on that evening were Plácido Domingo, Natalie Cole, Steve Martin, Edward James Olmos, Magic Johnson, and a host of other celebrities. Clint was in the entrance lobby of the hotel ballroom where the affair was being held. He was talking to a small group of people who had approached him. A photographer was taking a photo of Ann Marie Gillen and me. Ann Marie was the COO of Revelation Entertainment, an entertainment and film production company owned by Morgan Freeman and his partner Lori McCreaty. The photographer got the shots, and I noticed that Clint Eastwood was now standing alone. He was loose and approachable.

I walked over to him and introduced myself. When I told him that I was one of the co-founders of the organization whose students would be performing later that evening, he became more interested. I told him a little bit about the kids and how our program in Watts, Venice and East L.A. helped get most of our kids out of gangs, truancy, etc. I answered a few questions he asked about the youth activities we provided. By the time our brief conversation ended he was completely relaxed. He encouraged us to keep up the good work and said that he looked forward to the performance that our young people would give. The thing that impacted me most was how completely absorbed he became when I spoke of the work the kids had done to transform their communities.

At the time, I was not aware that he was into music. Some weeks later I was talking to a musician friend of mine, Cedar Walton, about the impression Clint left with me. Cedar informed me that Clint was a musician. And I understood. Other celebrities I met that night were nice, too, but when he shook my hand as I was leaving to get backstage, the subtle almost smile that showed on his face, informed me as to why he wears his legendary status so well.

The next time I saw Clint Eastwood was at an affair hosted by Linda Guber on the Warner Brothers Studios lot. When I entered the room, I thought, "Now how often will you see Clint Eastwood without a crowd of people surrounding him?" I walked up and said, "Mr. Eastwood, how nice to see you again." I could tell that he could not quite place me. I reminded him of our meeting at the Beverly Wilshire Hotel. When I mentioned that our kids had performed that evening, he remembered. He extended his hand and said he had gotten a kick out of watching the show the youngsters had put on. His Oscar winning film, "Bird," the story of the great jazz saxophonist, Charlie Parker, starring Forest Whitaker, had been released a few years prior. I was saying how much I enjoyed that movie as Linda Guber took the podium. I had to join my group, so I shook his hand and proceeded to find my companions. I can tell you that this second brief encounter re-affirmed my original feeling. That Clint Eastwood is solid and for real, with the soul of a jazz musician.

His artistic prowess is well known around the world. I am so glad that I respect, admire and enjoy his work as a filmmaker and actor. There are some artists who shall remain nameless whose work I admire, but when I meet them in person, I found myself almost regretting that I liked it at all. Not so with Mr. Eastwood; now that I know of his music connection, perhaps someday we can have a nice conversation. I place him on the upper shelf of cool, among the coolest people I know, such as Bill Cosby, my friend and fellow musician the great jazz pianist Cedar Walton, Dennis Weaver, Patricia Duff, Jeff Bridges and last but not least my nephew Kerry (KJ) Bell, who lives in Dallas. These are some of the coolest people I know, and Clint certainly belongs among them. That's why I'm offering **A Simple Thank You** to **Clint Eastwood** for caring about young people and for being so gifted, so powerful, so real, and so damn cool.

Chapter

F

Farrah Fawcett

American Icon

I met **Farrah Fawcett** for the first time at a conference, in Beverly Hills, that was sponsored by the "Show Coalition." That afternoon, my partners and I spoke to Farrah about becoming involved with our after-school youth organization. She seemed interested and wanted to know more about the group and its mission. Several days later, Patricia Duff made a phone call to Farrah and they spoke at length about the group and how the kids were helping to reduce the incidence of violence in the inner-city communities where they lived. Ms. Fawcett heard about the incredible effect that the program was having with the "Waging Peace" concept the students had developed, and it rang a bell with her. The more she learned the more excited she became. She was amazed that a group of neighborhood kids were actually accomplishing what the authorities, the media, many educators, and a growing number of community leaders believed to be an impossible task. This group of youths, many of whom were former hard-core gang members two years prior, had now embarked on a different mission. They had previously been a part of the problem, but now had a new lease on life.

Once they realized the unnecessary pain and suffering their gang affiliated activities were causing, they set out to make a difference. More and more they realized that they could have a positive effect because other young people listened to them and were thereby influenced to disengage from the destructive behavior. A growing number of youths not only joined "Colors United" but almost immediately became a part of the solution by being active participants in waging peace. They saw the favorable results that their community involvement produced and were therefore encouraged to do even more.

As the host of the event, Farrah got things off to a good start. The audience was impressed and delighted with her warmth, and totally taken by her still apparent southern charm. When she flashed that coveted Farrah Fawcett smile, photographer's cameras flashed away bathing the theater with flickering light that was reminiscent of a Fourth of July celebration, albeit without the sounds of random fireworks.

This was the first time that The Group's flag-ship presentation, "Watts Side Story" was performed at a well-known theatre in the heart of Hollywood. The Richard Pryor Theater is owned by Mitzy Shore who is also the owner/proprietor of the world famous Comedy Store which is located on the Sunset Strip. To have Farrah Fawcett's name associated with the event assured that the show was sold out. Every seat in the house was filled and some late-comers were turned away due to the lack of space.

The announcer's booming but mellow voice filled the auditorium when he said, "Ladies and Gentlemen, please welcome your host for the evening, Miss Farrah Fawcett. The crowd exploded with applause and when Farah walked on stage from the wings, the audience let out a collective gasp upon first seeing her overpowering beauty and grace. She was stunning to say the least. That night Farrah Fawcett was the defining image of a real Hollywood star. She welcomed the audience and thanked them for coming out to witness a wonderful theater piece that accurately depicts life in the inner-city of Los Angeles, and reflects the plight of countless young people in urban America. As Farrah left the stage to another round of thunderous applause the audience was ready.

The young actors had completed their preparation and now waited nervously backstage for their queue to take the stage. The curtain opened and two of the lead actors hit the stage with energy and focus. From that moment on, the audience sat riveted to their seats. Many were in disbelief that they were watching a troop of inner-city middle and high school students, delivering such a powerful portrayal of life as they experience it every single day. All three acts were professional-caliber performances and two hours later, the audience was on its feet applauding, whistling, and screaming Bravo! Bravo!

Farrah's interest in the young people did not end after the performance that night. She thoroughly enjoyed the evening and stayed around after the show congratulating and taking photos with the cast members and staff. One of the students asked if she would come to one of the Saturday classes. She told the students that she would love to visit the campus sometime. A couple of the kids showed her a few moves from a hip hop dance number that was featured in the show. Farrah picked up the moves surprisingly fast and by so doing, she got bit by the hip hop bug, so to speak. She wanted to learn more of the moves. They promised to teach her the complete routine when she visited the campus. That promise pretty much sealed the deal. We discovered that she loved to dance and I think she was quite surprised to have picked up on hip hop so quickly. Had the program continued I have no doubt that she would have visited the class fairly regularly as other celebrities did. All of us enjoyed her immensely and looked forward to her visit.

We extend **A Special Thank You** to **Farrah Fawcett** for sharing her valuable time and lending her legendary name to the young people in our after-school youth intervention program.   (See Farrah's photo page).

Morgan Freeman

American Icon

Morgan Freeman, as far as I am concerned, can do no wrong as an actor, and I believe him to be an incredible human being. The ease that graces this man certainly places him in the category of "cool" that accommodates the likes of those I named earlier such as Cosby, Bell, Bridges, Duff, Eastwood, Walton, and Weaver. We attended a screening of: "Cowboy Del Armor," the latest documentary film by gifted director and mutual friend, Michele O'Hayon. A number of celebrities attended the Beverly Hills showing but Morgan was clearly the star that everyone sought out. The way Mr. Freeman has conducted his life speaks volumes about his character.

I had a chance to spend a little time with him personally and I also watched from a distance the way he would greet and interact with an adoring public. His natural accessibility and openness makes one feel that he is totally interested in the person with whom he is engaged at that moment. Seeing him in this capacity made it easy to understand why most who have met him, leave feeling that Morgan is a friend for life.

He introduced us to his lovely daughter, Deena, who enjoys her work behind the camera as a hairstylist. We spoke for some time about one of his incredibly talented sons, gospel musician and singer/songwriter "extraordinaire," Alfonso Freeman, whose music I discovered quite by accident about a year ago. I believe that Alfonso's music will some day be known the world over because he is a fantastic artist in his own right. Most singers don't find it easy to spotlight another singer unless that newly discovered singer has something special and I am no different. I predict his great success because not only is Alfonso Freeman a fantastic singer/songwriter but the listener soon discovers, as did I, that the music he writes and performs is straight from the heart.

I sense that Morgan is one of those fortunate men who can successfully be a good and caring father and a best friend to his kids. He was interested in the various topics that we briefly spoke about, but he was most notably engaged when speaking about his family.

I watch him on a talk shows every chance I get, and I always learn something of value as an actor or as a human being. The last talk show I saw him on, I learned something about both acting and life. Morgan Freeman is the kind of man that makes you glad and thankful that he is successful, rich and so well-loved. I have said this to him personally; now I'll say it in writing so the world will have the chance to hear yet again, how special Morgan Freeman has become to so very many people around the world.

Morgan Freeman is a super talent and a great guy. He confirmed that his company has agreed to produce the film "Straight Up", a feature motion picture about the work we did with the kids in the Los Angeles inner-city. The film will be directed by Michele O'Hayon. Rumor has it that he might even consider playing me in the movie if the final script is solid. I asked him about that possibility and he just looked at me with a soft smile. I understood that. Like most actors who are both smart and honest he was not about to say yea or nay at this point. My fingers are crossed, and I am hopeful that this truly great actor will agree to play me in the film. From all of us who admire his work and appreciate his soulful spirit, I am sending **Mr. Morgan Freeman... a Simple Thank You.**

(See Morgan Freeman's photo pages).

CHAPTER
G

God

Thank You, to my beloved God, for giving me the ability to believe, and the grace to not judge, criticize, or condemn those who do not.

TRUTH'S SQUIRE AND MASTER
By

Kingston DuCoeur

Like the woman who wears infinity's nod
Like a pulsating vein in the bladder of God

Like endless oceans of time and space
that are but a furrow on an unaging face

More valid than beauty, more thorough than death
Yet I still command with one tacit breath

Where life and light applaud love and laughter
There she extols as Truth's Squire and Master

Heroes of Faith

In their own words

"When you shall know the truth the truth shall make you free."

Jesus of Nazareth

"Let my people go!"

Moses

"The ink of the scholar is more sacred that the blood of the Martyr."
Muhammad

Pervading nationalism imposes its dominion on man today in many different forms, and with an aggressiveness, that spares no one. The challenge that is already with us is the temptation to accept as true freedom what in reality is only a new form of slavery.
Pope John Paul II

"The way is not in the sky the way is in the heart"
Gautama Buddha

"Good human qualities cannot be bought with money, nor can they be produced with machines, but only by the mind itself"
14th Dalai Lama

"Meditation is concentration used to know God"
Paramahansa Yogananda
Founder of Self Realization Fellowship, in Los Angeles, CA

Gertrude Gipson
Personal Hero

Gertrude Gipson (Penland) was a nationally celebrated entertainment columnist who wrote for publications across the country. She was a true friend who helped many entertainers find their way to success and stardom. In Los Angeles she was an absolute icon and was loved, honored, and respected throughout the state of California.

I first met GG, as she was affectionately known, through a mutual friend, Jackie Gardner. Although I was not in the close-knit inner social circle, mutual friend Jackie was GG's best friend, and a founding member of Gertrude Gipson's Regalettes Social and Philanthropic organization. Like GG, Jackie was an extremely beautiful woman and although I have not seen Jackie in quite some time, I know she is still a beautiful woman, as is her sister Yvonne, who I did happen to run into around Christmas time in 2005.

When Jackie introduced Marcus and me to Gertrude, I remember how surprised I was that GG was so friendly. Sometimes really attractive women can be aloof and guarded when they don't know you. Gertrude was a major celebrity in her own right, but she treated everybody like she knew them personally. Wherever she went she was the toast of the town. Jackie, her lovely sister, Yvonne, and all the folks in their circle were fun-loving, respectable people who knew how to party, but always with dignity. Their whole crew, led by GG, always looked like they had just stepped out of a fashion page of Ebony magazine.

I knew who Gertrude Gipson was before we met because I came to California for one purpose and that was to become a star. I made the rounds to the many clubs around town, sitting in with the musicians and trying to connect with the local entertainment scene. I read the Los Angeles Sentinel's entertainment section religiously and was an ardent fan of GG's column. When I came to L.A. from Texas she was the manager/hostess of the Famous California Club at the time. I started to land a few freelance gigs, but nothing important beyond the fact that I was being hired as a singer in L.A. It was every entertainer's desire to get some ink in Gertrude Gipson's column. She was one of the most sought-after guests at parties and gatherings of the social elite, but she was also accessible, too, and just as gracious when she was with "everyday" people. I was fortunate to receive great reviews from GG at every stage of my career. Through the years I have kept them along with other pieces of memorabilia that I cherish. I have included some of those reviews in this chapter.

To readers who did not know this special lady, I have also included some facts about her remarkable life that were taken from her brief but revealing obituary. When you see the names of some of the people who participated in her memorial service, you'll get a little more insight as to who she was and how much she meant to so many people like me. Her obituary begins...

Funeral Held For Well-Known Entertainment Columnist Gertrude Gipson in L.A — Obituary

Services were recently held in Los Angeles for Gertrude Gipson Penland, well-known columnist for the Los Angeles Sentinel. She died after a battle with pneumonia.

Hollywood celebrities and statewide politicians were among those who crowded the Good Shepherd Baptist Church in South L.A. to say goodbye and celebrate the life of Gipson. Moving tributes were paid by Nancy Wilson, Sidney Poitier, Marla Gibbs, L.A. District Attorney Gil Garrett, L.A. County Supervisor Yvonne Braithwaite Burke, Frankie Beverly and Lou Rawls. Vocal tributes were paid by Linda Hopkins, Ernie Andrews and Howard Hewitt.

Rev. Gharah L. Degeddingseza, pastor of the Good Shepherd Baptist Church, officiated. Expressions of sympathy were delivered by Rev. O.C. Smith of L.A. and Rev. Frederick Haynes III of Dallas, Texas.

Born in Ocean City, NJ, she was raised in Los Angeles, attending Los Angeles City College. She married local journalist J.T. Gipson (now deceased) and began her own career in journalism. She was entertainment editor of the California Eagle, West Coast editor of the Pittsburgh Courier, West Coast editor of Sepia Magazine, and for many years, entertainment editor and columnist for the L.A. Sentinel. Her column appeared in numerous black newspapers across the country. She later married L.A. entrepreneur Elledge Penland, also now deceased.

Former California Gov. Edmund "Jerry" Brown appointed Gipson to the California Motion Picture Development Council.

She leaves behind two daughters, Reve Gipson and Shonte Penland Abraham, and a brother, Randolph Lomax

To Gertrude Gipson (Pendland), a gracious and elegant lady, we send a **Simple and elegant Thank You.**

(See G G's) photo pages)

CHAPTER

H

Edith Head
American Icon

Edith Head will be remembered as the most awarded costume designer in Hollywood history. For fifty years she designed costumes for some of the biggest films in Hollywood, and earned a remarkable total of eight Academy Awards. We watched her grace the stage of the Academy Awards ceremonies year after year.

Meeting Ms. Head was one of the most important encounters of my professional life, and it happened at a time when I needed the kind of affirming our chance meeting gave me.

It was during the week of my having been cast in my very first motion picture (which never got made). I was a singer at the time. An independent film maker, whose name was Nicky, had a script about a black cowboy.

This producer had seen me on the Mike Douglas Show that was co-hosted by the late Robert Cummings. The other guest star on the show that day was Polly Bergen, and, I believe Peggy Fleming, the Olympic ice-skating champion –although it could be that we appeared on the show with them another time.

Shortly after the Mike Douglas Show aired, I ran into this producer at a restaurant in Hollywood on the Sunset Strip. I was having dinner with a friend from Melbourne, Australia, Barbara White. Barbara had written a novel titled "Ebony Rising"; she and her husband Charley, were trying to get it made into a movie.

Barbara assigned the exclusive rights to me, and handpicked me to play the male lead. It is a novel about a white female screenwriter who falls in love with a black actor and the problems they encountered as a racially mixed couple in America. This was before Stanley Kramer's wonderful film, "Guess Who's Coming to Dinner," starring Spencer Tracy, Katharine Hepburn, Sidney Poitier, Katharine Houghton, Cecil Kellaway, Beah Richards, Roy E. Glenn Sr., and Virginia Christine, was released in 1967. Michael Sarne's film "Johanna," starring Genevieve Waite, Calvin Lockhart and Donald Sutherland (Sutherland's first film I believe), was released in 1968. After those two film releases, there was not a lot of interest in black man/white woman love stories; however, I do still own the worldwide rights to Barbara White's novel "Ebony Rising."

Nicky came to my house in the Hollywood Hills, brought a bottle of champagne, and assured me that I had the leading role in his film that would co-star Bo Belinsky, the ace pitcher for the newly formed Los Angeles Angels baseball franchise. Bo Belinsky later fell from grace as a major league ball player due to alleged gambling and other allegations. Nicky and I shook hands. He told me that he was going to New York to finalize the deal on his end, and would return to L.A. in a week. In the meantime he told me to go to Western Costumes, rent a cowboy outfit and have an 8x10 photo made of me in the western garb. He said he needed it to show the backers.

The next day I went to Western Costuming and rented the outfit. While I was browsing the cowboy section, I saw this diminutive lady who seemed to be in her early fifties. She was nicely dressed in what Hollywood refers to as "upscale" casual attire, standing across the aisle from me, perusing through that section of clothes. Having seen her so many times on TV at the Oscars ceremonies, I immediately recognized her as Edith Head. I have never been shy about meeting celebrities. I held to the practice of shaking hands with people that I admired with hopes of becoming more like them.

Being certain that the lady in the next aisle was Edith Head, I approached her and said, "Miss Head?" She turned to me with a most congenial expression and answered, "Hello." I told her my name and said that I have always admired her work—which was the truth. In my youth I had briefly entertained the idea of becoming a fashion and/or hair designer. How and why I came to think of those professions is a chapter for a different book, but basically I think it's because I am drawn to the creative aspect of things. I like to create my own style of a thing, and that's the thread that runs through most things that interest me.

She did not mention that she had seen me on TV, or in Vegas or anything of the sort. Having spoken of her to a number of people in the film industry since that fateful day I have come to understand, based on the response of those who knew her, Edith Head was a down-to-earth and good natured person who made everyone she met feel the way she made me feel that day. She made me feel like I belonged in the movies. I told her why I was there and what I was looking for. We chatted for about five minutes and I told her that I didn't mean to distract her, but I was glad to meet her. She replied, "Nice to meet you, too." I went back to my section and continued to look for an outfit.

I was still looking about ten minutes later, and to my surprise, I heard her call me by name; she had noticed a vest that I had selected. She looked at it and said, "No; that'll never do." She saw another vest, took it from the rack and said: "This one; take this one." I didn't think twice. I said: "Thank you." She said: "Come along." I followed her to the hats. She took a hat from the shelf, looked at me and placed the hat back on the shelf. I asked her, "Should I wear a white hat?" Without looking at me, she replied: "Of course not; forget that good guy white hat nonsense. You want to look good; a movie star's got to look good." She continued to look at various hats, glance at me, take another hat and then another until she picked up a black hat, stared at me briefly with squinted eyes and said, "This one, try this one." I put on the hat and turned towards her. She said: "Not perfect, but better than the others. If you trim your hair it'll be perfect." I looked in the mirror; to me the hat was perfect without trimming my hair. I said "Thanks, I like it." She said: "Not bad; but keep looking, and if you see one you like more get it, but not a white one, and you have to feel comfortable in it."

She started to walk away. I said to her: "Miss Head, do you think I can make it in the movies?" She turned, took a couple of steps towards me, looked at me for about two seconds and said: "Yeah, you can make it. You got an acting coach?" I answered: "No ma'am." She said, "Take some acting classes; you've got it in the eyes." She turned and went on her way. I thanked her; she kept walking, raised her hand about shoulder high and waved without looking back.

For weeks and weeks I wondered what she had meant when she said that I had it in the eyes. It was not until I started taking acting lessons some time later that I learned that acting (especially film and TV acting) happens primarily in the eyes, and with the ears. Eye contact and focus, listening and reacting naturally to what you hear, is what good acting is all about. It's not about voice inflections, or "emoting," if you have proper focus, and you listen well.

David Mamet says, "Don't spend a lot of time trying to figure out how to say a line. If you speak the line honestly, that will be the best line reading." I have found his words to be true.

I promised myself, that whenever I had the opportunity and the influence to determine who the costume designer would be no matter what the project, theme or the period would be, I would insist on trying my best to get Edith Head for the job. I only hoped the project would be important enough to have a budget that could afford Ms. Head.

Unfortunately, she passed away some years ago. Meeting her and hearing her say to me those words: "Yes, you can make it because you've got it in the eyes" was as important to me as any I had heard since T Bone Walker told me I could be a singer like him.

To the first lady of costuming, **Madam Edith Head,** Wherever her spirit may rest in peace, I send… a **Simple but fashionable Thank You,** for those fifteen minutes you gave to me, which helped move me forward to where and what I am today. (See Edith Head's photo page).

Marcus Hemphill
Personal Hero

Aurelius Marcus Hemphill was one of the most beautiful souls I ever encountered. I used the word "was" because Marcus, as he was called, died of cancer in 1987. He was a writer on the Bill Cosby show at the time.

I was angry with Marcus when he passed because he had refused to stop smoking more than two packs of cigarettes a day. That among other life choices had taken an irreversible toll on his young and promising life. Selfish though I may have been; his loss cost me the dearest friend I had made during my adult years. His life had promise because he was not just an employee of Cosby's; Marcus was a good and trusted friend of Bill's.

Many times after work, Bill and Marcus drove home together from the NBC studios in New York. Cosby would drop Marcus off in the Bronx before going to his own place in Manhattan. This of course caused jealousy among some of the people that worked on the show. I guess you might say they felt like it was a case of "teacher's pet syndrome." In this case, it was not at all a "teacher's pet" situation. As I stated in the Chapter C, The Bill Cosby Chapter, Marcus and I had been close friends with Bill since 1966. Like all human beings, Marcus was not perfect he had his flaws, but he was loyal sometimes to a fault. The bottom line is, to know Marcus was to love him. He would stand by a person whom he considered to be a "friend, even when that individual might have had less than honest motives.

His respect, appreciation and loyalty to Cosby were—like my own, absolute. I dare to suggest that the high esteem with which Marcus held Cosby was also equal to my own. In addition to those qualities, he had a winning personality that was far greater than mine. Marcus Hemphill was one of the most intelligent people I've known. We attended the same college, although at different times. Many people would have been surprised to discover that Marcus was seven years older than I, and six years older than Cos. His unaffected and youthful charm was genuine. Had it not been, Bill would have picked up on it very early in our association. His intelligence came not only from his formal education, but was due to his natural curiosity, and his open mind for learning. The "yin & yang" of it is that his intelligence was almost equaled by his astounding naivety. In many ways he could be extremely childlike. The case in point below occurred one day before we met Cosby. In fact, the story I'm about to share with you happened even before our first booking in New York.

We got booked at "Tikki Island"—a night club in inner-city Los Angeles. The day of the opening, Marcus went to the cleaners near the corner of Western and Adams Blvd. We had paid our rent, filled our car with gas, which in 1964 was about 26 cents a gallon and that left us with only $10.00 between us. The clothes at the cleaners cost about $2.50 to have both his wardrobe and mine cleaned and pressed. Marcus returned to the apartment beaming with that big broad smile that he was known for.

He came bouncing up the stairs with the clothes, fresh from the cleaners, his long legs taking the stair steps four or five at a time. I came to see what was up as he laid the clothes neatly over a chair and said, "Man this is our Lucky Day." I asked, "What is it?" and Marcus replied, "You won't believe what I just hooked up." Before I could speak, he pulled out two "gold" watches with "gold" bands and said, "Look man, I just got both of these for $5.00." The dude said he had found them in a box near the bus stop. Marcus showed me the price tags on these watches at $125.00 each. On the tags was printed "Boulova." At that time, if you had a Bulova watch, you had the top of the line as far at the black community was concerned.   He handed one of the watches to me and upon close examination, I discovered that the word Bulova was misspelled and not properly aligned. Upon closer scrutiny, I could see and pointed out the flaws to him. I said, "Marcus, this shit ain't real, they're fakes and not very good fakes." He was crestfallen. Marcus could not lie successfully because, like a child, his eyes and face would betray him. He was not a good liar and he knew it. So if he made an error, or came up short, he would eventually come clean because he would always get caught in a lie and consequently, he didn't often try to lie. I told him, "You've been had. How much money do we have left from the $10.00?" He handed over the crumpled money. We had a dollar and some change left and had not even eaten lunch yet. He genuinely felt bad but I was pissed.

Later that evening, when we got dressed to go the club, Marcus put on one of the watches and came into my room. He pulled up his shirtsleeve and he said, "It looks real don't it? Do you think anybody can tell its fake?" I shot him a look, and he said, "Want me to bring you yours?" I said, "Hell naw! I told you I ain't wearing that crap." They looked real enough for the stage; I probably would have worn it, but I'm allergic to any kind of metal jewelry, except silver and gold. Then I started to wonder if Marcus knew the watches were really fakes and was trying to scam me.

Over the years, I learned that he could be as gullible as a four year old. He was no fool, but he could be overly trusting. Even if he were trying to pull one over on me, that particular scam would have been weak. I'm not saying that I'm the smartest person on the block, but being raised on the mean streets of "Big D," I doubt that you could've pulled that weak scam on the average seven year old in Dallas.

There are long stretches of time when I miss Marcus every day. He was, without a doubt, the most generous person I've ever known. In the past his unsuspecting and good heart had cost him dearly. Marcus and I were both from Texas; he was from Ft. Worth and I grew up in Dallas. We had attended the same college in Austin, but when he attended the school it was called Samuel Huston College, and the college "across town" was named Tillotson College. By the time I enrolled some six years after Marcus, the two schools had merged and were named Huston-Tillotson College. Today it is Huston-Tillotson University. (HTU)

Marcus and I met in 1964 after my return to Los Angeles from Europe where I had served two years in the Armed Forces. I had a manager at the time named Kurt Hurt, and one of the nightclubs Kurt booked was a club in Santa Monica, on Second and Broadway named "The Zanzibar." The club was owned by an elderly gentleman, a retired musician, and his wife. His name was "Fiddler" Amsterdam; he was the uncle of the famous comedian Morey Amsterdam. Fiddler's wife was a former Vaudeville dancer named Gypsy.

On my opening night at the Zanzibar, filling in on bass with the trio that backed me was a tall skinny dude with a broad smile and friendly eyes. It was Marcus Hemphill. The Zanzibar became my "home-base," meaning I was the house vocalist and if I got a better paying gig, a private party, or an out of town booking etc., I could send a replacement singer, or Fiddler would hire a singer for the nights I'd be away. It would remain my home base gig, unless a new singer came in and "cut my head," meaning he was so much better than me and became a bigger draw. The gig was mine — period. For some reason, Fiddler and Gypsy liked me from the beginning. Perhaps it was because I always practiced something that Miss Billie had taught us many years ago. I always had good manners, plus, I would sit and talk with Fiddler and Gypsy every night for at least 10 or 15 minutes before, after, or sometimes during the evening. I told them dirty jokes that none of the other musicians would dare to tell them. The jokes were never out of taste or over the top, but they made them laugh and they liked it.

Fiddler was impressed with my military service because Kurt Hurt had told them that I had been a "James Bond" type operative. Fiddler loved to hear about my work with G-2 (espionage) and G-2 air. Plus, I packed the house for all three shows every night. Only one other singer had been able to do that. His name was Everett Mills, a hell of a singer/showman and the lover of Kurt Hurt. Kurt booked Everett in a fabulous top paying club in Portland, Oregon. He signed a long-term contract with the Portland nightclub. They both moved to Oregon, and I became the house vocalist at the Zanzibar. I knew that no singer could "cut my head." The singers that had even a remote chance of doing so, were already house vocalist at other clubs.

Some of the male singers that ruled at that time were the great jazz singer Ernie Andrews (who had recently signed with The Harry James Band), Lou Rawls who became a big star when he recorded "Tobacco Road." Then there was Mel Carter, who became a star after recording "Hold Me," Sam Fletcher was the house vocalist at "Memory Lane," Johnny "Guitar" Watson who was strictly a blues singer, and ZZ Hill, another blues singer. Johnny Guitar and ZZ Hill were already stars on the "Chittlin' Circuit,"— which means strictly small clubs in the black community. The house trio was the Gene Russell Trio. There were a number of dynamic female vocalists like, Damita Jo and Etta James, but I did not have to worry about them trying to take my gig because they were too famous for the Zanzibar, and back then, clubs either featured a male vocalist or a female vocalist. For example, The Zanzibar would book a male singer, a "shake dancer" (a stripper), and Fiddler would be the opening act with his violin.

Every weekend when I appeared at the Zanzibar, Marcus would be there. He would sit in with the trio. Fiddler would not hire him as a regular because Gene Russell had his own bass player. However, since Marcus was filling in on bass my opening night and it went well, I would ask Gene to let Marcus play on my sets; which was cool with Gene and his cats. I had been the featured singer at the Zanzibar for about two months and was packing the house to standing room only.

One Sunday night, near the end of the first show, two gorgeous women came into the club. There were no tables available, but Fiddler seated them at his and Gypsy's private table which was located in a corner near stage right. At the end of my set, I went over to them, introduced myself and they responded by giving me their names. One was a red head named Hope, and the other one was a blond who said her name was Angelica, pronounced "An-ge-lica," though her friends called her Gayle. I asked what I should call her and she said, "You can call me Gayle or An-ge-lica." I had never heard it pronounced that way so I said, "I'll call you Gayle, since that's what your friends call you, and maybe I can be one of them." She extended her hand and replied, "I'd like that very much." As I told Marcus later, her hands were softer than a newborn baby's hands, and she was definitely giving me rhythm (showing interest in me).

A party of four was leaving—Hope saw them and pointed to the table. When the four people left, Gayle and Hope moved to the vacated table. I sat down and asked them if they had any requests for my next set. Hope asked if I would sing "My Funny Valentine"," and Gayle asked if I knew "There Will Never Be Another you." I said, "Of course"; I love those songs, in fact they were two of my favorite songs—my "show stoppers" as it were. Marcus came to the table. I introduced him and told him that the ladies wanted to hear "Funny Valentine" and "There Will Never Be Another You." Marcus asked if they had been here before. Hope said: "No, but we heard there was a good band with a great singer playing here, so we decided to stop in."

The waitress came to take our orders; the ladies ordered two drinks that I'd never heard of even though I had been a singing waiter at the Artist of Dallas Club while I was in college. I had also managed "The Bronze Knight" —a private club in South Dallas that was started by a fellow named Tony Davis. Angelica ordered amaretto and orange juice and Hope ordered Tawaka and milk over crushed ice. The waitress knew that I usually ordered gin and tonic, and Marcus liked scotch and water. Fiddler gave me two free drinks each night, and the musicians got one. Anything above our freebies, were charged half price. Marcus was not a hired musician and he had to pay full price, so I told the waitress to put Marcus' drink on my comp.

I had never seen red hair the color of Hope's hair, and the blonde's hair was long and in the style of Mary Travis (of Peter Paul and Mary), except that it looked almost like silk —not thin, but fine and soft looking. Marcus asked Hope if they were hair models to which she replied, "Nope."; I asked if they were actresses; again Hope answered, "Nope." Then Gayle added, "Just think of us as girls who like good music." Hope added, "And good people." For some reason, they both seemed to get a kick out of their remarks.

The trio's fifteen minute intermission was over, and they were returning to the bandstand. Fiddler would open the set by playing two songs on his violin; the trio would play a song and Fiddler would introduce the shake dancer, and she would do a fifteen minute routine. When she finished, the trio would play two songs, and Fiddler would introduce me; I would do my three song set and usually one, sometimes two, encores. The trio would play four songs and close the show.

Marcus and I sat with the two ladies until the shake dancer was about halfway through her act, and I said I better get ready to go on. We stood up to leave and Hope asked, "Would you guys like to go a fun place with us when you finish here tonight?" I asked, "Where?" Hope said, "At the "Cliff House." Marcus lived in Santa Monica at the time and was familiar with the place. He said, "The Cliff House on PCH in Malibu?" Hope replied, "Yes, have you played there?" Marcus said, "No, but I'd like to." Gayle said, "I'm sure you will someday."

Marcus and I went into the men's room; I was relieving myself at the urinal, and Marcus was doing likewise at the toilet. A guy was washing his hands when we walked in, and when he left Marcus said, "Which one do you want?" I said, "I'll take whichever one you don't want." Marcus: "I like redheads." Me: "The blond is kind of quiet." Marcus: "You know what they say about the quiet ones; they're hot to trot." Marcus: "Hope requested 'My Funny Valentine' and Angelina 'There will Never be another you' That's your bread and butter" (meaning that those were two of my killer songs). I corrected his mispronouncing of her name. Me: "An-ge-li-ca Gayle, and the redhead's name is Hope; that's easy to pronounce." Marcus: "It sure is because I want some Hope (pun intended), and I need some hope; Just a little dab of Hope will do." Me: "You know what to do, get down with the music and you might get some 'Hope' tonight." We washed our hands and Marcus said: "I know you gon sing your ass off this set, right?" Me: "Damn right I am."

We went into the dressing room and waited for the dancer to finish. When we heard Fiddler say, "How about another round of applause for Jo Lean, Jo Lean, the dancing machine" we left the dressing room and stood by the curtain that led to the stage. Fiddler continued, "Now ladies and gentlemen, it's time for the star of our show; he has recently returned from Europe where he appeared with Chet Baker and Anita O'Day at "La Chat qui Pez" in Paris France, and In Copenhagen, Denmark at "Monmarte" with the great Oscar Peterson. Let's hear it for Kal Craig." My manager, Kurt Hurt, had convinced me to change my first name from Carl to Kal, saying it would read better on the marquee. Back stage, Marcus and I shook hands and I said, "Come on man; let's go cop these chicks." Marcus: "Right on."

We hit the stage beaming. One of the things that Mrs. Bailey had taught me in high school was that the first thing the audience should see when you take the stage is the most beautiful smile you can show, because a nice smile gets them to like you as a person before you ever sing a note. She also told me: "Show those dimples; you'll be surprised what a positive effect your dimples have on people." I tested her theory from time to time —it was true. I noticed that if I went on stage without a smile the initial applause would be lukewarm, but when I had a big toothy smile the applause was at least twice as loud. I have passed this knowledge on to the hundreds of students I have taught over the years. Marcus had an easy, naturally captivating smile and his eyes would light up, especially when he was "mackin" (trying to get the girls) and he knew how to pour it on. When we later formed The Pair Extraordinaire our roles onstage and off would be that Marcus brought the charm, I provided the wit and humor; together we created the perfect balance.

On stage, as I passed the piano player, I told him. "I'm opening the set with "S'wonderful," in E flat, followed by "My Funny Valentine," and "There will never be Another You." I counted off an up-tempo beat, and I was straight out "macking" when I sang:

"S'Wonderful, marvelous, that you should could care for me.

I sang the song through once, and called Marcus' name for him to take a sixteen bar solo. This was one that had been in my repertoire since high school, and we had done it a few times at the Zanzibar, but I never heard Marcus play the solo the way he did that night. He was so cookin' that after his sixteen bars, I yelled over my shoulder to him, "Gon N' play. Marcus." He continued his solo for the full thirty-two bars, and when he finished the audience applauded him like we had never witnessed. I came back in at the beginning of the song and sang another complete chorus. We swung the hell out of that tune, and the crowd loved it and they let us know they did. The two gorgeous ladies were really digging it. At the end of the applause I said: "How about that smoking solo by Marcus Hemphill?" The audience acknowledged him with another round of applause, I looked back at Marcus and winked; he understood.

I continued: "Ladies and Gentlemen, I'd like to dedicate my next two songs to two of the loveliest ladies in the house tonight. The first song is "My Funny Valentine" and I'd like to dedicate it to Hope. My buddy Marcus said to me in the dressing room, that I'd better sing this song super good because he needs Hope, and would love to get some tonight." The audience laughed, and the two ladies laughed, and Hope's face turned slightly pink as she blushed with laughter. Then I said, "And the last song of my set I want to dedicate to Gayle. It's called "There Will Never Be Another You." I continued: "Ladies and gentlemen, I have recently become a member of the Audubon Society; I am a dedicated bird collector, and right now, I would give anything for a Night N Gale." The crowd erupted with laughter, and both Gayle and Hope were beet red and writhing with laughter.

Those jokes went over so well that we made it a routine to ask audiences if there were ladies present who were named Hope or Gail. If there were, we would use those jokes and if not we would say, "If you see Hope and Gail, tell them their husbands are outside in the car flirting with Delores and Alma." Then Marcus would chime in over his microphone and say, "Naw man, I said they were flirting with divorce and alimony." These jokes always went over well and got huge laughs.

I followed with "My Funny Valentine" and ended my set with " There will never be Another You" sung in ad lib tempo the first time through, then we swung the socks off the last two choruses. I gave each musician a solo and everybody cooked. We left the stage to thunderous applause and calls for encore. For my encore I sang a very funny song written by the late great Oscar Brown, Jr., entitled "But I Was Cool." The two women laughed so hard at the song that when Marcus and I got in the dressing room, I told him, "We cooked and I think we're going to score with these chicks."

We joined Hope and Gayle at their table for a moment to make sure they had not changed their minds about going to the Cliff House. They said they would wait until Marcus packed up his bass, and I settled up with Fiddler. By the time I got paid, Marcus had put his instrument into the dressing room and was sitting at the table with the ladies. I joined them and we discussed how to get to the Cliff House. I suggested that we all go in one car in order to prevent parking problems. Hope said they were in a little two-seat sports car, and the only way to go would be to take two cars. She said they were parked on the street in front of the club. Marcus said, "The hotel at the Cliff House is probably booked solid this time of the year, and parking is gonna be a hassle." Gayle said, "Don't worry, we always get good parking spots." I said, "You got connections huh?" Angelica said, "As a matter of fact, we have very good connections," and again they laughed about her remark. I said, "I'll pull around front and we'll follow you to the Cliff House."

At that time, I drove an aqua blue 1956 Mercury with white leather seats and matching interior. For a nearly ten year old car it ran good. I had purchased it at a used car lot on the corner of Venice Blvd. and Motor Ave. in LA. My car payment was $30.00 per month, which I was paying off at $7.50 a week. It had been a well kept automobile by its previous owners. The only problem with the car was that sometimes the tumbler in the ignition switch would fall and I would have to jiggle the key for a couple of minutes before I could turn the ignition key and start the car. It rarely happened, so I had not bothered to get it fixed. I kept it clean and it was not dented up, so it was a decent looking set of wheels. I pulled around in front of the Zanzibar and the ladies were parked directly in front of the club.

They were in a 1955 Classic type T Bird Convertible. The most interesting thing to me about the car was that it was almost the same color as my 1956 Mercury, and it also had white leather seats and interior. I pulled alongside them and they pulled off slowly, I followed. We headed west on Broadway and turned right on Ocean Ave., and proceeded down the California incline to PCH. As we drove, Marcus started to tell me about the Cliff House. It was a high class hotel with a world class supper club, and a room downstairs called the "Bare Foot Room". Marcus said "I hope they're not taking us to the Bare Foot Room because that's a surfer boy room with sawdust on the floor, and featured loud, loud amateur sounding rock bands."

The four of us walked into the Bare Foot Room and it was just as Marcus had described it. It was filled with what appeared to be college students and maybe some teen age students with fake IDs. Pepperdine University was located around Seventy-Ninth Street and Vermont in South L.A. at that time and the university would not move to Malibu until some ten years later. I'm sure a lot of the kids in the Bare Foot Room were mere teens. Marcus and I looked at each other with bewilderment. We spotted a table near the front and debated if it was too close to the band, which was playing louder than loud. We decided to look for another table. Hope pointed to a table where people were leaving, and we moved quickly towards it. We waited about five minutes for a waitress to take our orders. Hope said: "Will you guys play a song?" Marcus and I looked at each other this time with utter disbelief. I said: "We don't have the rest of our musicians." Hope said "I'll bet you can borrow this band's instrument." Marcus said: "You gotta be jiving." Gayle said, "Oh please, please just do one song; it will make us so happy." I said, "I can't sing without musicians, and these guys can't play our music."

Another five minutes passed and still no waitress took our order. I said, "I'll go to the bar and order a couple of drinks. Would you ladies like the same as before?" Hope said, "Yes please," and she reached for her purse and I said these are on us. They both said thank you. I repeated their drinks because I wanted to be sure I pronounced them correctly. ME: "amaretto and orange juice," and Hope answered, "Tawaka and milk over crushed ice." Marcus reached into his pocket and said, "Scotch on the rocks with water back." I waved off his money, and made my way to the crowded bar repeating the names of the ladies drinks because again, I'd never heard of Tawaka or amaretto. I had been waiting at the bar a few minutes when Marcus walked up to me and said: "These chicks say they're going to leave if we're not going to do a song." I said, "They must be nuts; how can we play without musicians? And I'm not bout to try to sing with that band." Marcus said: "Man, but let's don't blow it with these babes; they seem hot to trot." Me: "Are you crazy? What are we gonna do?" Marcus: "I don't know but let's do something, even if it's wrong. Just let's not blow it with these chicks." I ordered the drinks, and Marcus and I carried them to the table. As soon as we sat down the band finished a very bad attempt at playing some rock song, and announced an intermission. Hope immediately went to the bandstand and started talking to the bandleader. Suddenly the band leader said: "Ladies and gentlemen we have some guest musicians in the house. They play at the Zanzibar club in Santa Monica. Give them a big hand"; it was like nobody even heard him. Hope beckoned us to come forward. Before I could protest, Marcus was on his feet headed toward the bandstand. I reluctantly followed. Hope gave Marcus and me a hug and said: "This is gonna be great"; she was smiling like she had just won a million dollars.

Marcus picked up the electric bass and began to check the tuning; no one even paid any attention that we were on the bandstand. Gayle and Hope were standing at our table with excited anticipation. I looked at Marcus and said, "What the hell we gon do?" Marcus said "Do the blues, in G." He started to play the intro. Still the room was noisy, but by the time Marcus finished playing a twelve bar intro the room was quite a bit less noisy. I started to sing a Joe Williams song and I was straight out "mackin" to Gayle and Hope as I sang:

Well alright, OK, you win… I'm in love with you.
Well alright, OK, you win… so baby what can I do
Anything you say I'll do, long as it's me and you.

By the time I got through the chorus, you could hear a pin drop in the Bare Foot Room. Marcus' specialty was the blues, and he whipped up on that electric bass. When we finished the song the room exploded with applause and yells for more. Marcus and I were stunned by the almost overwhelming response. The next song we did was "S'Wonderful"—the George and Ira Gershwin song that I had opened my set with at the Zanzibar for Gayle and Hope. I finished with "But I Was Cool." The room was filled with laughter throughout the song, and at the end of the three songs they went wild with applause. The bandleader returned to the bandstand and asked if we wanted to do some more songs; of course we declined. We would quit while we were ahead, miraculously far ahead.

We went back to our table where Hope and Gayle were glowing with excitement. They each gave Marcus and me big hugs and kisses on the cheeks. The bandleader had asked us our names before we left the bandstand. He was now saying to the crowd, "Wow! How about that? Let's hear it again for Kal and Marcus." The applause and yells were unbelievable. We sat down and Hope said, "See, I told you they would love you guys." Marcus and I had a new outlook on things where the girls were concerned. The ladies excused themselves and went to the powder room. I said to Marcus: "What the hell was that we just did?" He replied, "I don't know, but I think its gon git you a 'Night N Gayle,' and looks like I might even get some Hope." We shook hands and toasted each other and sipped our drinks with horny anticipation.

A fellow walked up to our table and asked if he could buy us a round of drinks. We declined and thanked him. We didn't want him to be there when the girls returned from the ladies room. He asked if he could sit until our dates came back. I said, "You can stay a minute." He said his name was Duffy. Then he said, "Don't look now, but see that woman at the table over there by the wall? She's wearing jeans and an orange blouse." My partner and I sneaked a peek. Duffy said, "I'm trying to score with her, and I told her that I was you guys' manager. Will you guys play along with me? I work here in Malibu and I know this place like the back of my hand. I'll do the same for you if you ever need it. She wants to meet you guys; that's why I told her I was your manager." Marcus and I looked at each other for a second or two and agreed to play along with him. Duffy thanked us and offered again to buy us a drink—this time we accepted his offer and he left for the bar.

Shortly thereafter, Hope and Gayle returned and I asked Gayle if she wanted to dance. She was eager to get on the dance floor. Marcus was talking to Hope when Duffy brought two drinks to the table. While I was on the dance floor I saw Duffy and the woman he was trying to hook up with go upstairs to the supper club. Hope and Marcus joined Gayle and me on the dance floor; we danced for two more songs. People on the dance floor were complimenting us for doing a great job when we did the three songs. I was amazed that the crowd really dug us.

We returned to our table and a couple of minutes later Duffy and his lady came to the table. He introduced the woman whose name was Sarah. Then he said that the owner of the supper club, a man named Norm, wanted to talk to us about booking us with the "Ink Spots," the world famous singing trio. Marcus and I went upstairs and met Norm. Lo and behold, our fake manager, Duffy, had convinced Norm to hire us as the opening act for the Ink Spots. He had done it to impress Sarah, but as it turned out Norm, having heard other customers talking about what a hit we had been downstairs in the Bare Foot Room, agreed to hire us.

The first thing Norm said to us was, "OK, you're hired; I need an act to open for the Ink Spots in two weeks." He continued, "But like I told your manager, I'll pay you $100.00 a night for the both of you and not a penny more." Duffy said, "Guys, I tried to get the $150.00 you asked for, but Norm won't budge. What do you guys say to the $100.00?" Norm said, "It's a take it or leave it offer." Marcus and I looked at each other and Duffy said to Norm, "Give us a few minutes to think it over, and we'll let you know before you close tonight." Norm said, "Take it or leave it." Duffy, Marcus and I went outside to discuss the offer.

I had never in all of my years as a professional singer been paid more than $25.00 for a gig, and that was when I sang at fraternity, or sorority affairs and private parties like Bar Mitzvahs, etc., and as a musician Marcus had never been paid more than $15.00 a night. We got outside and Duffy asked, "Well what do you guys think?" I said, "Hell yeah we'll do it!" Duffy said, "Great. Let's go downstairs like we're talking it over. You guys don't have to pay me a commission for this, but if I get you any more gigs, you can give me ten percent—agreed?" We agreed.

We returned to our table, to find Sarah sitting alone. I looked at the dance floor; Gayle and Hope were not there. I assumed they had gone to the powder room, but before I could ask where they were, Sarah said, "The ladies had to leave but asked me to give you this." She handed me a note which read:

Dear Kal and Marcus;

Please don't be upset; we had to leave, but we promise you will see us again. You guys are wonderful. Thanks for a really great time.
Love,
Gayle & Hope

I was shocked as was Marcus, but we played it off like it was no big deal. We thought for sure they would come back to the Zanzibar the following weekend. Night after night, for the next two weekends Marcus and I anticipated seeing those two gorgeous women walk into the club but they never did.

The Pair Extraordinaire was created
At the end of the evening, Duffy, Marcus and I went upstairs; Duffy told Norm that we would take the gig for $100.00 a night for the two weeks. Duffy added, "If you want them longer than two weeks they'll take an extra $25.00 each per night." Norm said. "It's just for two weeks; if it goes longer than that we'll see." Marcus and I had work to do —on Tuesday night two weeks from now we would open at the "Cliff House" in Malibu with the world famous "Ink Spots," and that was a really big deal. I loved the Ink Spots; they had appeared at Huston-Tillotson during Activities Week my junior year. I had gotten their autographs. Appearing on the bill with the Ink Spots meant that we had entered the "Big Time" for real.

The next day I drove to Marcus' house on Twenty-Sixth Street in Santa Monica. I told Marcus that we needed a thirty-song repertoire. We both knew hundreds of songs, and it was not a problem to select thirty of them. I knew that a thirty song repertoire would allow us to perform ten songs per show since we had an hour to fill. With thirty songs, we would not have to repeat any song unless the audience requested it. We agreed to rehearse every day for the next two weeks in order to be ready. We were trying to think of a suitable name for our act. Joe and Eddie were a famous duo on the folk music circuit at that time, and we briefly considered calling ourselves Marcus and Kal, or Carl and Marcus but we were not impressed with those choices.

When I drove back to my apartment in L.A., I drove out on Santa Monica Blvd. —the 10, Santa Monica Freeway, had not been completed. I drove East on Santa Monica Blvd. I noticed two towers that were being constructed on Little Santa Monica Blvd. and Century Park East, in newly developed Century City. The construction sign advertising the twin towers read: "The Prestigious Pair Coming Soon." I noticed the sign and immediately thought, that would make a good name for our duo. By the time I got home I was convinced that the name was right, except I would drop the word prestigious and just use "The Pair." It was perfect. I called Marcus and told him about the name and he liked the name as much as I did.

We rehearsed every day as planned, and began to realize that we had something unique, but never imagined we would become as successful as we did. One day when Marcus came to my place to rehearse, he showed me a word in his French/English dictionary. The word was "extraordinaire." Marcus said, "How about The Pair Extraordinaire? It has a nice ring to it." It did have a nice ring, plus, it described our act as being unique and special. So, when we opened at the Cliff House we were billed as "The Pair Extraordinaire"

Opening night was incredible—the audience loved our act from the very first song. We opened with the Gene McDaniels hit, "A Hundred Pounds Of Clay" and cooked for an hour, from the first song to the last encore, which was a very funny version of the old Country Western Song "I'm An Old Cow Hand." The entire engagement went so well that although the Ink Spots left after their two weeks were done, The Pair Extraordinaire became the Headliner at the Cliff House, and remained there for six months.

One evening on the way to our gig at the Cliff House, I stopped for a red light at the corner of Chautauqua and PCH and while waiting for the light to change, a burgundy-colored Cadillac convertible stopped alongside us. The gentleman driving the caddy noticed the fingerboard of Marcus' bass fiddle protruding out the front passenger window. He called out to us and asked, "Where are you guys playing?" I answered, "The Cliff House; we're at the Cliff House on PCH." Marcus recognized the driver as the star of the TV series, "Maverick" and said to me: "That's Maverick, James Garner!" I looked and realized that he was right. It was James Garner. When the light changed, James Garner said, "The Cliff House? I'll stop by later."

Well Mr. Garner did not make it that night, but Peter Gowland, who was one of the top photographers to the stars at the time, came in regularly, as did a number of other celebrities. Marcus' mother moved out of her two-bedroom apartment on Hobart near Adams Blvd., in LA and moved in with an elderly lady in Santa Monica to take care of her. Marcus and I took over his mother's apartment on Hobart St. As soon as we moved in, we started rehearsing eight hours a day —four hours in the morning and four hours in the evening. We got our act really tight.

We had been at the Cliff House for five out of the six month run. One night, about three weeks before our closing night, a guy named Al Charles and his lady-friend whose name (like Fiddler Amsterdam's wife's name) was Gypsy. They came to the Cliff House to celebrate his birthday. After our first show that evening, Al invited Marcus and me to join him and Gypsy for a drink. We had not seen too many black people attending our shows, so we were eager to have a drink with Al and his lady. This turned out to be another incredibly lucky meeting. Al Charles was a delightful individual, and Gypsy was an extremely beautiful woman with a winning smile and great personality. They had dinner and stayed for all three shows. We spent all three of our intermissions at their table and by the end of the evening the four of us had become friends. Al was so completely engaging that I gave him the nick name "Tom Jones," which had nothing to do with the singer with that name, but rather it was the name of one of the biggest movies that summer —a film staring Albert Finney and Susannah York. In the film, Albert Finney's character, "Tom Jones," was an adventurous, womanizing, completely adorable free spirit in eighteenth century England. It was the perfect name for Al, and he loved it because he and Gypsy had recently seen and enjoyed the movie.

I shall always remember Al, not only for his fun loving and generous nature, but also because of the really wonderful people that were his friends. Through Al we met and became friends with a lady named Jackie Gardner who would introduce us to Gertrude Gipson (who you read about in Chapter G). Jackie, Yvonne (Jackie's sister), as well as Al's two brothers, Edgar and Vernon Charles became friends. These were golden days; in fact, I wrote a song that became one of the pair's all-time favorite songs to perform. The name of the song is "Where Is The Money" and it was inspired by one of the many catchy and memorable statements that Al used to make in conversation. Al's older brother Edgar Charles owned "The Caribbean Lounge". Al and their younger brother Vernon worked there as bartenders. Edgar and Vernon were great guys, but as far as I'm concerned there will never be another Al "Tom Jones" Charles. Al got "The Pair" booked into the "Caribbean Lounge" just as he had promised to do the night of our first meeting when he and Gypsy came to the Cliff House to celebrate his birthday.

Our opening night at the Caribbean Lounge was two weeks prior to our Tikki Island booking which was on the night of the day when Marcus had picked up the fake gold "Bulova" watches. From there we started playing at high school assemblies, college engagements, and the likes. Shortly thereafter we began to get booked into the top folk music venues such as "The Ice House," "The Golden Bear," "The Mecca," "Warehouse Nine," "The Troubadour," and other top local clubs. Less than a year later we were appearing on a nationally syndicated TV show called "Hollywood A-Go-Go."

The days at the Zanzibar and Cliff House were now fond but distant memories and thoughts of Duffy, Gayle, and Hope, had all but faded. We had landed a record contract on Liberty Records.

I woke up early; it was a red letter day. Today was a day that Marcus and I had no idea would come so soon after forming our partnership. This was the day that "The Pair Extraordinaire" would sign our record deal. The magic hour was set for 3:00pm when we were to be at the record company on Sunset blvd. and Orange in Hollywood. Marcus had gone to visit his mother in Santa Monica the night before and spent the night. He called and said he would be at our apartment by 1:00PM in order to have ample time to get dressed, and be in Hollywood by three.

By now we had signed a management agreement with a fellow named Mitchell Tableporter whom we met through a songwriter friend named Sue Quickle, and her real estate agent husband, Court. Just before 2:00PM the phone rang; it was our manager, Mitch. He informed us that Don Blocker, the head of Liberty Records, had asked him to have us wear one of our stage outfits to the signing because media photographers would be there to get some press shots. We assured Mitch that we would be at Liberty Records offices at ten minutes before three, properly dressed for photos. It was now just after two. We decided to wear black trousers and our paisley roll collar shirts, which would be fresh from the cleaners for the photo shoot.

At 2:15, we left the apartment to pick up the paisley shirts and we put them on and struck out on the twenty minute drive to Hollywood in order to be at the record company by ten minutes to three at the latest. We got our shirts from the cleaners, and got into the car at approximately 2:25, right on schedule, but, would you believe, of all the days for my spotless clean aqua blue 56 Mercury to act up, it acted up then. Why today, and at this time? This had not occurred for several months, but to my utter disbelief, the tumbler in the ignition switch had fallen and I could not get the key into the ignition. Marcus had a confused look on his face, but I reassured him that we would be OK. I tried to put the key into the ignition, but to no avail. I tried for ten minutes; I talked to the car, I pleaded with the key to go in, but no dice. Marcus looked at his fake "gold" Bulova and it was 2:35 and panic time. I said to Marcus, "Is there a locksmith nearby"? He replied, "Not that I know of."

I said, "Let's call Mitch and tell him what happened." There was a phone booth at the Watkins Hotel near the corner of Adams and Western Ave. Marcus said he would take the other side of the street and look for a locksmith. I'd make the call and look on this side of the street for a locksmith.

I was trying my best not to panic. I did not want to be late for the most important event of my career, and perhaps blow this opportunity by being tagged as unreliable. I knew that Marcus was feeling the same vibe. We took off in opposite directions. I walked about ten steps as Marcus was waiting for the light to change so he could cross to the other side of the street. I saw a man approaching. He had a lunch box in his hand. Out of desperation I asked him, "Excuse me, sir, do you happen to know if there is a locksmith nearby?" The guy looked at me and with the happiest sounding voice I ever heard he said, "*I'm* a locksmith." I could not believe it. The light changed but Marcus did not cross the street —instead he turned and started to walk towards the locksmith and me.

The locksmith inserted what looked like a long but narrow fingernail file into the ignition, wiggled it around for about five seconds, and told me to try the key. I got behind the wheel, inserted the key, which went in effortlessly, turned it, and the motor turned over.

That was the sweetest sound I could have heard at that time. I asked how much I owed him; he said, "Don't worry about it; just pass it on by helping someone else in need." I insisted on giving him a five-dollar bill and said, "Please, let us buy your lunch." But he said, "No, really it's OK. See I know you're good guys," and he went on his way. Marcus got in the car, and I waited for traffic to clear so I could pull away from the curb. We heard a car horn honking, and both looked in the direction of the honking. Coming towards us in the opposite direction was an aqua blue '55 Thunderbird convertible. Behind the wheel was Gayle and in the passenger seat Hope. They continued to honk as they drove by smiling and waving at us. We could not believe our eyes. We drove to the record company trying to figure it out. Marcus said, "I'll bet they've been out of town and are back." I asked, "But what are they doing in this part of town?" Marcus: "We can ask them when we see them, cause they'll show up now that we're on our way to becoming big stars." We never saw them again.

We walked into the lobby of the Liberty Records office, and the clock on the wall behind the receptionist desk was at straight up 3:00PM sharp. We signed our contract, had our photos taken, and drove back to the apartment without a hitch. Marcus called his girlfriend, I called my girlfriend and that night we went to the Cliff House and celebrated. Before leaving for the Cliff House, I called my mother to tell her about the record contract. The phone rang, my mother answered, "Hello." I said, "Mudear, guess what?" She replied: "You're gonna make a record." Me: "How did you know that?" The next thing she said took my breath away: "I had a dream; in the dream two very beautiful women were sitting at my kitchen table and we were drinking coffee. They had flaming red hair." I told my mother to hold on just a minute and then I told Marcus to pick up the extension in his bedroom; he picked up the phone, and I said, "I got my mom on the phone and you got to hear what she just told me." Marcus spoke into the phone, "Hi mom, did he tell you the good news?" Me: "She already knew." Marcus: "I mean did you tell her the news about our record deal?" Me: "I'm telling you she already knew about it. Mudear, tell Marcus what you just told me."

Mudear: "I had a dream that two very beautiful women with red hair were sitting at the kitchen table having coffee with me. The youngest one looked to be about nineteen or twenty years old". She said to me, "Your baby is going to be very famous and make all your dreams come true. He's going to make a record you know." The other one was maybe twenty-four or twenty-five, just sat there smiling; she hardly spoke at all." I asked my mother, "What color did you say their hair was? Was one of them a Blonde?" She replied, "They both had beautiful red hair. I have never seen hair that color of red. The dream was so real that when I got up this morning I went straight to the kitchen to see if the coffee cups were still there, but there was no sign of the cups or any coffee being made. That's the reason I know it had to be a dream. Did y'all make a record yesterday?" Marcus: "No ma'am, but we signed a recording contract with Liberty Records today around three o'clock."

I proceeded to tell her the whole story of how we had met Gayle and Hope, and how we had not seen them for nearly a year until today when my car wouldn't start. Marcus said, "The whole thing was strange from the very beginning. How they disappeared that night after Duffy got us hired to open for the 'Ink Spots,' and the locksmith thing." He told her about the locksmith appearing out of nowhere. When we finished telling her the whole story my mother said: "They were Angels." I said, "Angels?" Mudear said: "I know you might find it hard to believe, but they were Angels, no doubt in my mind." Me: (Still a bit skeptical), "Are all angels white?"

Mudear: "I don't know the answer to that, but I believe God don't discriminate." She said to me, "Honey, don't you even think about that; just thank God for watching over you and making your dream come true."

Marcus: "The locksmith wasn't white, he was black." Then he asked, "Mom did they say anything else?" Mudear "The only thing the older one said was that you're good friends and they see you all the time." Marcus: "We haven't seen them but twice." Mudear: "That don't mean they don't see you." She continued: "Now don't y'all go around telling everybody about this. Folks will think you're crazy and you'll get nothing but ridicule. Don't stop your blessings —Jesus said, 'Cast not your pearls before swine.' This is between you and God, and that's how y'all need to keep it." When we got off the phone Marcus called his mother, who was a deeply religious Christian woman. We told her the whole story, and when we told her what my mother had said about the women being angels, she agreed and also told us not to talk about it for the same reason my mother had given.

That night at the Cliff House Marcus ordered amaretto and orange juice and I ordered Tawaka and milk over crushed ice. When our dates tasted our drinks, they never ordered anything else for as long as we dated them. Over the years, I have ordered amaretto and orange juice or Tawaka and milk over crushed ice only for the women that I was serious about. And true to my mother's words, I have not spoken to anyone else about "Gayle" and Hope.

We never saw those women again although we were on the lookout for them at every performance. The years passed, and strange things would happen from time to time. It became second nature for Marcus and me to attribute anything unusual to Hope and Gayle. We spoke about it only to each other until one day I saw Donna Summer on a talk show. I'm not sure if it was on Oprah or the Tonight Show or Arsenio Hall, but I'm almost certain it was Donna Summer. Ms. Summer was telling a story that goes something like this:

After months and months of pounding the pavement of New York trying to get a break to no avail, she was on the brink of giving up her dream of becoming a successful singer. One day she was walking down Broadway feeling dejected when a man whom she had never seen before started to walk along beside her. According to Donna Summer, the man started to talk to her. The stranger told her to go to a certain building at a particular time of day and she would meet someone who would help get her career moving in the right direction. Then all of a sudden the man was gone; she said it was as though he had vanished. She looked in every direction for the man who had spoken to her just a few seconds ago, but he was nowhere to be found.

Being almost desperate to get a break, and feeling that she had nothing to lose, Ms. Summer went to the building at the time the stranger had suggested. While entering the building, she met someone who became instrumental in making her the huge success that she later became. Like each of the chapters in this book, the Donna Summer episode is written from my recollection, and might not be exactly word for word what Ms. Summer said, but the bottom line of her story is exactly what she communicated to the talk show host that day. Donna recounted this incident and said that she was convinced that the vanishing stranger that had told her where to go, and when to be there, was an angel.

Ever since that TV show, I have wanted to meet Ms. Summer, not only because of her talent as a singer, and her celebrated work as a fine artist, but mostly to share our story of angels being directly responsible for the formation and the success of "The Pair Extraordinaire." I have heard other such stories, but to hear a public figure like Donna Summer share her belief with a national television audience must have been reassuring to others like myself who have had a similar experience. Our "guardian angels" encounter began that fateful evening at the Zanzibar and led us to the Cliff House and the "Ink Spots" gig. It culminated with Marcus and me seeing Gayle and Hope driving by and honking at us during the locksmith incident on the day we signed our record deal. I have not physically seen the ladies since that day, but I know that somebody up there likes me, and

I choose to believe that Gayle and Hope have a lot to do with it. In January 1965, we recorded our first album on Liberty Records, "The Pair Live at The Ice House."

Three years later, when we were preparing to record our fourth album on the Liberty Records label, we received a phone call from Jack Tracy, our record producer for that album. Jack told me that he had a song that he wanted us to listen to. He said the moment he heard the song we were the first artists to come to mind. Jack said he would stop by our house tomorrow and play it for us. Marcus and I shared a huge house at 7927 Hillside Ave. at the top of Fairfax in the Hollywood Hills. The next day Jack Tracy came over and played the demo. He placed the acetate on the turntable and explained that the song was written by Barry Mann and Cynthia Wild. When he said that the title was "Angelica," pronounced An-ge-lica, Marcus and I looked at each other but said nothing. When I heard the first two bars of the song I knew we would record it. The opening lyrics were: "Each night I meant to say/I miss her through the day," Halfway through the song I said, "I love it." Marcus said, "This song was written for The Pair."

The head of Liberty Records was now Bud Dane. He was married to our neighbor, the talented singer, Jackie DeShannon at the time, and had told Jack the song was not right for her. Jack Tracy said if we did not want to record the song he would shop it to Johnny Mathis. I felt that if Johnny had gotten hold of the song he probably would have recorded it and no doubt would have done an excellent job with it, but I knew that An-ge-lica was my song. Marcus and I both believed that nobody could perform that song as well as us. We believed, and I still believe that it was sent to us by our angels, Angelica Gayle and Hope. If I ever run into Barry and Cynthia, I want to ask them where the idea for that song came from. I attended a lot of ASCAP—(American Society of Composers, Authors, and Publishers) meetings and gatherings but have not run into them, as yet.

We recorded the song and it was the only song that we performed every single night, in every show for as long as The Pair Extraordinaire was together. We felt sure that sooner or later Hope and Gayle would show up at one of our shows. They never did, but to this very day it is still one of my all-time favorite ballads—written by an artist other than myself. When I think of the recordings we made, it is one of the first songs that come to mind. The song still haunts me, and ever since I started to write this chapter that song has been in my head every day and every night. Unlike other songs by other artists that occasionally get stuck in my mind until I get tired of hearing them in my head, I happily embrace the soothing melody and the beautiful and moving words to Angelica.

After we gained popularity across the board (i.e., live concerts, Las Vegas main showrooms, record sales, and television appearances) I began to get approached by record company executives, producers, managers and related industry people. They would tell me that I should leave the Pair Extraordinaire and break out on my own. Their main rationale was, "Why share your fame and money with another person? After all, you're the singer and the Pair's fans will follow you." I never took their advice because I did not want the headache of putting up with bands on tour after seeing bands demanding more money or quitting, and leaving you on the road, trying to use a pick up band, or having the tour canceled.

I have never been motivated by greed, but I did not strike out on my own mostly because traveling with Marcus was fun. We connected on so many levels. We had our squabbles for sure, but they did not overrule the fun we had on and off stage. We could rely on each other and we did not have issues over things like women, and egos or jealousy —the thing that caused most groups or duos to split up. We had only one dispute over money. Here's what went down. As I stated before Marcus was the most generous person I've ever known, plus he was notoriously extravagant. One evening while we were on tour with Cosby, I arrived at the arena where we were appearing. I went to the dressing room. Cosby was getting dressed. I walked in and said: "What's up Bill?" Bill looked at me and didn't respond. At first I thought he was going to pull a joke or something, but then I picked up his vibe and knew that something was bugging him. So I asked, "What's going on man?" He looked at me with that icy stare and replied: "So you don't want to pay me back my money huh?" For an instant I just thought he had to be pulling something on me. So I said, "How much money do I owe you? Now, I could see that he was dead serious when he said, "You know how much money you and Marcus borrowed, and Ron (Bill's road manager) said that he was going to deduct it from you guy's check and you refused to agree to his taking the $1500 that you owe on the debt." I was baffled because I have never borrowed money from Cosby or anyone else associated with Bill. I asked Bill. "When did I borrow any money from you or Ron?" Cosby: "You and Marcus borrowed three thousand dollars last week, and were supposed to have it deducted from your pay this week". ME: Bill, I don't have a clue what you're talking about." Cosby was staring at me with that look that I never wanted to see in his eyes. I said: "Let me talk to Marcus, and find out what's going on because I don't borrow money from people," I added, "But if I owe you money I'll pay it so don't sweat it". I left the dressing room and went looking for Marcus. He and I had come to the arena together, so I knew he was around somewhere.

I caught up with him back stage near the wings. I was so angry that I was shaking. ME: "Marcus, what's this bullshit about you borrowing three grand from Bill, and telling Ron that I was going to pay half of it back?" Marcus: --seeing the state I was in quickly explained: "It was a mistake man. I never told Ron that you were going to pay half the money back."

ME: "With the money you're making, why are you borrowing from people?"

Marcus: I just needed to… ME: (interrupting him) "I don't give a damn what you needed or why you needed it. But don't you ever, include me in your dumb ass schemes. You got Bill pissed off at me for some bullshit that I know nothing about whatsoever." Marcus: "I'm sorry man; it was a mistake."

ME: "You bet your ass it was a mistake, and I don't appreciate it one damn bit. Come on! Go in there, and tell Bill the truth and melt that ice that's in his eyes." Marcus: "I'm really sorry man; where's Bill?" ME: "He's in the dressing room pissed off at *me*. Come on and clean that bullshit up".

When we got to the dressing room Cos was not there. We looked around for him, but couldn't find him. I told Marcus that he needed to find Bill and set things straight. I went for a walk inside the arena because the show would start in about an hour, and I knew I could not go on stage with the feeling that was coursing through my body. I went back to the dressing room about thirty minutes later. Marcus was not there, but I know he must have straightened things out because when Cos came in, the ice in his eyes was gone, and there was no lemon in his voice. Things went on as usual and Bill never brought it up again. Marcus later told me that when he explained what had happened about the money he had borrowed without my knowing about it, Cosby just looked at him, shook his head and said, "Pi-ti-ful. That was the one time that Marcus and I clashed over money.

A year or so later Marcus and I were laughing about the incident. Marcus said to me: "Do you remember that night in Winnipeg when you got pissed at me for borrowing money from Cos, and Ron thought you were going to pay half of it back?" ME: "How could I forget that?" Marcus: "You were so pissed off that if you had not taken a walk and cooled off before show time, you might've gone on stage and subconsciously said something like 'Ladies and Gentleman I want you to sit back and relax while I put foot to Marcus' ass.' Then I asked him, "Marcus what were you doing with your money?" Marcus: "Man I was just partying, and when I spent all my money the fools that I was partying with could not be found" I Looked at Marcus, shook my head slowly and said—in my best Cosby imitation, "Pi-ti-ful. We had a good laugh over it.

There were some issues between us later on when we finally called it quits, but we split before it irreparably damaged our friendship. Eventually, however, I discovered that drugs were becoming a problem with Marcus. I now had a family, and I knew I could not trust or rely on a druggie.

In 1976 when I was on my way to Dallas to bury my beloved mother (may God bless her beautiful soul, and may she rest in peace), I boarded the plane at LAX. I was seated in the first class section. Before take-off, to my surprise, Marcus boarded. We talked briefly and after take-off I went back and sat with him. He explained that he had to get out of L.A., and away from the crowd that he had fallen in with. I asked him if he was "sprung" (meaning addicted to cocaine) and he said, "If I'm not, I gotta get outta here or it's bound to happen." I had seen major signs, which is one of the reasons I split from the duo. He was genuinely sad that my mom had died and was rather hurt that I had not told him about it. The truth is, when he started hanging with his new crowd I did not see or talk to him much. His mother, Mrs. Thelma Brown-who I called mom, treated me as her son and my mother who Marcus called mom, treated Marcus as her son, as well. He had to change planes in Dallas in order to get to his destination, New York City. He was going to stay with his sister, Sandra, and get his life back on track and thankfully he did.

Marcus wrote a play that ran on Broadway for twelve weeks. The name of his play was "Innocent Black and The Five Brothers," starring Melba Moore, with music by the Whitehead Brothers, and produced on Broadway by Gloria Hope Shear. It should have run longer because the black churches up and down the eastern seaboard had pretty much booked it solid for another six months, but I hear that New York politics can be brutal. I attended the opening in 1983 and thoroughly enjoyed it.

When the flight landed in Dallas we stayed in the airport and went into United Airlines Million Mile Club Lounge and had several drinks. We reminisced about the past and talked about the future. We talked about the great ten year run we had enjoyed together from 1964 to 1974. We spoke at length about our good fortune of hooking up and becoming friends of Bill and Camille Cosby. We talked about my family, and Marcus repeatedly told me how lucky I was to have a beautiful wife and two wonderful sons (my youngest son had not yet been born). We then talked about his mother and his dad and stepmother, both of whom I knew well. We continued to drink and share memories. His two-hour layover seemed to go by in 30 minutes. It was a sad but hopeful parting. Sad because my mom had died, and sad because we knew that it was final: The Pair Extraordinaire had officially ended.

When his flight was announced we shook hands and embraced. When we looked at each other there were tears in Marcus' eyes, and I could a feel a tear running slowly down my face. It was a hopeful parting because he recognized that he was sprung, and realized that he did not want his life to end as a drug addict. After he got married he cleaned up and never looked back. A few years later, Cosby contacted Marcus and hired him as a writer on "The Cosby Show."

His family thanked me profusely for the way I represented myself. His wife told me she would always cherish the poem I wrote that was read at his funeral. His parents felt the same way, and expressed it to me. The statement I made earlier in this chapter is true: some days I think of the time we shared on this earth and I miss him. In life, I did not know how much our friendship and our time on stage together meant to me.

In 1987 a friend of mine that lived next door to Marcus in New York came to visit me at my home in Altadena, California. He was the first to inform me that Marcus had only a short time to live. I gave him a CD that I was working on at the time. One of the songs on it was a song that Marcus and I wrote. It was our first hit record. The name of the song is "In the Beginning." When my friend, Casey Daniels, returned to New York he called me and told me that when he gave the CD to Marcus, Marcus grabbed it from his hand almost viciously, and clutched it to his chest, and did not say another word. Before Casey left Marcus' apartment, he said that Marcus was lying quietly. His breathing was labored, but he seemed somehow soothed by having received the CD, even though he had not yet heard it. Three weeks later Marcus died.

The Cosby show that aired the week after his passing ran a statement to Marcus from Bill. It said, "In memory of Marcus Hemphill, See you later, Man." Marcus would have loved it.

To my musical partner and dear friend **Aurelius Marcus Hemphill**, I send to you thoughts of friendship and love, and deep into the quiescent realm of expanding eternity where you rest in peace I send... **a Heartfelt Thank You.** (See Hemphill photo pages).

CHAPTER

I

INVICTUS
By
William Ernest Henley; 1849-1903

Out of the night that covers me,
Black as the pit from pole to pole,
I thank whatever gods may be
for my unconquerable soul.

In the fell clutch of circumstance
I have not winced nor cried aloud.
Under the bludgeoning of chance
My head is bloody, but unbowed.

Beyond this place of wrath and tears
Looms but the horror of the shade,
And yet the menace of the years
Finds, and shall find me, unafraid

It matters not how strait the gate,
How charged with punishments the scroll,
I am the master of my fate;
I am the captain of my soul

CHAPTER

J

Joe Jackson

Unfortunately, not all fathers who are well known get the recognition they deserve. One such father, in my opinion, is a man whose very name will ignite controversy, and will likely cause venomous words of protest and outrage to be spewed across the pages of this book. That man is **Joe Jackson,** the father of "The Jackson Five." Before you storm off to the refrigerator in ravenous disgust, let me explain from the point of view of a black man, who is a father, a teacher, and a modestly **celebrated artist.** `

I am prepared for the typical reaction that I get from almost everyone when I say that I respect Joe Jackson. When I explain why I respect him, most will admit that my reasons make sense, but their initial reactions usually run the gamut from snickering, to guffaw, to howling belly laughs, to outrage, and disgust. These are typical responses from my friends, be they black, white, brown, yellow, red or whatever. Here are my reasons; may you be the judge. We often hear about the stern discipline under which he raised his children, but most people do lip service to the lack of discipline that is often found among kids in much of the black community nowadays. Worse yet, many of those same people have absolutely no idea what it takes to raise a male child in the inner-cities of America. I do not like to use the word "ghetto" because that particular word should not apply to African-American communities, no matter how deep the suffering, how bad the squalor, the meanness, and human degradation black folks encounter from both within and outside of their community.

Excuse me if I digress, but the word "ghetto" is a misapplied and, sadly, accepted concept that belonged to another oppressed people at a time of rampant and legalized attempts to exterminate, under the fear and hate mongering regime of Adolph Hitler. The attempted genocide that was perpetrated upon the Jewish people occupies a different chapter of the same hideous book that includes the malignant slave trading practices that were the most lucrative and sinister tools of commerce ever known to man.

It is a well known historical fact that long before the continent of Africa began to lose her sons and daughters to European and Western commerce, the Jews had been enslaved by the Pharaohs of Egypt. Long after their great spiritual leader Moses gained their freedom they were and, still today, are hated and maligned. Some say it's because of their approach to dealing with the Palestinians, who in my opinion also deserve to have a place to live on this earth, free from occupation. Some say it is due to the "throw a rock and hide the hand" antics that some Jews have been accused of using to exploit unsuspecting people.

I believe that many Jewish people today are feared and hated because of their creative and enterprising spirit, their focused hard work, and relentless determination to succeed. To believe that the Jewish people as a whole are thieves defies logic, and flies in the face of reality. No doubt some people of Jewish persuasion are thieves, just as some Italians are murderers, some blacks are stupid, some Latinos are rapists, some Asians are corrupt, some Native Americans are drunks and so forth and so on. I think it is obvious to most that any type of individual you find in one race you'll find in every race of people.

I am willing to honor their excellence, I am open to learn from their suffering and I will even acknowledge and, where possible emulate, their triumphant "go for the jugular," type of business acumen. Blacks especially, should emulate this aspect, but not in a radical way. But by no means should we accept the legacy of their misfortune, by calling the black community a "ghetto." Jewish people themselves have distanced themselves from the notion of ever living in a "Ghetto" again. The mere suggestion would evoke an automatic cry of "Never Again," as well it should.

In my view, the state of the inner-city in America, as it stands today is worse than were the ghettos of Eastern Europe before the syphilis-carrying madman's, almost successful attempt, to dehumanize and destroy an entire people. It would be wise to emulate the fact that nearly every dollar in the Jewish community touches at least seven different Jewish hands before it leaves the community. According to a published report from the "Black Think Tank"—a television show hosted by Tavis Smiley on CNN during Black History Month, every dollar in the black community leaves the community the first time it is spent.

No matter how poor a Jewish neighborhood might be in today's world, the Jews that inhabit them do not live in ghettos. They have long since thrown off the mental shackles that the word ghetto so subtly applies. You may say, "well it's just a word," but I say that while it might appear to be just a word—that a word, any word in itself, has little or no meaning—it is the idea behind the word that resonates in the psyche, and transports the sustenance that gives it meaning. So why should African-Americans accept the psychological defeat that is inherent in the very image of living in "The Ghetto"? They should not, because there is no good, productive, or uplifting reason to do so.

I began this chapter by stating that I respect Joe Jackson as a father. Whether or not he is a complete or good father will no doubt be debated well into the future, but now let's deal with the facts as we know them and the truth as I believe it to be.

Joe Jackson did not just raise a child he raised six boys and three girls in Gary, Indiana—a city that was known for its less than savory, less than safe places in the areas where most African-Americans lived. In fact, for decades it was purported to be one of the worst cities in America when it came to crime, violence, and poverty. I distinctly remember when Gary, Indiana was considered the "Murder Capitol of The World," according to the broadcast media in the 1970's. Imagine what it would be like to raise six male black sons in Watts, Compton, South Side Chicago, Detroit, Dallas, South Bronx, or any of the urban centers that are located in inner-city America, which some still call "ghettos."

As a father, Mr. Jackson needs to be commended for doing whatever it took to make a life for his family, and for keeping his boys out of the slave camps which we know are called penal institutions. Many, if not most successful black men got spankings or whippings. One of the most beloved and successful entertainers in the world, Stevie Wonder, refers to this in his great song, "I Wish."

'Trying your best to bring the water to your eyes /thinking it might stop her/from whipping your behind/I wish those days/could come back once more/ why did those days ever have to go, cause I loved them so.'

Here again, I am not saying that you should or should not spank or use corporal discipline on your child. That is not a decision I'm qualified to make for anyone other than myself. I am, however, qualified to state the obvious, which is that young men today need strong leadership that is put forth in a way that will inspire them to accept (and in later years appreciate) guidance, correction, and self discipline. Mr. Joe Jackson is one who dared to provide that type of "tough love." In spite of all the criticism from the media, the public, and even from his own children, he stands firm, facing it all in a manner that is unwavering and consistent. Some will ask, "What about his wife, why have you not mentioned her role in keeping vigil over her brood?" My answer to that question is simple. There is nothing that needs be said about that gracious and gentle lady. She is, in my eyes and in the eyes of many in this often mean-spirited world, above reproach.

Is she some kind of angel? Why not? If there are angels among us, her character and quiet dignity through all she has had to endure as the mother of the most famous African-American family in the world, I think that Mrs. Katherine Jackson would be among the most worthy to qualify for such an honor. That in itself also speaks for the good fortune, and unsung, and perhaps peculiar wisdom of Joe Jackson.

There seems to be at least one undeniable fact about him, and that is, when his children have had to face the "slings and arrows of outrageous fortune," so to speak, or the "firey darts" of a gluttonous media, or even the ridicule from some of his own family members, he has not dodged the attempted slander. He has not hidden from his accusers, nor has he whimpered and caved in to the various kinds of pressures that would have put all but the strongest among us on a fast train to Camarillo. Mr. Joe Jackson, in my opinion, is the kind of man that every father (albeit with certain modifications) wants to be. Even as he stands today, he certainly is a man, and one that African-American men and women in particular should respect and admire. When The Jackson Five were young, they were prime targets for routine exploitation by the expert exploiters in Hollywood whose reputation and *raison d'être* were notoriously vicious. Joe Jackson and Berry Gordy stood in the gap against the malevolent exploits that thrived on the young, talented and unprotected.

Their often criticized and maligned stewardship was the primary reason that The Jackson Five did not suffer the cruel and humiliating fate that was the rule rather than the exception for far too many successful African-America entertainers. We know the long list of those who died penniless and broken. The mansions that were built, the exotic cars that darted between Hollywood, Beverly Hills, and the sand and surf of Southern California beaches, were enjoyed by those who used them up, burned them out and tossed them aside like empty bent beer cans that are crushed and collected by the homeless.

Through the years, it came to be that not all of these merchants of exploitation needed the Palm Springs sun to maintain the dark chocolate skin color they were born with. Joe Jackson, and the iron hand with which he ruled, kept Michael and Janet safe from the ravenous exploitation that they themselves must now realize, was the historical destiny that awaited every fresh and gullible "star." To have entered the backbiting, money-grabbing, spirit-breaking fray without someone who is savvy and honest, or "crazy" enough to not be conned or intimidated, would have been predictably tragic. Joe Jackson should be given the "Golden Crazy Award" for protecting his gifted kids until those kids themselves knew that they were adult enough to move on without him, and against his will, if necessary.

When his son, Michael, went through the recent trial, Joe Jackson was there, wanted or not. When he walked with his pressure-ridden family into that courtroom every day, it was clear to me that Joe Jackson was ready to take a bullet for his son without hesitation, and that nobody was going to mess with Michael. That's the kind of father I'd want to be, should (God forbid) I ever have to face similar circumstances.

So then, **Mr. Joe Jackson**, who I have never met, or ever (to my knowledge) been in the presence of, wherever you are, whatever you are doing, I wish you, your dear wife, and your family all the best, all the time, and I hope you will read this book, and accept from me **A Simple, Though knowingly, Controversial Thank You**, for being who you are.

Chapter

K

John F. Kennedy

John Fitzgerald Kennedy, thirty-fifth President of the United States of America.

November 1963 was a memorable month in the minds of most Americans who are over forty years of age. The most common memory we share is the assassination of President John F. Kennedy in Dallas on November 22 of that year.

I have memories not only of the assassination, but I also recall the whole atmosphere around the killing. My interests were immediate and compelling because —although I did not witness the actual shooting, I was there, in Dallas, at the parade, when it happened. More importantly, as things unfolded, it turned out that I knew some of the people and places that were involved. I had ties to the Texas School Book Depository, where Lee Harvey Oswald was said to have fired the shot that some folks believe killed the president.

My sister Frankie Roland was the pharmacist at Parkland Hospital, and her pharmacy was located right next to the emergency room where President Kennedy was taken. She witnessed his arrival and the hysteria that followed.

Frankie described the tremendous grief and uncontrollable panic that gripped Jackie Kennedy. She said that Governor Connally was conscious when he arrived, and Mrs. Connally was in total control and comforting her husband. To be fortunate enough to have a sister who was an eyewitness to the chaotic hospital scene has yielded some much appreciated first-hand information.

My late boyhood friend, John Henry Johnson's, stepdad was named Thomas "Sheeby" Shields. Sheeby, as everybody called him, was the warehouse "straw boss" at the Texas School Book Depository. Mr. Shields would sometime give his stepson John Henry fifty cents an hour to unload and stack books. John Henry got his stepdad to hire me one summer when we were in high school. Sheeby told John Henry and me to meet him at the back entrance of the Texas School Book Depository on a Saturday morning at 7:30 AM. Our job was to unload the books from the push-baskets and stack them wherever Sheeby told us to stack them and to box the loose books that were already stacked. We would be paid two dollars for four hours work. John Henry and I took the bus to downtown and waited at the rear door as directed. Who could have dreamed that years later this building would be the site of a plot to kill the president of the United States?

We waited for Mr. Shields an hour and a half but he still had not arrived. John Henry called his mom and told her that Sheeby was not at the depository. She informed him that Sheeby was still asleep. She said she had tried to wake him but he would not wake up. She said that he stayed out late and had come home drunk. We were told to come back home because he would probably need to sleep off his drunk. We went home and sure enough Sheeby was still asleep, and would sleep for most of the day.

I don't know if John Henry ever went back to the depository to work. I did not go back because Sheeby never asked us. That next summer I started to get a few singing jobs and when I went off to college I was not available, nor was I interested in stacking books at the Texas School Book Depository.

The other personal and direct connection to this tragic and life changing story is with Jack Ruby the man who shot and killed Lee Harvey Oswald on national TV. Jack Ruby was a night club owner, whom I had met as a young man. It is tragic for obvious reasons, and life changing for me, because I had recently been hired as the house vocalist at a fabulous little nightclub, "The Galaxy." My plan was to sing at the Galaxy for a year then return to L.A. and resume building my career which had been making progress when I was drafted into the Armed Forces.

The pain I felt and the confusion and heaviness that gripped the city caused me to change my plans. Instead of staying in Dallas for a year, I left for Los Angeles on January 5, 1964, a month and a half after the assassination.

Jack Ruby hired a lot of black musicians. Joe Johnson, was a local musician with legendary status, and had the House band at Ruby's Club

Vegas out on Oak Lawn near Lemon Ave. Almost all of the nightclubs jobs, private parties, and other social gatherings hired black musicians except for country music dance clubs and bars. The truth of the matter is, until the Beatles came along, there were not very many young white musicians except classical, country western, bluegrass, and big band players. This started to change after the Beatles set the tone, and white kids began to learn to play "rock and roll" guitar and other instruments.

My relationship with Jack Ruby was as a waiter to customers, and musician to club owner. It began after Jack Ruby had heard me singing at a private night club called "Artist of Dallas Club"—a club that was primarily for musicians and other professional entertainers. I can't recall who the owner or owners were. I think it might have been owned by a group of musicians, or maybe, by the local musicians union. I worked there one summer as a singing waiter. I only saw Jack Ruby three times. The first time was the night when he, another man and two women came to the Artist of Dallas club. I took their order and when I went to the bar to fill the order, the other waiter-a white guy whose name escapes me, said to me: "You know who that is don't you?" I replied, "A famous musician?" He said "That's Jack Ruby so take good care of them." I knew who Jack Ruby was, but I don't think I had ever seen him. Local musicians usually know who the club owners are. I knew that he owned the Carousel Club in downtown Dallas and the Vegas Club out on Oak Lawn near Lemon Ave. It was well known by all the local musicians, and I can tell you straight up, that Jack Ruby was definitely a gangster, and he didn't mind letting it be known. Joe Johnson, a tenor saxophone player, had the house band. And according to Joe, and some of the musicians that worked with him regularly, Jack Ruby was moody and temperamental. Some nights he would greet you cordially, and some nights he might not say anything.

The two songs that he especially liked were, "When the Saints Go Marching In," and "Straighten Up and Fly Right." He ran his clubs like a mother hen over her chicks. If he liked you, you were in, but if he did not like you, you just stayed away. He liked musicians in general and was liked by the ones that worked for him, and always paid them well--$10.00 per night when the going rate was $7.00. It is also rumored that he was close to Candy Barr, and Chris Colt and her Colt Forty-Fives—the two most famous strippers in the history of Dallas. Jewel Brown said that they came into the Carousel Club from time to time, but they never came in together, even though it is said that they were good friends.

That night at the Artist of Dallas Club I took Jack Ruby and his party's order; the guy at the table handed me a bill, and told me to keep the change. The drinks they ordered cost $2.50 each, making a total of $10.00. The lighting in the Artist of Dallas club was subdued and I assumed that the guy had given me a twenty dollar bill (a good waiter never counts a tip in front of the customer), but when I got back to the bar to fill an order I'd taken from another table, I realized that the man had given me a hundred dollar bill. I had never been given a hundred dollar tip before so I took extra good care of them, making sure that I kept their ash tray emptied and wiped clean. Each time I went to my tables I would use a little catch phrase that the customers liked. I would say, "Please excuse this extra good waiter while I tidy up a bit for you." I kept an eye on their drinks and at the appropriate time I'd go to their table and say, "Excuse this extra good waiter but would you like another drink?" I served them two round of drinks before the band took an intermission. Jack Ruby paid for the second round and gave me a three dollar tip.

Just before each intermission I would go to the bandstand and sing my three song set. Then the band would play one song and announce the intermission. When I finished my set I would thank the audience for their applause and announce my own name. Then I would say," How about a round of applause for this marvelous band." Just before leaving the bandstand my closing remarks were; "Drink hearty, be with the party, and don't bother nobody." It drew warm applause and laughter. Then I would make the rounds to my tables and take care of my customers. This was the time when most people would order another drink. They would chat with me, saying how much they enjoyed my singing, etc. They usually tipped better after I sang. I went to Jack Ruby's table to refresh their drinks after my song, and the gentleman that had paid for the first round of drinks asked me what bill he had given me when he paid for the drinks. I told him he had been most generous to this extra good waiter; "You gave me a hundred dollar bill." He replied. "You are an extra good waiter and a pretty good singer, but not that good. I intended to give you a twenty dollar bill when I told you to keep the change, not a hundred." I said, "Sorry sir." I took the hundred dollar bill from my wallet and gave it back to him.

Jack Ruby and the two women never spoke during this exchange. I thanked the man and said I was sorry for the mistake; he said, "Not at all, it was my mistake not yours." He took out a twenty dollar bill, handed it to me, and said give me a ten. I gave him a five and five singles. For the remainder of the evening I made it a point to take extra good care of them, and kept a good attitude. During the evening various people stopped at their table and a couple of them sent drinks to them. The musicians returned to the bandstand, Ruby and his party stayed throughout the set. Just before I was to sing my second set I went to their table, and asked if they had any special request. Jack Ruby said, "Do you sing 'When the saints go marching in?' I said "Yes sir I do." The hundred dollar bill guy asked me, "Do you know who this is?"

I replied, "Everybody knows who Mr. Jack Ruby is." This seemed to please Ruby; he took out a five spot placed it on the table and said, "That song makes me happy, sing it good for me". I said, "For you Mr. Ruby, I'll do my best rendition."

I finished my set and proceeded to make my rounds to check on my tables. When I got to Jack Ruby's table they were getting ready to leave. Their entire party was now in a good mood. Jack Ruby asked me if I knew where his night clubs were located. I answered in the affirmative. He asked me if I knew Jewel Brown; I said yeah, Jewel sings at your Carousel Club. She's a friend of mine. JR: "Yeah she's a great singer and a great gal" I agreed. Then he said as they were standing up to leave, "Come see me at the Carousel, I like your style." ME: "Thank you, when should I stop by?" Jack Ruby: "Tuesday, come by Tuesday night around seven o'clock." ME: "Will do, and please say hello to Jewel for me." He nodded indicating that he would. I thanked them all for coming and asked them to come back and sit in my station, so I can work on getting that $100 tip. The hundred bill guy said, "You're gonna have to clean a lot of ash trays." They all laughed, and I joined in. As they left the club, people stopped them and you could tell that Jack Ruby enjoyed all the attention. The next time I saw Jewel Brown she told me that Jack Ruby mentioned that he might hire me sometime. She said she would put in a good word for me, and keep me on his mind.

The following Tuesday night I went by the Carousel Club as requested. I walked in right at seven o'clock; the place was practically empty except for a few people at the bar. The waiters were setting the room for the dinner crowd. I told one of the waiters my name, and said that I was here to see Mr. Ruby. Jack Ruby was seated at the corner of the bar. When he heard his name mentioned he looked in my direction, recognized me, and beckoned me forward. I went to the bar and without looking up from his paper work he patted on the empty bar stool next to him indicating for me to sit. Again without looking up he said, "Give me a minute." I said "Sure, I didn't mean to interrupt." He didn't respond, but he called to the waiter who was backing the bar and told him to bring me a drink. I told the bar backer I'd like a gin and tonic. He brought me the drink and I sat quietly waiting for Jack Ruby to complete his paper work while I sipped my drink and surveyed the room.

The Carousel was a very nice little supper club, with globed candles on the tables, napkins and silverware neatly placed, sparkling clean water glasses, the usual fare, but with a touch of class. Approximately five minutes passed when Jack Ruby put his pen into his shirt pocket, placed the paperwork in a neat pile, looked at me and said: "How you doing?" I replied, "I'm doing good; thanks for asking"—that's a phrase I picked up from a movie, and used especially when I wanted to make a good impression; it worked, Ruby seemed surprised but pleased with my response. I quickly asked, "Is Jewel working tonight?" I knew the answer to that question but I wanted to make a friendly connection. He replied,

"She's in on Thursday, Friday, Saturday and Sunday." ME: "That's right today's Tuesday." JR: "I got nothing for you right now but I might have a couple of nights coming up at my Vegas club; you know where that is?" ME: "Oak Lawn and Lemon area." He nodded and said, "Finish your drink. I gotta take care of some things." He stood up and said as he started to leave, "Check with me from time to time and I'll also tell Jewel if something comes up." ME: "I will, and thanks for the time and the drink." JR: "Enjoy your drink." He went into the kitchen area. I downed the rest of my drink, and left. When I stood up to leave, I said to the bar backer "Thanks." He said, "Yeah, anytime". I understood what he meant. The Carousel was a white only club, as was the Club Vegas and all of the clubs in Dallas at the time. The only black club in downtown Dallas in the 50"s and 60's was the "Waiters and Porters Club," but that's the way it was all over the South and in many places "up North."

The next time I saw Jewel Brown I told her about my meeting with Jack Ruby at the Carousel Club. She told me that he had mentioned it to her. She said, "Jack likes you. He said you seem like a good kid; I told him that you are a very nice person and a good singer." ME: "Thanks Jewel." Jewel: "I know you'd do the same for me." ME: "Damn straight I would." Jewel: "Just take good care of him and his friends when they come to The Artist of Dallas club. And don't piss him off; you might be the first colored male singer to work the Carousel." Me: "You think so?" Jewel: "I told you he likes you. I might be going on the road with ZZ Hill for two weeks. If that gig comes through I'll drop a lug (put in a good word) for you with Jack as my replacement." ME: "Cool, that'll be real cool."

The third and last time I saw jack Ruby in person, was towards the end of that summer. He came back to the Artist of Dallas Club. That time he was with a really pretty woman, but was seated on another waiter's station. When I did my three songs at the end of the second set I acknowledged him by saying: "Ladies and gentleman I would like to end this set by dedicating my last number to one of the premier night club owners in the city of Dallas, and in the whole State of Texas; How about a big round of applause for Mr. Jack Ruby." The audience applause was warm but not overwhelming. Ruby loved it. He waved his hand in the air, and at me. I started to sing "When the Saints Go Marching In." Jack Ruby and the woman he was with clapped loudly, and did the same when I ended the song.

I left the stage and before I made my rounds to the customers seated in my station, I asked the waiter in whose section Ruby and his date were seated, if it was ok if I stopped by Jack Ruby's table to say hello. The waiter said yeah, it's Ok. My asking his permission was more than a courtesy. I don't know how it is nowadays but back then, if you had a big tipper or an important person seated at one of your tables, a lot of waiters did not want other waiters talking to their special customers. Since I was the only black waiter working at the Artist of Dallas Club—which was in itself a big deal, I did not want to break any unwritten rules and cause problems for myself. That was one of the coolest gigs I had. The pay was something like $3.00 a night, but as a singing waiter my tips were grand, and the other employees-all of them white, were cool with me.

I approached Jack Ruby's table and said: "Mr. Ruby, I hope you are having a good time this evening." JR: "We're having a great time" He gave me a five dollar bill. I told him that he is not seated on my station, and the waiter would not like it if I took tips from his customers. JR: "Take it; I'll take care of him, too." I took the five, thanked him and said, "I just wanted to say hello. I'd better make my rounds to the customers on my station." JR: "Keep in touch" ME: "I'm going back to college next week and probably won't be home again until Thanksgiving." JR: "You're a college boy huh?" ME: "Yes sir." JR: "Good for you; keep it up." Me: "I will, and I'll check with you when I come home. I'd better check on my customers."

I took drink orders from my customers, and when I got back to the bar, I showed the five spot to the waiter that served Jack Ruby's table. I told him that Jack had given me five bucks for singing "When the Saints Go Marching In" and said that Jack said he would take care of you. I added, if you don't get a good tip from him I'll split the five with you at the end of the night." He agreed. I really dug working at the Artist of Dallas club. It was my first time being a singing waiter, and I loved it. Jack gave the other waiter a $3.00 tip, and I did not have to split my five dollar tip with him.

Musicians are usually so cool to be around. Although Dallas was a totally segregation enforced city at the time, most of the white musicians were cool. The waiters, bartenders, parking attendants, hosts etc. at the Artist of Dallas Club were themselves performers or musicians looking for a gig, as was I. And what better place to stay in the know about gigs and future gigs than the place where all of the musicians—local and out of town performers hung out? My fellow waiters applauded when I sang and were friendly with no signs of jealousy or racial hang-ups. This was at a time when earlier that summer I was in downtown Dallas talking to a white musician that I knew from the Jazz sessions at the Woodman Auditorium. A white traffic cop stopped directing traffic, walked up to the white musician and me and told us to break it up and move on. As we split and went in opposite directions, the cop said, "This here ain't New York City". As far as I was concerned, working at the Artist of Dallas Club was like being in another world.

I went back to Huston-Tillotson College –in Austin, and the following year I transferred to Texas Southern University in Houston. In January 1960 I took a greyhound bus to Los Angeles. I saw Jack Ruby three years later when I, along with the whole Country, saw him shoot and kill Lee Harvey Oswald on national television.

My most vivid recollection of November 22, 1963 is, naturally, the assassination of President John F. Kennedy. I was a young man, twenty-five years old, and recently honorably discharged from the Armed Forces, where I served in G-2 as an Intelligence operative at the 2nd Military Intelligence Battalion at Kaiserslautern, Germany. I was also assigned to G-2 Air, with the 17th Tactical Air Force, Strategic Air Command (SAC) Base at Toule Rose, France. My experience while serving in United States espionage units was fascinating, and is a story that I will explore in depth in my memoirs.

I returned to the states from Europe in early October; I visited my friend Gloria Trammel and her husband, Clifton Mitchell for several days at their Washington, D.C. home. Then I met up with some friends in New York, who had also been discharged at the same time. We stayed in New York for a few days before continuing to our individual destinations.

I arrived in Dallas on November 20, 1963, and discovered that President Kennedy was coming to Dallas/ Ft. Worth that week. The following night, November 21^{st,} I auditioned and was hired as the house vocalist at a fabulous little club called "The Galaxy" which was owned by a man named Leon Iris.

The morning of November 22, 1963 was a cool but clear day. It was unseasonably warm day for late November. I got out of bed, turned on the TV, and found out that the President was leaving Ft. Worth, and on his way to Dallas. I was excited about seeing President Kennedy because he had done some remarkable things for Civil Rights. Before his presidency no "negro" had been allowed to serve in the Intelligence sector of the armed forces.

It was JFK who issued an order that inductees that tested in the top ten percent, regardless of race, creed or color would be automatically placed into Military Intelligence and sent to Ft. Holabird, MD. I was selected and trained at Ft. Holabird —known in the Intelligence community as "Cloak and Dagger" school. This was one of the reasons why I appreciated and respected JFK. The other reason –and perhaps the main reason I revered him is because two months after my twenty-fifth birthday I heard President Kennedy's speech on Civil Rights.

Try to imagine if you can, how it felt to hear for the first time *ever,* an important white man say something positive, or making non-derogatory statements about black people in America. John F. Kennedy did it on National radio and TV. Please think about this! I was a twenty-two year old, college educated, so called "cream of the crop" (as we were referred to at Fort Holabird) adult, who had *never before* heard an important white man speak publicly about the legalized and entrenched injustice to which black people in America were subjected. That's how systemic and in-grown, bigotry had been allowed to contaminate a "Free" society for more that three hundred years—until 1965, when black people in America were finally allowed to exercise their most fundamental right—the right to vote.

JFK's speech in June 1963 was a call to the conscience of an entire nation to take a serious look at what America had become in the eyes of the world. It was that historic speech that brought tears of joyful disbelief to my eyes, and his words rang like bells of hope in my equally disbelieving ears. What vision it took for an Irish Catholic white man from Massachusetts to rattle the chains and tug at the still unbroken links that held a heroic and noble people in bondage and servitude for more than three hundred years. It does not matter a wit to me whether his was an act of courage, conscience, or self-serving political ambition. What JFK did that day in June 1963 was to rescue an acquiescing America from the shame and hypocrisy that had covered her with the dross of spiritual, moral, and political corruption. Relive that incredible moment with me as I sat in Kaiserslautern, West Germany with friends, listening to the speech that freed the slaves from the self-deprecating doubts and fears that second-class citizenship had so thoroughly imposed on the average "negro." What follows is President Kennedy's speech in its entirety…

In his own words

Good evening my fellow citizens:

This afternoon, following a series of threats and defiant statements, the presence of Alabama National Guardsmen was required on the University of Alabama to carry out the final and unequivocal order of the United States District Court of the Northern District of Alabama.

That order called for the admission of two clearly qualified young Alabama residents, who happened to have been born Negro.

That they were admitted peacefully on the campus is due in good measure to the conduct of the students of the University of Alabama, who met their responsibilities in a constructive way.

I hope that every American, regardless of where he lives, will stop and examine his conscience about this and other related incidents. This Nation was founded by men of many nations and backgrounds. It was founded on the principle that all men are created equal, and that the rights of every man are diminished when the rights of one man are threatened.

Today we are committed to a worldwide struggle to promote and protect the rights of all who wish to be free. And when Americans are sent to Viet-Nam or West Berlin, we do not ask for whites only. It ought to be possible, therefore, for American students of any color to attend any public institution they select without having to be backed up by troops.

It ought to be possible for American consumers of any color to receive equal service in places of public accommodation, such as hotels and restaurants and theaters and retail stores, without being forced to resort to demonstrations in the street, and it ought to be possible for American citizens of any color to register to vote in a free election without interference or fear of reprisal.

It ought to be possible, in short, for every American to enjoy the privileges of being American without regard to his race or his color. In short, every American ought to have the right to be treated as he would wish to be treated, as one would wish his children to be treated. But this is not the case.

The Negro baby born in America today, regardless of the section of the Nation in which he is born, has about one-half as much chance of completing a high school as a white baby born in the same place on the same day, one-third as much chance of completing college, one-third as much chance of becoming a professional man, twice as much chance of becoming unemployed, about one-seventh as much chance of earning $10,000 a year, a life expectancy which is 7 years shorter, and the prospects of earning only half as much.

This is not a sectional issue. Difficulties over segregation and discrimination exist in every city, in every State of the Union, producing in many cities a rising tide of discontent that threatens the public safety. Nor is this a partisan issue. In a time of domestic crisis men of good will and generosity should be able to unite regardless of party or politics. This is not even a legal or legislative issue alone. It is better to settle these matters in the courts than on the streets, and new laws are needed at every level, but law alone cannot make men see right.

We are confronted primarily with a moral issue. It is as old as the scriptures and is as clear as the American Constitution.

The heart of the question is whether all Americans are to be afforded equal rights and equal opportunities, whether we are going to treat our fellow Americans as we want to be treated. If an American, because his skin is dark, cannot eat lunch in a restaurant open to the public, if he cannot send his children to the best public school available, if he cannot vote for the public officials who will represent him, if, in short, he cannot enjoy the full and free life which all of us want, then who among us would be content to have the color of his skin changed and stand in his place? Who among us would then be content with the counsels of patience and delay?

One hundred years of delay have passed since President Lincoln freed the slaves, yet their heirs, their grandsons, are not fully free. They are not yet freed from the bonds of injustice. They are not yet freed from social and economic oppression. And this Nation, for all its hopes and all its boasts, will not be fully free until all its citizens are free.

We preach freedom around the world, and we mean it, and we cherish our freedom here at home, but are we to say to the world, and much more importantly, to each other that this is the land of the free except for the Negroes; that we have no second-class citizens except Negroes; that we have no class or caste system, no ghettoes, no master race except with respect to Negroes?

Now the time has come for this Nation to fulfill its promise. The events in Birmingham and elsewhere have so increased the cries for equality that no city or State or legislative body can prudently choose to ignore them.

The fires of frustration and discord are burning in every city, North and South, where legal remedies are not at hand. Redress is sought in the streets, in demonstrations, parades, and protests which create tensions and threaten violence and threaten lives.

We face, therefore, a moral crisis as a country and as a people. It cannot be met by repressive police action. It cannot be left to increased demonstrations in the streets. It cannot be quieted by token moves or talk. It is time to act in the Congress, in your State and local legislative body and, above all, in all of our daily lives.

It is not enough to pin the blame of others, to say this a problem of one section of the country or another, or deplore the fact that we face. A great change is at hand, and our task, our obligation, is to make that revolution, that change, peaceful and constructive for all.

Those who do nothing are inviting shame as well as violence. Those who act boldly are recognizing right as well as reality.

Next week I shall ask the Congress of the United States to act, to make a commitment it has not fully made in this century to the proposition that race has no place in American life or law. The Federal judiciary has upheld that proposition in the conduct of its affairs, including the employment of Federal personnel, the use of Federal facilities, and the sale of federally financed housing.

But there are other necessary measures which only the Congress can provide, and they must be provided at this session. The old code of equity law under which we live commands for every wrong a remedy, but in too many communities, in too many parts of the country, wrongs are inflicted on Negro citizens and there are no remedies at law. Unless the Congress acts, their only remedy is in the street.

I am, therefore, asking the Congress to enact legislation giving all Americans the right to be served in facilities which are open to the public—hotels, restaurants, theaters, retail stores, and similar establishments.

This seems to me to be an elementary right. Its denial is an arbitrary indignity that no American in 1963 should have to endure, but many do.

I have recently met with scores of business leaders urging them to take voluntary action to end this discrimination and I have been encouraged by their response, and in the last 2 weeks over 75 cities have seen progress made in desegregating these kinds of facilities. But many are unwilling to act alone, and for this reason, nationwide legislation is needed if we are to move this problem from the streets to the courts.

I am also asking the Congress to authorize the Federal Government to participate more fully in lawsuits designed to end segregation in public education. We have succeeded in persuading many districts to desegregate voluntarily. Dozens have admitted Negroes without violence. Today a Negro is attending a State-supported institution in every one of our 50 States, but the pace is very slow.

Too many Negro children entering segregated grade schools at the time of the Supreme Court's decision 9 years ago will enter segregated high schools this fall, having suffered a loss which can never be restored. The lack of an adequate education denies the Negro a chance to get a decent job.

The orderly implementation of the Supreme Court decision, therefore, cannot be left solely to those who may not have the economic resources to carry the legal action or who may be subject to harassment.

Other features will also be requested, including greater protection for the right to vote. But legislation, I repeat, cannot solve this problem alone. It must be solved in the homes of every American in every community across our country.

In this respect I want to pay tribute to those citizens North and South who have been working in their communities to make life better for all. They are acting not out of a sense of legal duty but out of a sense of human decency.

Like our soldiers and sailors in all parts of the world they are meeting freedom's challenge on the firing line, and I salute them for their honor and their courage.

My fellow Americans, this is a problem which faces us all—in every city of the North as well as the South. Today there are Negroes unemployed, two or three times as many compared to whites, inadequate in education, moving into the large cities, unable to find work, young people particularly out of work without hope, denied equal rights, denied the opportunity to eat at a restaurant or lunch counter or go to a movie theater, denied the right to a decent education, denied almost today the right to attend a State university even though qualified. It seems to me that these are matters which concern us all, not merely Presidents or Congressmen or Governors, but every citizen of the United States.

This is one country. It has become one country because all of us and all the people who came here had an equal chance to develop their talents.

We cannot say to 10 percent of the population that you can't have that right; that your children cannot have the chance to develop whatever talents they have; that the only way that they are going to get their rights is to go into the streets and demonstrate. I think we owe them and we owe ourselves a better country than that.

Therefore, I am asking for your help in making it easier for us to move ahead and to provide the kind of equality of treatment which we would want ourselves; to give a chance for every child to be educated to the limit of his talents.

As I have said before, not every child has an equal talent or an equal ability or an equal motivation, but they should have an equal right to develop their talent and their ability and their motivation, to make something of themselves.

We have a right to expect that the Negro community will be responsible, will uphold the law, but they have a right to expect that the law will be fair, that the Constitution will be color blind, as Justice Harlan said at the turn of the century.

This is what we are talking about and this is a matter which concerns this country and what it stands for, and in meeting it I ask the support of all our citizens.

Thank you very much.

That is the speech that helped to bring our country into the light of a new day. The question now becomes: are we losing the hard fought-for gains towards equality that JFK initiated with that speech? Have we squandered a generation of hope? Have we, as African-Americans, allowed the signposts that point to our very survival to be up-rooted by our own diminished sense of brother- and sisterhood towards one another? Have we abandoned the road to reason that JFK, MLK, gave their lives to help us secure?

Where are we now? Do we know? Do we care? Or, are we content to live with the illusion of freedom? That would be the ultimate distraction—if we were not aware and vigilant enough to guard, protect, and if need be, regularly refurbish the truth of its meaning. I was proud and grateful to have experienced the joy of knowing that someone in power not only understood the plight of our oppressed people, but was willing to expose it to that silent majority that had been all too willing to participate in the maintenance of an evil that had prevailed for so long a time. President Kennedy did his part; Dr. MLK and others have done their part. Now, we must do more to begin to help ourselves and our young people to understand these days and times in which we live. Somehow we must help them to see, to recognize, and to understand the dark and baleful handwriting on the wall.

To **President John Fitzgerald Kennedy,** for the enlightened and uplifting speech you delivered to the nation and the world on June 11, 1963, it is with profound gratitude that I acknowledge your courage and your greatness with **A Simple yet profound Thank You.** (See JFK photo pages).

Martin Luther King Jr.

Dr. Martin Luther King Jr.
January 15, 1929 — April 4, 1968

In his own words:
"Our lives began to end the day we became silent about things that matter."

"Our greatest sin of our time is not the few who destroy, but the vast majority who sit idly by."

"In the end we will remember not the words of our enemies, but the silence of our friends."

"We must learn to live together as brothers or perish together as fools."

"Nothing in the world is more dangerous than sincere ignorance and conscientious stupidity."

"Everything that is done in the world is done by Hope."

"I have a dream!"

Coretta Scott King
April 27 1927- January 30, 2006

In her own words

"I support the non-discrimination act of 1994 because I believe that freedom and justice cannot be parceled out in pieces to suit political convenience.

"My husband, Martin Luther King, Jr. said: 'Injustice anywhere is a threat to justice everywhere.' On another occasion he said: 'I have worked too long and hard against segregated public accommodations to end up segregating my moral concerns; Justice is indivisible.'

"Like Martin, I don't believe that you can stand for freedom for one group of people and deny it to another."

Press conference on the Employment non-discrimination Act of 1994, Washington, DC   June 23, 1994

*A Simple and profound Thank You to
Dr. Martin Luther King Jr., and to Mrs. Coretta Scott King, wife of
MLK, slain Civil Rights leader.*

Chapter

L

Maurice Lacy
Personal Hero

Wilmer Maurice Lacy was the most brilliant person I've ever known personally. We met at the age of thirteen during our freshman year at Lincoln High. That first meeting was, to this very day, the most embarrassing moment of my entire life. It happened on orientation day, the first official school day of the year. The freshman class was gathered in the auditorium, and I was seated about five or six rows from the front. At one point I turned around to look at the clock on the back wall, and looked into the dancing eyes of an albino kid. I don't think I had ever seen an albino before, and I sure had never seen one close up. It scared the hell out of me. I let out a scream that must have sounded like a pre-teenage girl who's just discovered a mouse in her lunch pail. I tried to play it off like I was kidding around, and some of the kids bought it, but Lacy knew it was a real scare type scream.

Maurice was totally cool about it. We started to talk, and by the time the principal, Professor T.D. Marshall, took the stage, Lacy and I had traded a few jokes, and shared a couple of laughs. From that day on we were best friends. At the age of thirteen, he was the most talented individual any of us had ever seen. He was no dilettante—when I say talent, I mean he had real talent. As a singer his idol was Frankie Laine, and he could sing "Jezebel," "Jealousy," and "That's my Desire" so well that if you closed your eyes you might think it was Frankie Laine himself. His talent for drawing and painting were head and shoulders above even the most noted art students at Lincoln at the time. Maurice was a gifted, self-trained classical pianist but his real musical passion was for the conga, and the bongo drums. His main gift, so to speak, was his writing. The poetry and prose he wrote in high school still rivals many of today's seasoned professionals.

On my fourteenth birthday Lacy gave me a book that changed my life: "The Prophet," by Kahlil Gibran. I loved it, and I understood it on a spiritual as well as an intellectual level. By the time I was sixteen, I had read Albert Camus, J.D. Salinger, Herman Hess, and dabbled into, Kierkegaard, Spinoza, and Friedrich Nietzsche (of which I understood little and recall even less). "Thus Spoke Zarathustra," "The Catcher in the Rye," and "The Stranger" made it an interesting and worthwhile endeavor.

By the time we graduated' we were both very much into Emerson, Thoreau, and Walt Whitman.

One day after school, some kids were fighting and I wanted to watch, but Lacy kept saying *C'est la sacre du savage*. I asked him what it meant and he said, "It's French for "It's the ritual of the savages."" Thus began my fascination with French and other languages which were reinforced by Mrs. Bailey.

When I reached high school age I had only heard of the Milky Way and the moon, that is, until I met Maurice Lacy. He told me about Alpha Centauri, pointed out and explained the constellations, and astral projection (out of body experiences). He was one of only two people I knew at that time who believed that man would go to the moon during our lifetime. The other guy is George "Billy" Gipson, Little Gip's older brother. Like Lacy, Billy Gipson or Big "Gip" (as he was sometimes called) was also a gifted artist, but he was three years our senior.

I gained so much from Lacy. He expanded my mind and my consciousness. Because of him I developed a love for books and authors, and I started writing prose, poems, essays, and, of course, music. I became President of the "Scribblers" Club, our high school creative writing club. I also developed a life-long appreciation for fine art. The only thing I could teach him was how to develop a "hip" or a "cool" walk and when he joined ROTC, I taught him the drill commands and how to march. In my high school if you did not have a cool walk you were not with it. For weeks on end, everyday Lacy and I would spend our lunch period in the boy's restroom practicing his cool walk, which he was never able to master although he did learn the ROTC drills and commands.

There was nothing shallow or narrow about Maurice Lacy. He was, as he might have said about someone like himself, replete with fecundity, although he would never have said it about himself. His modesty was genuine, and his wisdom was natural and sage-like. Being an etymologist, he and my English teacher, Mr. Berry, got me well acquainted with Webster's Dictionary. We spent long hours after school at my house in the projects, talking about things that were light years over my head, but were absolutely fascinating and stretched my imagination, and I loved it.

Lacey's pseudonym was "Cloud" and mine was "Bird". We had our secret language with which we could hold a complete conversation in code that no one else could understand. He mostly came to my house, but I did visit him at his home a few times. His parents seemed to be the intellectual type. His mother and father were soft-spoken and semi-friendly. His mother was a beautiful woman, and he had a younger sister whose name I believe was Sharon. We graduated high school and Lacy left for Los Angeles the following week. The night before he left he came to my house and stayed until the next to the last bus ran. Ordinarily, when Maurice came to visit I would walk him to the bus stop and wait with him until the bus came and when the bus pulled away I'd go home. But on this night, we both were happy because Lacy was going to the West Coast to pursue his dream, and at the same time we were sort of sad that we would no longer be in the same city. The bus arrived and I boarded it, but when the bus driver pulled away, I was still on the bus. I rode all the way to Lacy's stop. He got off and stood waving as the bus pulled away with me aboard. I rode to the end of the line, and back to the projects in Bon Ton.

Maurice and I vowed that we would always keep it touch, which we did. I was going to college and he was doing his thing in L.A. He had a book of his poems published by the "Three Penny Press" that I kept with a number of other items that were important to me. When I was drafted into the military, I shipped my things home. My mother kept all of it, but when she died (may she rest in peace), most of it was misplaced—including my most cherished book of poems by W. Maurice Lacy.

In 1960 I made my way to Los Angeles. Maurice had been in L.A. for four years and we had kept in touch. He was now living in Venice, CA and had made a name for himself as a Venice poet. The day after my arrival in Los Angeles I went to Venice to meet Lacy. It was good to see him again and he was glad to see me as well. We spent all afternoon and into the night on Venice beach at the various coffee houses and clubs that Lacy frequented. He was living with a cute little lady named Nikki and to my surprise Maurice told me that he and Nikki were moving to San Francisco in a week. I was disappointed that he was moving away just when I came to town, but we hung out a lot while he was still there. Through the years we lost touch, but I always believed we would run into each other somewhere. Whenever I saw an albino I would call out Maurice Lacy's name, but it never turned out to be him. A friend, who was also my attorney when I lived in Pasadena, knew Lacy in Dallas. They grew up on the same street. His name is William Turner. He told me that he had visited Lacy in L.A. and said he would get me Lacy's phone number, but never did.

I had made up my mind to find Lacy if he was still in LA. I wanted to read his poems, view his art, jam with him, and just see him again. I was excited in 1996 because I had decided to attend our class reunion. I felt sure that he would be there, or someone would know his whereabouts. My heart dropped when his name was called as the obituaries of classmates were being read. I have selected some prose that he wrote while we were at Lincoln High. I have saved and cherished them. To think that a kid in tenth and eleventh grade wrote these would be hard to believe were it not for the fact that I was there, and I am willing to have the paper tested to prove the age of this writing. Take a look at the prose written by a fifteen year old named, Wilmer Maurice Lacy, the "Cloud"

Despair

A beggar am I? Then a beggar I shall remain throughout this venture.
For my thirst is unquenchable, my hunger unending.
My heart opens to the song of truth, and as fruit, it ripens in its intensity.
The painful revelations stun me, often with horror, and I lay obsessed
thru the night.

Declaration of Love

I stand in the midst of a crowd with its needless chatter; still I'm alone,
and thoughts of you that wound me and set my passion aflame are truly
the cause of my seclusion.
For who among those mannequins and fools could appreciate or
nourish my deepest feelings?
"Fool" that I am they say; "why does he leave our gaiety? With his idle
thoughts does he think himself better than we?"

My love, if I could dwell with you and share the hours of the day and
night, I could dispense with desire and need.
I must desert those thoughts and their sweet pain, and become a
mannequin.
And I must strengthen them and become one of them in order to do so.

Love me hypocrisy, that I may veil my nakedness with deceit, and with
joy, speak with their tongues, with words which they hear and language
which they understand.

Were I to go to them and speak of my love for you, I would be as the fool
that cries into the night for sunlight.

Rescue me O truth—for I cannot dwell in falsehood. Now you are my
Joy and my Sadness, my Love and my Hate, my Desire and my Scorn,
and if I would possess any two I would have naught to do but thirst for
you—and an hour... with

Therefore I shall live and be uplifted and give my soul wings... But if
this be an impossibility, I yield, thus letting my heart's hell invade my
soul's heaven.

Rebellion

*The wings of night have enfolded swiftly and the bosom of day nourishes
the world with splendor, with truth.
And I am rushed from the realm of sleep by the cares which society
imposes upon the loveliness of day:--Rushed into a seasonless and
massive confusion—the city.*

*The day blooms on, its sultry excitement serving not as a balm for the
restlessness it enfolds.
Lost: The beauty, the ardor so designed to be remembered is wasted by
academic blunderers. The potion, so unique, so apart of life is denied
the young by elders who think themselves wiser than the gods.*

*Predictions of disaster are the diseases of their mouths. Bunglings of the
past, pain their nights and they awaken embittered, determined to guard
and guide their young to material wealth that they themselves cannot
afford.
Damn the flowers that bloom in the wild, they shall be uprooted and cut
and placed in your house. But hasten now, forget the day, the song of
birds, and the changing skies; be not lazy. Learn of numbers and
business and people and languages.*

*"Forget the way of nature, there are snakes in her tresses and thieves
lounge in her groves." The elders continue, "Hasten faster, faster; for
alertness and swiftness and the cunning of the hunter Fox award you
the booty.*

*And the redemption of their mistakes is now in motion. The offspring of
the fool will be wise says the fool, "I will make him wise for he is mine."*

*Oh Lord, I shall deny in my youth little of the eccentricities of thy hand
for potentialities are fruitless without inspiration.*

To: Love

Love! Thou who are the redeemer of time and flesh, I pray thee, breathe but lightly upon my scribbling, that Charlotte might be mindful of thy presence, and thus render her song unto the day.

W. Maurice Lacy
"The CLOUD"

To Mr. Wilmer Maurice "The Cloud" Lacy, the most gifted, honest, cherished and influential classmate and friend I have ever known. I send you **a loving Thank you.** (See Lacy's photo page).

CHAPTER

M

Nelson Mandela
International Icon

One of the few regrets I have in life is a missed opportunity to meet a consensus Icon, President Nelson Mandela; it was no fault of mine but rather a last minute change that was beyond my control. In 1996, Sony studios held a reception for President Mandela. Because of a close association with the studio at the time, my partner and I were placed on the invitation list along with four outstanding students from the youth group we ran. Naturally we were excited and looked forward to meeting the great man and hearing his speech. Alas, it was not to be.

Two days before the reception, our office was notified that regretfully, our names were removed from the guest list; due to the fact that so many high powered individuals from the Hollywood scene had virtually demanded additional tickets. These were highly influential figures from the film, and entertainment industry whose request had to be honored by the planners of the event. With sincere apologies our names were removed. The disappointment weighed heavy on my heart, but there was nothing to be done to prevent the situation, although we tried every possible avenue of influence available to us.

Still, I hold out every hope that I will someday meet this man who stands alone in modern history. Most people know the story of Nelson Mandela, and we marvel at the realization of what he endured, overcame, and finally accomplished. His soul, his spirit, his resiliency, as well as his graceful and even-handed use of the power he gained, has made his place in history equal to the great biblical figures of the Old *and* New Testaments.

My renewed longing to meet and shake Mandela's hand is embedded in the trenches of my rekindled hope and most fervent desires. This newly awakened excitement came about six weeks ago when I was in Dallas, TX for an annual affair. I was invited to dinner at the home of Joe Ashmore Jr. and his lovely wife, Jane. These are folks who I consider to be dear friends. I look forward to seeing or talking to them whenever I'm in Dallas, if time permits. They have been staunch supporters of the Maurine F. Bailey Foundation –of which I am founder. I appreciate their involvement each year, but I value their friendship even more than their most welcomed participation.

Before I relate the wonderful story about Nelson Mandela, I want to briefly state who the Ashmores are and why I consider them special. Joseph E. Ashmore Jr., is a retired State judge who served twelve years on the bench in the state of Texas. He now heads up a highly successful law firm under his name. It is a family business consisting of Joe, two of his four talented children and staff.

His son, Gary Ashmore, and his daughter, Lori Peters, are partners in the law firm. His daughter Mary Elaine is an educator, and his other son Joe Ashmore III is a weapons designer for the US Government. I call his wife Janie, the "Queen Mother" because of her elegant and fun-loving spirit. Mary's two children, Ryan and Kristen, round out this active and successful family. The love and respect they have for Janie, Joe and their siblings are evident and no doubt well deserved.

With few exceptions, of the people I write about in this book, Joe is the most recent of my acquaintances. It is hard to imagine that it has been ten years since first meeting Judge Ashmore. I enjoy listening to his stories about some of the hilarious things that he has witnessed in court over the years. I could write a whole chapter on his personality, and perhaps someday I will.

Back to the story of Mandela which was recounted by a close family friend of the Ashmores. Because of the nature of his association with President Mandela, I have tried several times to get his permission to use his name but have not received a response to my request. Out of respect for his privacy, I will refer to him simply as "Padre", since he is a member of the clergy. Padre himself is quite an engaging figure, with a delightful sense of humor. He kept us laughing at dinner, and his keen insight into world affairs was enlightening and thought provoking to say the least.

He shared a wonderful personal experience he had with the former President. It happened when Padre and others lived in South Africa, and worked to help build the new government when Mandela was elected. A number of interesting things happened during this transitional period. The most captivating and revealing incident pointed to Nelson Mandela's commitment to freedom and justice for all South Africans. The president announced that he was opening South Africa and welcoming Africans from across the continent to come to South Africa and participate in the newly established democracy.

As with all such invitations, not everyone who answered the call was of the highest character. Some were not content to live and work in harmony with the citizens of the host country. Small bands of trouble-makers formed and began to commit unlawful acts in upscale neighborhoods. President Mandela took not only a serious leadership interest, but he took a personal, active interest that is unique in the annals of modern governance.

According to Padre, one morning around 1:00AM while most residents of the upscale neighborhood where Padre and other officials and their families lived were sleeping, there came a knock on Padre's door. He sent his house man to see who was at the door that time of night. The house man returned upstairs and informed Padre that he had looked through the peephole, and there was a man at the door that looked sort of like President Mandela.

Padre went down stairs, looked through the peephole and to his utter amazement, there stood President Mandela on his front stoop. Padre opened the door and the president was there with a squad of armed officers. He did not enter Padre's house; he stood there and explained to Padre that he was going door to door, checking with the residents to see if his posted guards, and policemen were conducting themselves appropriately. Padre said that he and the other families in that neighborhood as well as other areas of the city where Mandela had visited in the middle of the night were more than impressed. The concern that President Nelson Mandela showed for the safety and well-being for the citizens that memorable night was unprecedented.

That single act caused Padre and his colleagues to strengthen their resolve to support the president's efforts to unify South Africa. What a story! What a memory for those who experienced a visit by the president in the middle of the night. I join with each of them in chanting "Long Live Nelson Mandela."

Many of us might never have the opportunity to meet this august figure, and I consider myself fortunate to have a friend like Judge Ashmore. Because he and Janie invited me into their home that evening in August 2006, I had the pleasure of meeting a gentleman who worked with President Mandela and experience his compassion first hand. Padre himself is obviously a special individual. I hope to see him again.

I want to say a special thank you to Joe and Jane Ashmore, for their friendship and support. Please allow me to continue to acknowledge Nelson Mandela's wisdom by sharing the following.

Nelson Mandela, in his own words

"Education is the great engine of personal development. It is through education that the daughter of a peasant can become a doctor, that the son of a mineworker can become the head of the mine; that the child of farm workers can become the President of a great nation. It is what we make out of what we have, not what we are given, that separates one person from another."

"Only free men can negotiate; prisoners can not enter into contracts."

"No one truly knows a nation until one has been inside its jails. A nation should not be judged by how it treats its highest citizens but its lowest ones."

"To be free is not merely to cast off one's chains, but to live in a way that respects and enhances the freedom of others."

"I learned that courage is not the absence of fear, but the triumph over it. The brave man is not he who does not feel afraid, but he that conquers that fear."

"I detest racialism because I regard it as a barbaric thing, whether it comes from a black man or a white man."

"A good head and a good heart is always a formidable combination"

(See Mandela's photo pages)

Nathalie Mathis

My beloved mother

(Motherhood)

Motherhood in its purest form is, (next to life itself) God's greatest gift to humanity. I have my own dear mother (may she rest in peace) to thank for bringing us up in such a way that I now understand what a mother is meant to be. Webster's definition of the word mother is, among other things: "A female that gives birth to a plant, animal, or a human."

This, and other definitions may adequately put forth the general idea, but it does not begin to reveal the importance of the role of a true mother. The noble attributes of a true, or should I say a "complete," mother is beyond any word, group of words, or language itself to fully demonstrate the profundity of its meaning. A mother can be a fortress, a cocoon, redeemer, and a treasure to the child that is fortunate enough to be born and raised by such a one.

The heroic aspect of my mother's life is depicted in one harrowing episode that began one winter night before we moved to Dallas. In fact it happened before I was born. Over the years during my childhood this particular story was told by many different relatives, some of whom were eye witnesses. They always inspired and reinforced the love, honor and filial respect that my siblings and I had for Mudear (the endearing name we called our mother) until the day she died, and it still exists in our hearts and minds to this very day.

It was a cold wintry night. My mother, my father, my two sisters and my brother lived in a shotgun shanty on Baptist Hill, in Gilmer Texas. Just after 10:00 PM (my mother, as did everybody on Baptist Hill) kept accurate time by the morning, afternoon, and night time freight trains that ran on the tracks less than a hundred yards from our wood-framed share-cropper type shanty. My father was working a late (4: 00 PM to midnight) shift at the steel mills. The whistle on the ten o'clock train had blown, and Mudear put my two sisters and my brother to bed, and turned in for the night. No one could ever remember how it happened but some how the shotgun shanty went up in flames. My mother hearing the neighbors screams, woke up to find the house fully engulfed in flames.

She grabbed my oldest sister Faye and my older brother Billy, and ran from the house. She dropped them on the ground where the hysterical crowd picked them up, and carried them away from the rapidly crumbling house. As Mudear started back into the house to get my sister Tharsell (Honey), the house literally started to disintegrate. Three or four men and women grabbed hold of my mother telling her "You can't, you can't go back into that house." My mother's voice could be heard over the frantic and panic stricken crowd. She was screaming, "My baby, my baby's in that house," but the people holding her back would not let her go.

Years later, Mudear told us that all she could remember was calling out to God "Save my baby." The next thing she remembered was scooping my sister from the burning bed. My two year old sister's face was engulfed in flames as Mudear carried her seemingly lifeless body from the exploding structure. The minute her feet touched the ground, the house exploded blowing her and the baby cradled in her arms half way across the yard. Mudear told us that people said that she took the hem of her night gown and put out the flames that were still burning on my sister's face. The only thing my dear and beloved mother could remember about the whole tragic event was, waking up to screaming voices, taking Faye and Billy out of the burning house, and calling out to God to save my baby. Then she remembers waking up in my grandmother's house on Vinegar Hill.

Anytime someone would mention the word Hero when talking about what Mudear had done that night, she would not allow such talk. She would say: "There was nothing heroic about it." She said any mother would have done the same thing under the circumstances. Her definitive statement about the whole thing was always, "All I did was to cry out to God to save my child and he heard my cry and answered my call."

For three consecutive years, every night without fail Mudear would bathe my sister's horribly scarred face with butter milk. Growing up, my sister Tharsell (Honey) had a terrible scar over almost three quarters of her face. When she first started school, kids could be cruel and made fun of her. They called her "Scar Face" but her personality along with the love, support, and self esteem that our mother instilled in her helped her through. Nobody called her names when her siblings were around. My oldest sister on my mother's side, Norma Faye, and my oldest brother on my mother's side, Billy, would take care of anyone who dared to call 'Honey' "Scarface" or any other mean name.

My sister, Honey, reminded me of an incident that happened when I was seven years old that pretty much put and end to the mean-spirited teasing of my sister. There was a girl in Honey's class that hated her, (Nobody ever hated Honey, because she has always been a genuinely sweet and kind person). Most people today don't know that her real name is Tharsell Remar Watson. Her entire life she has been known as Honey and deservedly so.

One girl who seemed to hate her, was named Lola Mae Hunter. One day we were playing dodge ball on the park in the Bottom. There were lots of kids around. Lola Mae ran up to my sister and called her Scarface. The game stopped. I got in Lola Mae Hunter's face and screamed at her saying

"At least she's got a reason for her face, but what's the reason for that Opossum looking face you are wearing." The twenty or more kids that were present fell out laughing. They laughed so hard and so long that Lola Mae ran away in tears. I don't remember anyone else ever calling my sister names again.

Today she is a beautiful woman inside and out. The scar is hardly visible, if at all, and most people agree that her skin and complexion are worthy of a magazine ad. The young people in her church call her "Mama Honey." She is a true matriarch of the Faith. I am so proud to be her baby brother.

Mudear was a living example of a good and noble mother. After moving to Dallas she raised four children as a single mother. I can not recall a time in my youth when my beloved mother did not struggle to make ends meet. When we moved to Dallas my sister Faye was nine, my oldest brother, Billy was five and my sister, Tharsell was four, I was two. In Dallas, we moved in with my Aunt Porter who was a care- taker for an octogenarian widow named Mrs. Thorhammer. About three months later Auntie moved into Mrs. Thorhammer's home to provide twenty-four hour care for her.

We took permanent residence in Auntie Porter's house and shortly thereafter, Mudear took a job with a white family as a domestic. She worked five and a half days a week, ten hours a day, and was paid two dollars a week. She worked more than a year at that job. She then got a job with a different family that paid four dollars a week.

When I was five years old she started working for the Dees family who paid her five dollars weekly. Mrs. Dees adored my mother, and one day Mrs. Dees said to my mother, "Nathalie, you are like my best friend." By this time my mother was earning seven dollars a week. Mr. and Mrs. Dees had two sons. The older boy's name was Bean Bakedbeans Dees. That was **his real birth name.** They obviously had a wicked sense of humor to name their first born, "Bean Bakedbeans Dees", (BB Dees). Bean was about twelve years old. Their younger son was named Calvin; he was one year younger than me which made him four years old.

The Dees used to ask Mudear to please bring me to work with her. During the summer, when kindergarten was out I would go to work with Mudear. They were wonderful to me. Calvin and I really hit it off. He was the first white kid I'd ever known. I liked him and we got along well. Calvin would often start to cry when my mother got off work and it was time for me to go. Every morning I was eager to go to work with Mudear, I was excited about playing with my new friend.

Although Calvin was a white kid and I was black, the thought of being different never entered our minds. That is until one day Calvin and I were eating lunch on the back porch. I finished my sandwich and Calvin being eager to please me went into the kitchen and returned with another sandwich which his mom had cut in half. He offered one half of the sandwich to me, but I was full. I wanted to go back to playing whatever game we were playing when his mom had called us to lunch.

Calvin wanted me to share his sandwich but I refused again because I was full. Calvin started to plead with me to share his sandwich. I continued to refuse. Calvin started to cry which usually got him his way. But I was not about to eat anything when I was full. Mudear had taught us to not be greedy, and eating when you are not hungry, especially when your stomach was full is being greedy. I continued to refuse the half sandwich and Calvin continued to cry and beg me "please, please, please eat it." I shook my head no. Then Calvin yelled at me, his face turned beet red and he yelled Eat it! Eat it nigger, I said eat it. I refused. Mrs. Dees and Mudear were sitting inside at the kitchen table also having lunch.

When they heard Calvin call me a nigger, they rushed outside, Mrs. Dees followed by Mudear. Mrs. Dees demanded that Calvin apologize. After crying a bit longer young Calvin whimpered out an apology. His mother admonished him to never use that word again, and sent him to his room. I understood the full implication of what had happened, and I did not like it one bit. Mudear stood in the kitchen back door way and never said a word. I could tell by the look in her eyes that she was very displeased with what Calvin had said to me.

Maybe thirty or forty minutes had passed and I wanted to play. So I asked Mrs. Dees if Calvin could come back outside and play. She said "That was a bad thing that Calvin had said to me and he would have to stay in his room for at least an hour before he could come outside to play." It seemed like five hours had passed before that hour went by. My mother still never said a word.

Calvin came back outside I didn't like him calling me a nigger, but I still liked playing with him. The rest of the day passed and we played together as though nothing had happened. When the work day was over we boarded the street car (trolley) and Mudear moved the "white only" sign toward the front. We took a seat behind a white man. Mudear was unusually silent as the street car rattled along. As usual, just before we reached our stop, Mudear let me reach up and pull the cord.

The buzzer sounded, and just before the street car stopped to let the passengers off, Mudear said, "You know you're not going to work with me tomorrow don't you?" I shrugged my shoulders the way that little kids do when they don't know how to answer. We walked down the hill from the street car stop toward our neighborhood –"The Bottom" and Mudear continued. "Baby, that wasn't right for Calvin to call you that name. "You are not a Nigger, and you never will be." And anybody call you that, especially white folks, you just get away from them and stay away. Do you understand me?" I said "Uh-huh."

We continued down the hill to The Bottom. A few moments passed in silence and Mudear said, "I think I'll make a meatloaf for dinner, would you like that?" We loved her meatloaf and she knew it. I sensed that she was trying to make me feel better so I tried to push it by asking, "Will you make a banana pudding too?" (Banana pudding was my favorite food; I loved it). She shot me a "don't push it" look, and said, "Maybe Sunday I might make a banana pudding, IF, you don't get on my nerves." That was good enough for me. I knew that we'd have meatloaf tonight and banana pudding on Sunday and I could hardy wait.

The next morning I was aching to go play with Calvin. I got dressed and was eating a bowl of cereal when Mudear asked, "Where you getting ready to go?" I said, "Can I go with you?" She replied, "What did I tell you last night? Did you think I was playing?" I was really sad and started to pout. Mudear: "No need to give me that sad sack look either." "I told you that you're not going up there with me no more." Those words really hurt. I liked Calvin, not because he was white but he was fun to play with, and he had so many toys. I tried to defend my point of view by saying "Miss Billie said, if somebody makes a mistake and apologizes we're supposed to forgive them".

Mudear: "Miss Billie is right about that, and as wonderful as Miss Billie is, there are some things that are my responsibility to teach you, and this is one of them." My eyes started to tear up and I said, "But he apologized." Mudear heaved an exacerbated sigh, and walked into her bedroom. She told me to come in there. I got up from the card table that doubled as our kitchen table and went to my mother's bed room. She was sitting on the side of her bed. She told me to sit beside her. I sat and she took my hand and said: "Miss Billie is right. It was a good thing that Calvin apologized for calling you that terrible name. But it was a worse thing for him to call you that in the first place." I was looking down at the floor. She said, "Look at me son" I looked at her eyes and she continued. "Carl, this is not about Calvin; he's just a baby, like you. This is about you and your self respect. If you let folks treat you like nothing, pretty soon you might start believing that you're nothing." She said, "Now you listen to me, you are a child of God. You are smart, you are intelligent, and you are a good person. Don't you ever let anybody treat you like you're dirt. Do you understand what I'm saying?" I nodded yes.

She continued. "It's not Calvin's fault; Calvin heard that from somebody else." He might've heard it from his daddy, or his mama, or from Bean. I don't know who he got it from, but all I know is you got to have self respect or nobody else will have respect for you. I know you like playing with Calvin and I know he's going to pitch a fit when you don't' come with me today, but I got to let Mr. and Mrs. Dees know that nobody can disrespect me and my family, and get the chance to do it again just cause they apologize afterwards. I work for them because I need to work and they have been good folks to work for. But I don't have to bring my child up to their house for my child to be happy. So you play with the kids here in the Bottom today. What about Little Gip, and Toogie, and John Henry, and Philmore? They're your friends and I bet they miss you -especially Lil Gip. Every time you go to play with Calvin I know they miss you".

When Mudear left for work she told my sister Honey to be sure to make us some lunch. I never played with Calvin again although I sometimes thought about him. Mudear said that every day he'd ask about me but after the first week he stopped throwing his tantrum over my not coming to play.

My mother told us one evening that Mrs. Dees explained to Calvin that he had lost a playmate because he said a really mean thing, and he must never use that word again. The Dees' were good people and I still think of Bean and Calvin as part of an unfortunate, but fond memory. Wherever Calvin is, I hope he's OK and happy.

The foregoing represents a small but accurate expression of motherhood that was not even the tip of the iceberg when it came to the nurturing, care, and guidance that my dear mother provided for her children.

The distinctions that are drawn and the labels assigned to a mother (i.e. a good or a bad mother) are designed by human thought and conveyed by human expression. They are attempts to inform the masses about the complete or the incomplete state of human consciousness. As a youth growing up, to hear the words: "A bad mother" was rare, and would be considered, in etymological terminology, a "contradiction in terms."

This is not to say that there were not childbearing women whose motherhood was incomplete, but even they were not considered "bad mothers." In my view this was so because if a child was neglected by its parents, someone in the neighborhood would see that the child received basic necessities, and acceptance by the children of the surrogate parents. Here again is the evidence of the often scoffed at phrase "It takes a village to raise a child."

I recall in our own home, a woman asked my mother to watch her two children, Sonny and Golda Faye for the weekend. She showed up two years later to get them. My mother was furious, but she never complained, or, was unkind to those kids. They were good kids, having good manners and respect for adults, and I can not recall ever being angry or upset with them. This proves that even this "bad" mother had raised her children to have these good qualities.

I am not making excuses for women who have children irresponsibly, and then blame the kid's bad behavior on the fact that the child's father (or rather the male that impregnated the woman) is not around. I realize that what I'm about to say will draw criticism from many women, but the fact remains that in our country, the system of checks and balances where men and women are concerned has gone astray. Not withstanding the injustice that women have been subjected to, and are still suffering from in many parts of the world. We take not lightly the inequities that remain part of America's corporate, political, and religious landscape.

In certain American cities and states the pendulum seems to have swung too far. It is not politically correct to engage in healthy and honest debate regarding the glaring imbalance that in some cases not only favor women, but often encourage some to pursue and win incredibly unfair advantages. Some of my friends say, and I can not dispute the reality, that the pendulum perhaps swings necessarily too far in order to find true and equal balance. As natural as it may seem, and as necessary as it may appear, it is still fraudulent that this is allowed to persist. Unfairness is still a form of bigotry, and should not be applied against one gender or the other in the name of retribution or correctness.

I personally don't know any man who disputes the right of women to earn equal pay for equal work, but in some instances, that too, is becoming misapplied. For example, when a female firefighter who is not physically able to carry a sixty pound hose up twelve flights of stairs, receives hundreds of dollars in bonus money simply because the truck from her engine company arrives at the scene of a fire two or more minutes sooner that an engine company that is all male. The question I would ask these women and men who are proponents of this type of ludicrous policy is this: "If you and your infant, toddler, or disabled child were trapped on the twelfth floor of a burning building, who would you rather arrive at that scene first, a female firefighter who cannot carry the sixty pounds of fire equipment up the twelve flights of stairs, or a firefighter that is fully capable of carrying the equipment up the twelve flights of stairs?"

I believe that the honest answer would be obvious to even the most ardent proponent of women's rights, and I am an ardent proponent. I believe that the honest answer would be the same if the firefighters were two men, and one of them was not physically able to reach you and your child, and the other one was capable and able to reach you. I believe the honest answer would be the same, no matter what the gender of the two firefighters might be. So the larger question is: Why is the incapable firefighter paid more money simply because he or she arrives on the scene a few minutes sooner? You might say that it is not possible that such an example could be so. If you check with certain fire companies in Southern California, you will discover that it is absolutely true. This type of frivolous attempt at equality makes a mockery, and is certain to cause a backlash against the reasonable efforts towards equality of men and women in the workplace.

Ask the judge, politician, or voting public which of the two firefighters mentioned above would they want to go into that burning twelve story building to rescue them and their child; I think the honest answer would be obvious, political correctness not withstanding. You might say: "Well that's just an isolated case." I say, there is no such thing as an isolated case of injustice for whoever is trapped on the twelfth floor of a burning building.

As an African-American who has been subjected to inequality as a matter of law, both written and unwritten, I deeply believe in the equality of all people. I do not believe that a person who has a GED and no experience or credentials, should be made the chairman of a Fortune 500 Company just for the sake of diversity, no matter what his race, gender preference, religion, etc. might be.

I believe that women have the same innate mental and spiritual capacity as men, but is it equality for a woman to receive $30,000 more than a man for winning the Boston marathon? To acquiesce to such injustice in the name of equality is to eventually invite hostility and resentment from those who do believe in, and stand for, full and honest equality for women. There are women who have made a cottage industry out of entrapping unsuspecting men who fall victim to a court system that can sometimes be destructive and malicious towards men by some judges—most of whom are males. Some of them hand down "one size fits all" decisions that are sometimes mean-spirited and by rote. They are decisions often based on misguided and erroneous interpretation of the law.

I firmly hold that a "Deadbeat Dad," by design or circumstance, ought to be held accountable for the well-being of any child that he creates. I am also aware that not all men who do not support their children would do much better if this paint-by-numbers coloring book of laws were not the cause of flight. When I worked with inner-city kids for nearly ten years, I learned some things that changed my thinking about parents, both male and female.

It is true that a disproportionate number of African-American households are without a father in the home. This sad fact is often worn like a badge by sympathy-seeking women and shortsighted, sharp dressing, ignorant men whose male prowess is based upon how many babies he can make. Unfortunately these guys become role models to many young men who grow up believing that becoming a player is some kind of salvation. Many black and Hispanic teen-age males seem to think that making a baby is their right of passage. This self-perpetuating trap is well laid and enticing to far too many of our youths. The other side of the coin is the scheming type female who knows that if she gets pregnant by Johnny "Fly by Night" that she will automatically have assured access to Johnny "Fly." Becoming a "Baby Mama" will assure her, with or without Johnny Fly, a baby to love and maybe be loved by. Plus, there's the bonus of a welfare check for as long as she remains eligible. This is an equally sad mindset. The combination of thought by Johnny Fly and Baby Mama is lethal to the very concept of the human dignity that we should all be heir to.

Perhaps the next scenario is saddest of all. It's the one where a young couple start out trying to make a life. They drop out of school, get married and have a couple of children, only to discover after a few years that his job at Taco Bell and her job at the nursing home are not enough to make ends meet. She gets a new job at Rite Aid, earning three dollars an hour more than at the Nursing Home. She now makes $10.00 per hour, and after another year at Taco Bell he gets a raise. He now earns $8.50 per hour. They both earn enough money and manage to buy a used car, some furniture at the swap meet, and upgrade into a two bedroom apartment. They are excited and both talk seriously about going back to school and getting a high school diploma.

One carefree night she gets pregnant again, and since most Latinos don't believe in abortion, they have the baby. They have been married for three years, and now they have three children which they both love dearly.

They both work hard, and she keeps a neat house, but alas, they realize that the $280.00 he grosses weekly yields $170.00 after taxes, and the $300.00 she grosses only yields $220.00 after taxes. No matter how hard they try to budget they see no way to progress. They start to argue; she starts to remind him that if she can earn $10.00 per hour, why can't he "be a man" and find a job earning at least as much as she does. He tries to join the military, but discovers that he has an irregular heartbeat and is not accepted. He starts to drink more, which she hates. She starts to nag, which he uses as an excuse to drink even more.

The arguments increase and after a year of mutual discontent they separate. He moves in with his mom, and she keeps the apartment. They try to reconcile, but the drinking has gotten worse. He tries to stop drinking, but he can't seem to quit. He gives her more than half of his paycheck every two weeks, but still it's not enough. He shows up with alcohol on his breath one time too many and is fired. Her frustrations are overwhelming. He can't find a job that pays more than minimum wage. She starts to call him a loser who couldn't even get accepted in the Army.

The drinking continues; she tells him not to come around for the kids and if he wants to see the kids, she will drop them off at his mother's house, and pick them up after their weekly visits. He goes to AA and stays sober for three months, hoping to get back with his family, but one Saturday while he was with his kids, one of his friends tells him that he had seen Maria at a club with a dude. Jose confronts her about it; she tells him that she is seeing a guy that works with her. He starts back drinking, and two months later Maria informs him that she wants a divorce.

After six years of marriage, they divorce. Two months later she shows up for work to find out that the guy she was dating left her a letter saying he was going back to Ohio; she is devastated. Jose goes from one minimum wage job to another. Maria applies for welfare, but because she now grosses over $300 a week is not qualified, and can only get food stamps. Maria has no choice except to file for child support. Jose is ordered to pay 30% of his $250 gross pay per week, per child. Out of about $190.00 take home pay he owed $180.00, $90.00 a week more than he earned. He is picked up for missing his payments and spends three weeks in the L.A. County Jail. He had never been arrested before, and L.A. County Jail is more than he is willing or able to endure. Upon his release from jail he leaves town and no one has seen him since.

Maria was not a bad mother—she was in fact a complete, or a good, mother and wife. Jose was not a deadbeat dad—he set out to be the best dad he could be. The realities of minimum wage America captured them and caused Jose to become a run away father, and Maria a struggling food stamp single mom. That is the fate that awaits most if not all teenage kids that "fall in love," drop out of school, and become not a bad mother, but a lost mother and not a deadbeat dad, but a defeated father.

Any child who is blessed to have a complete (or good) mother to raise him or her has experienced extremely good fortune and the unfettered grace of God. I am blessed to have had such a mother. As I said before, my dear mother Mrs. Nathalie Mathis worked for $2.00 a week flat when she first moved to Dallas in 1941. When she passed away in 1975 she was head of staff in the home of Herbert and Stanly Marcus (the original owners of Nieman-Marcus department stores) at their Highland Park home in Dallas. I think she was paid about $85.00 a week, which was top dollar for a domestic worker in Texas during the 1970's. She never had enough money to send us to college, but she gave each of us children the best of herself. She was Love personified, fun to be around, a fairly strict disciplinarian who gave me encouragement, taught me to respect myself and others, and to believe that I could become whatever I wanted to be if I worked hard at it and stayed out of jail. I never heard my mother use a curse word.

I thank God that she lived to see me appear on every major television show, including three times on the Tonight Show starring the late great Johnny Carson. She heard my records on the radio, and broke bread with Bill Cosby and his beautiful family. I mention this again because that was one of the true highlights of my dear mother's life.

She shaped my awareness of what a profound and unequaled gift the blessing of motherhood truly is. My sister Tharsell "Honey" Watson is a good or complete mother, married to my brother-in-law for almost fifty year. My late sister, Norma Faye Bell was an unusually good/complete mother. She raised six children as a single parent after her husband died unexpectedly of a heart attack.

To my beloved mother, Mrs. Nathalie Mathis who is in Heaven, and to all the mothers (living or dead) who have maintained the high calling of motherhood, for the good and noble work you do, I honor you with… an **Eternal Thank You.** (See Mom's photo pages).

CHAPTER

O

Edward James Olmos

Edward James Olmos is not only a dedicated "champion" of young people in general, but he is particularly concerned for the plight of Latino kids. E.J. can always be found at conferences, enclaves, schools, and programs that are designed to encourage and empower youth. In fact, I believe him to be a tireless advocate for such causes. I am aware that he has faced some serious challenges and dangerous encounters as a result of his advocacy. Still, he continues to do what has become his most noble avocation. When I worked with the students and other young people in Watts, Venice, and East L.A., rarely was there a time when, if called upon, did he not respond with his time, and often his private generosity.

Edward James Olmos believes in the children, and they trust and believe in him. When he talks most young people listen. He shares truths from his own experiences, struggles from his own life, which Latino youths, Asian students, black kids and young people no matter what their ethnicities resonate to. He seems to be able to pin point the issues that affect young folks and speak to the heart of the matter. I have been present on occasions where he inspired youngsters to commit to doing their best in whatever walk of life they choose.

E.J. has clarity and a vision of America that is justified, and in my view, realistic. I have heard him say time and again that the idea of America as a "melting pot" is misleading and injurious. It stifles the very possibilities that form the American dream. He has said that he sees America not as "melting pot," but rather as a salad in which there is, and ought to be, different mixtures whose ancestral, cultural, ethnic and religious/spiritual differences are brought together to create a gourmet dish that is digestible, productive, and cooperative. This salad that relieves the hunger, satisfies the appetite, and distills the juices that quench the thirst of each participating person. This salad is made of human beings, respecting and honoring who they are, and those around them, from which comes an aroma and a taste that satisfies the palate of God. However, as the song says: "Its gonna take a lot of Love to change the way things are."

Here again, I do not claim to speak for Mr. Olmos. He is an effective speaker who speaks for himself. I am merely voicing my opinion as to why I feel he is, and deserves to be, appreciated by America in general. Following the civil unrest after the Rodney King verdict, I was among other concerned citizens—some famous, some ordinary people, who appeared on a panel at "FAME" First African American Episcopal Church in Los Angeles hosted by the senior pastor–at that time, Rev. Cecil "Chip" Murray.

E. J. knew of the work our group was doing in Los Angeles to help contain the restless and agitated youth at Jordan High School in Watts. We spoke briefly before the conference started, and when the meeting was over, Edward James Olmos introduced us to Peter Ueberroth.

Mr. Ueberroth had come to L.A. at the request of Mayor Tom Bradley, to head up "Rebuild L.A.," an organization with a mission that was synonymous with its name. Primarily because of Patricia Duff, Peter Ueberroth, Edward James and others, the young people in our group were supported in their efforts to keep a lid on the violence at Jordan High School. Since that meeting we were involved in many efforts to promote peace and increase opportunities for "at risk" children throughout Los Angeles County.

I remember hearing Edward James speaking to a group of students about the importance of perseverance. He said: "Once you have made up your mind, go after your dream, whatever it might be. Staying the course is one of the things you need to do in order to fulfill that dream."

He gave an astonishing example from his own life. One young lady in the group said that she wanted to be an actress. He replied, "Study, and learn everything you can about the art and craft of acting, and stay with it." Then he said "It took me eleven years before I got my first audition. I stayed with it, and now I earn seven figures per movie." Eleven years before his first audition? Everyone—students, instructors, and I—believe that all present understood the importance of perseverance, commitment, staying the course, hanging in there, never giving up. That is one of many profound ways he communicates with audiences young or old alike. It is a foregone conclusion that he is a fabulous actor, I think it is safe to say that helping youth is his personal mission. It is, without a doubt, the reason that I give a **Simple, focused, thank you… to Edward James Olmos**.

(See E.J. Olmos photo pages)

CHAPTER

P

Rosa Parks
American Icon

In her own heroic words:

"No! I will not give up my seat to that white man."

Mrs. Rosa Parks, the mother of the Civil Rights movement, for your courageous refusal to acquiesce to the hideous Jim Crow doctrine that forced Black people to live and suffer as second and in some cases third class citizens of these United States of America, We uplift your very name and extend to you and your memory…an everlasting Thank You.

Sidney Poitier
American Icon

Sidney Poitier, the Prince of Elegance and Grace. A year had passed since we first met Sidney and Harry in Greenwich Village.

Once again we appeared at the Philharmonic Auditorium with Cosby. It was a fun trip back to N.Y. Marcus and I saw Thelonius Monk at "The Five Spot," one of the famous jazz night clubs in the Village, the night before the Lincoln Center concert. We were eager to explore the "Big Apple" for the third time, but we were on a 10-day tour and had to be in Toronto in two days. I'd seen Harry when he appeared in concert at the Greek Theatre in Hollywood during the summer of the previous year. I had not seen Sidney since our first meeting at "The Bitter End."

On the night following this second Lincoln Center concert with Cosby, I got together with some friends, and they took me to what was at that time the hottest club in Manhattan. The name of the club was "The Salvation." It was the first of the super exclusive dance clubs in the city. When it closed down a few years later, Club 54 became the rage.

My friend was a drummer named Jimmy Brown. We had worked together in Europe. He and his Scandinavian wife Merna, wanted to introduce me to a lady named Wanda, who lived in Queens. I agreed to meet her but told them not to mention my connection with Cosby. When we got to Wanda's place I was introduced as a friend of theirs from L.A. Wanda was a striking female and right away her attitude let me know that she felt like she was too good to go out with me. In fact, they actually had to persuade her to keep her date with me. As we drove from Queens to Manhattan Wanda looked out of the window and pouted all the way. I tried to strike up a conversation with her, but she was curt and uninterested. I felt bad for Jimmy and Merna, but was completely turned off by Wanda. Merna tried to start a conversation that included Wanda and me, but Wanda was still being snooty. We rode the rest of the way in silence; I could feel Jimmy and Merna's embarrassment.

We walked into "The Salvation," and when we were seated and placed our order, Merna asked Wanda if she needed to go to the powder room. When they returned, Merna was a bit peeved with Wanda, but Wanda was still aloof and uninterested. Merna commented that they had seen Sidney Poitier walking out of the men's room. I looked around the club and spotted Sidney, Harry and his wife Julie, and Cosby in a corner booth. I excused myself, and walked over to the booth where Sidney et al were seated.

Cosby, Sidney and Harry were glad to see me and invited me to join them. I told them that I was with friends at another table. I added that the woman I came with was very beautiful but a complete dud. Sidney laughed, Harry chuckled softly, Harry's wife Julie was silent and Cosby did his famous eye roll toward the sky as if to say "What have you gotten yourself into?", and made his all-purpose one word comment that you might recall from the Cosby chapter, which is: "pit-ti-ful." I went back to my table and told Jimmy and Merna that I was going to join Sidney, Harry and Bill, and I told Jimmy to put the drinks on my tab. I did not even look at Wanda, although she was now smiling broadly at me, and trying to make eye contact. I absolutely hate it when people treat you like crap, and when they discover that you are somehow celebrated, start trying to suck up.

I'm not the only one who feels this way; every celebrity I know resents it. I ignored Wanda, and went back to join Sidney's group. To see Bill Cosby, Harry Belafonte and Sidney Poitier, hanging out together is a gift; it's a memory that will last forever. They truly dig each other and are genuine friends who keep you laughing as they tease each other at every opportunity. You can tell that they have the highest respect and admiration for each other because when a serious topic comes up, they each listen attentively to each other's point of view without interruption. They afforded me the same respect whenever I commented.

Anyone who has been around Sidney is aware of the majesty and power he has both on and off the screen. Like Bill and Harry, he is highly intelligent with incredible depth and insight without trying to come off as some "hoity-toity intellectual." Perhaps the most delightful thing about Sidney is his easy flowing and infectious laugh. Few people enjoy a good laugh the way Sidney Poitier does. I think that's what keeps him so youthful, and Belafonte and Cosby keep him going when they're together.

When they did those incredibly funny movies directed by Sidney, "Uptown Saturday Night" and "Let's Do It Again" with Richard Pryor, they lit up the talk show circuit on their promotion tour. Anyone who saw those talk show appearances will no doubt remember the absolute hilarity and side splitting laughter that literally had Sidney in tears. Overall the most enduring image of Mr. Poitier is that he fully enjoys life.

As an artist, what can be said that has not already been recognized by film-goers and movie makers, the press and media in general? As an actor he ranks with the truly great ones like Bogart, Spencer Tracy, Brando, Jack Nicholson, Robert DeNiro, Al Pacino, Sir Lawrence Olivier, etc. As an

African-American actor he stood on the foundation that was laid by Paul Robeson, Woody Strode, and William Marshall, and built a monument to them all.

His films "The Defiant Ones" and "Blackboard Jungle" were a complete and powerful awaking agent for yours truly. Every black man, woman and child who had ever been made to believe that the "real world" of Hollywood filmmaking was out of reach, was given a realization and hope that single-handedly shattered over three hundred years of an inferior mindset that had psychologically paralyzed nearly a whole race of people. Every film he made was significant, enlightened and timely. His work in "Guess Who's Coming to Dinner" and "In the Heat of the Night" serves to highlight his pattern of excellence. I've had the pleasure to be in his company on a few occasions, although I do not claim to be on his phone list. Every time I have been around him, Sidney has consistently left me with the impression that my assessment of his noble character, is, and will always be accurate and well founded.

One of my most embarrassing moments

It happened during that visit at The Salvation when I joined Sidney, Harry and Julie, and Bill at their table. On the Learjet flight to New York, I had mentioned that I would love to meet Lena Horne. Bill said it might be possible because he would probably see Harry Belafonte, and that Lena Horne was Harry's neighbor, and he would see if he could hook it up. I was excited by the possibility of actually meeting the great Lena Horne.

During the one hour or so that I spent at Sidney, Harry and Bill's table I danced with Harry's wife Julie a couple of times. I did not know at the time that she had been a professional dancer. When we got on the dance floor I saw that she was a great dancer. We danced to an upbeat song and whatever move I made she was right in step. I was thinking that not only does Lena look younger than I thought she would, but she knew all the latest dances i.e. "the Boogaloo," "the Jerk," "the Swim," etc.

When the song was over we went back to the table. A few minutes later, a song came on that Mrs. Belafonte apparently liked because she started to move to the music while seated at the table. I extended my hand across the table and said, "Lena, I dig this tune. Do you care to dance again?" All conversation stopped at the table, there was an awkward silence and all eyes were on Julie. After a beat she said "Lena? What do you mean Lena? I'm not Lena; Lena Horne is my neighbor and my friend but I am not Lena; I'm Harry's wife." I can only imagine the look that must've been on my face as I sat there with my hand extended, and several cartons of egg on my face. Finally, Sidney couldn't hold it anymore and he started to laugh. Harry tried not to, but couldn't hold it and joined in, and Cosby was chuckling when he looked at me and rolled his eyes toward heaven and mouthed the unspoken word, "pit-ti-ful." Julie started to laugh. I started to apologize and Mrs. Belafonte who, seeing my utter embarrassment, was still chuckling softly when she said something like: "Well, do you still want to dance?" I said, "Yes". Again Sidney led another brief course of laughter.

As Sidney, Harry, and Julie enjoyed a good laugh on me, Bill looked heavenward and shook his head. Was I ever the goat! On the dance floor I apologized again. Harry's wife said, "Don't worry about it. It's not the first time it's happened." When we got back to the table, she said, "You're a good dancer." I often wondered if her comments were designed to easy my lingering embarrassment or had she really been mistaken for Lena Horne before. I stayed with them for about another 20 or 30 minutes and it was as though my "faux pas" had never happened. By the time I left the booth to join the friends I'd come with, I felt like I had been initiated into the "your behind will get teased if you goof up around us" club. I shook hands with Sidney, Harry and told Cos I'd see him tomorrow back at the hotel. I said to Julie: "Well now you know, Julie; sometimes the only time I open my mouth is to change feet." She laughed as did the others, and I felt somewhat vindicated. When I returned to my original table, Wanda was a completely different person. She complimented me on my clothes, said I was a good dancer, and for the rest of the evening was willing to do whatever I wanted. I never called her when I went back to N.Y.

Once while in Vancouver, Canada, "The Pair" was appearing at a club named "Marco Polo." In the hotel lounge after our show, we were having some drinks with Kenny Rogers and Mickey Jones who were with the folk-rock band "First Edition." We were with the same management team, "Ken Kragen and Ken Fritz". They had booked Kenny Rogers and the F E in a club across town called "The Cave." Kenny was with his second wife, Margo, at the time. We had knocked back a couple of drinks before Kenny and Margo retired to their room. Shortly after, one of the other band members came into the lounge, and he and Mickey left to get Chinese food.

Marcus and I were finishing our drinks when this very British lady dressed in evening clothes approached our table. She was probably in her mid-to-late forties. She reminded me of a character straight out of a Noel Coward play. She said, "Excuse me gentlemen, but have you ever met Sidney Poitier?" I nodded yes; Marcus said, "Yes, we know Sidney." The lady placed her hands around her throat as though she were going to strangle herself, closed her eyes, threw her head back, and said, "Oh Sidney, Sidney, Sidney, there's nothing more compelling than Sidney Poitier dressed in tails." With that, she turned gracefully on her heels and returned to her table to join what appeared to be her husband.

About five minutes later the waiter arrived with a bucket of iced champagne and two glasses, and informed us that the couple towards the rear sent this with regards. Then he handed me a note that read "Thank you gentlemen, for knowing Sidney Poitier." We looked back and waved thank you to the Noel Coward couple, they waved daintily back. Marcus quipped to me, "Damn, next time let's tell them we're Sidney's cousins; maybe we'll get a Rolls."

Some years later I saw Sidney on TV wearing tails, I recalled that night in Vancouver. The Noel Coward lady was absolutely correct; there is nothing more compelling than Sidney Poitier wearing tails.

Five weeks ago, I participated in an all-male celebrity Fashion Extravaganza at the Hollywood Renaissance Hotel. It was hosted by The Regalettes, a philanthropic and social organization. Sidney was the guest of honor, and received the 2005 Gertrude Gipson Penland Humanitarian Award.

He was not wearing tails for the occasion, but seeing him in a super-sharp grey silk suit, a pink and grey silk tie, and his dignity and charm reaffirmed his iconic status. The way he has elevated us as a people, as a race, as a nation, forces me with inflated gratitude to offer **A Grand Thank You,** to the Prince of elegance and grace, to **Mr. Sidney Poitier**

(See Poitier photo pages)

Richard Pryor
American Icon

Today is December 11, 2005. It is a sad day because today the world lost a true king of comedy. The great Richard Pryor passed away from heart failure. For years he had struggled with the debilitating disease—MS (Multiple Sclerosis), his wife, Jennifer was by his side when he lost his battle with his long illness. I had not reached the chapter in this book that I was going to write about my association with Richard. It was mostly, but not always, the smooth relationship that it had once been. Although I was angry with Richard for a time, I am grateful that we had the opportunity to resolve our differences, and the last time we spoke we relived some of the fun and crazy times we had together. Like his many devoted fans, I will miss him, and like those who worked and played with him, I shall remember him with fondness.

Richard Pryor was notoriously unpredictable, light-hearted and fun to be with. Those were the days when fame had not yet fully caught up to Richard. The first time we met was at a party; then we occasionally ran into each other at various clubs around town, but did not get to be what I consider friends until we appeared in Lake Tahoe during the same week. Richard was booked at the Sahara, Marcus and I, were appearing with Cosby up the street at Harrah's. Some nights after our show we would go to Richard's late show and hang out. The next night Richard would catch our last show, and we'd all hang out at Harrah's. It was great fun; sometimes Cosby would take over a blackjack table and deal for maybe an hour. Richard, Marcus and I did not gamble at the tables where Bill was dealing. We would watch and cheer as Cos dealt a winning hand to every player at his table no matter what cards were dealt. He would pay out thousand of dollars to casino customers, while Bill Harrah, the hotel/casino's owner stood near by Cosby enjoying the whole thing.

One week Camille came to town, as was her custom from time to time, to spend a few days with Bill. By now we had gotten to know Richard pretty well, having partied a few times in LA, when he lived in Baldwin Hills. Our agencies had talked about putting together a package featuring Richard and The Pair. The deal was for a string of tours at mid-level college campuses that paid real good money, but couldn't afford to pay the "top of the heap" stack of money that Cosby could have commanded.

On the first night of Camille's visit, after our show at Harrah's, Bill asked us to tell Richard that he'd catch up with us later. Marcus and I walked the short distance to the Sahara. When we got to the show room Richard was still on stage. He was co-headlining with Shani Wallace –an English singer/actress who was riding the waves of the 1968 Academy Award winning movie "Oliver." We sat near the back of the showroom and watched the last part of Richard's act. That night was the first time we had ever heard Richard use a swear word on stage. He had been performing for years and was on the rise as a comedian; his total act was clean and without any x-rated words. One of his funniest bits at the time was "The first man on the sun."

Just before leaving the stage, Richard looked into the wings where Shani Wallace was standing, waiting to go on, and said over the mike something like: "This broad (referring to Shani) is standing in the wings bugging me to get off stage; I say screw her, I get off stage when the fuck I please." There was nervous laughter in the room because no one was expecting that kind of language, and was taken completely by surprise. Richard stayed on a couple of minutes longer, and left the stage. Marcus and I moved through the show room on our way backstage. We reached the front row and the late great Pearl Bailey (God rest her soul) was sitting at one of the tables with some friends. We said hello and proceeded on backstage when Pearl asked me if Cosby was coming by to see Richard. I told her that Camille was in town and Bill had asked us to tell Richard that he would catch him later. Meanwhile Marcus had continued back stage while I spoke with Pearl Bailey for a couple of minutes.

On my way to Richard's dressing room, as I turned the corner, an English fellow almost bumped into me. He apologized, shook my hand and proceeded to compliment me on our show, which he had seen the previous night. I don't know if he was Shani Wallace's husband, manager or what. I thought he was a fan. While I stood talking with the guy who was still shaking my hand, and going on about what a great and unique act we had, Richard stepped out of his dressing room into the hallway. He saw the English guy and me talking, and went back into his dressing room. When

I got to Richard's dressing room, he was in his inner dressing room with the door closed. Marcus was sitting in the outer dressing room where I was.

Approximately ten minutes passed when Richard opened his inner door, stood in the door way and said, "I'm not hanging out tonight; tell Cos I'll catch him later." I said (jokingly) "That's what Bill told us to tell you." Richard turned and went back into his inner room. Marcus stood up and said to Richard through the closed door, "If you change your mind, we'll be at the tables." We left Richard and went to the casino.

This was the final weekend for Richard Pryor and Shani Wallace's booking at the Sahara, but we had another week at Harrah's. The previous night Richard had said that when we get back to L.A. we should get together. He said he would come by the house. When we closed the following weekend and returned to L.A., I waited a couple of days, and called Richard. A lady answered the phone. I asked for Richard and told her my name. She said "I'll get him," then she left the line. A few minutes later she returned to the line and said "Richard is busy right now. Call back later." I thought nothing of it, so I waited a day or so, and I called him again. Still he did not come to the phone even though he was home. Marcus had gone to San Francisco to be with his girlfriend who lived in Daly City. A week passed and I had not heard from Richard, so I called a third time, and this time I left a message asking Richard to return my call. Still I didn't get a call from Richard, so I decided that I would not call again.

A week later, a girlfriend and I went to the "Club John" on La Cienega's Restaurant Row. As we stood behind the ropes waiting to be seated, I spotted Richard and a lady seated at a table for four and there were only two of them. I gave the maitre'd my name and asked him to inform Richard that my friend and I would like to join them. To my utter surprise, the maitre'd returned and told us that Mr. Pryor said he did not wish to have us join him. He didn't say why, so I explained to my companion that he and his wife were probably having a private conversation. It was rumored that they were having some issues, and things were not smooth between them. The maitre'd seated us at a table some distance from Richard and the lady. I had planned to get seated and go over to Richard's table and say hello, but as soon as we sat down Richard and his lady got up and left. He never looked our way, never waved or acknowledged us in any way. He just left. I was confused as hell, but played it off.

When Marcus returned from San Francisco, I told him how Richard had not returned my calls, and told him what had happened at Club John that night, and how he just left the club without saying a word. I said I know Richard can be a little strange, but I don't understand what's going on. Marcus replied, "I know what it is; I talked to Richard just before I left for

San Francisco. I left you a note saying that I would be back in a few days, and said for you to call me at Nyla's house, but you didn't call." I told Marcus that I didn't call him because he was spending time with his lady and I figured if it was important he would've said so, or called me back. "So what's with Richard?" Marcus said, "Do you remember that night when I told you that I walked into Richard's dressing room and that English dude had Richard pressed against the wall and threatened to kick Richard's ass?" I said, "Yeah," I remember." Marcus continued, "I told you when I walked in the guy took his hands off Richard and told him that, if he ever spoke to Shani Wallace that way again he would break Richard's face." I said to Marcus, "Yeah, but what the hell's that got to do with Richard acting funky?"

Marcus: "Richard told me that when he looked out into the hallway he saw you acting all lovey-dovey and shaking hands with the dude that had slammed him against the wall." Me: "How was I supposed to know that he had been hassling Richard?" Marcus: "I tried to tell Richard that the guy probably realized that the three of us would kick his ass, and he was trying to be buddy-buddy with you before you found out what he had done to Richard." At first I was pissed at Marcus for not telling me sooner, but he reminded me that he had only found out about the misunderstanding when he talked to Richard before leaving for San Francisco. Then he added, "I told you to call me at Nyla's. I would have explained it to you then." Marcus was right. There was nothing else for me to say, but I was still angry with Richard. I tried to call him two or three more times but he would not take my calls.

When I found out though our agent that Richard had opted out of the college gigs that were being lined up, it really made me furious because we missed a lot of money over something that I had nothing to do with. As a result, Richard and I did not talk for years.

In 1998 we finally got a chance to clear things up when Arsenio Hall brought Richard to the Laugh Factory one Saturday afternoon. The kids from Watts, Venice, and East L.A. were attending a Comedy Camp that Jamie Masada started and ran. Arsenio had told Jamie Masada that he would agree to participate only if Richard Pryor could come and speak to the kids. It was a special moment for everyone, especially me. At the end of the class Richard said a few labored words to the students, after which Arsenio wheeled Rich off the stage.

I approached Richard and told him who I was. He looked at me with such tenderness and said "I remember you and your bass playing partner." I said, "We were in Tahoe together." Richard said "Tahoe. Yeah Tahoe." Then I said to Richard, "Rich, that misunderstanding between us really broke my heart." He replied "I know it did, but that wasn't me, I was somebody else back then." I told him that it was so good to see him out and about. He asked: "But we had fun, too, didn't we?" I said, "Man, we had so much fun. You kept the party hopping."

Richard's van pulled up out front and Arsenio wheeled Richard to the sidewalk near the chair lift in his van. Richard's wife/manager, Jennifer was supervising the operation and preparing the van for Richard. I knelt down beside his wheel chair and told him, thank you for coming here today. I had no idea that he would be there, but it was a gift from heaven that allowed me to make things right between us. I told Arsenio, "Thanks for bringing Rich here today." I know that Richard meant the kind words he said to me, and I was delighted that he remembered us; I will always remember him as one of the greatest. To **Richard Pryor**: for all the laughter you made, we will be forever grateful. You showing up at the Laugh Factory that day, allowed me to smooth out some things between us that had been much too lumpy for far too long. I appreciate that I can send to you two things: The first is a deeply sincere "Rest in Peace" and the second is...**a Simple Thank You**

CHAPTER

Q

Quincy (Jones)

Quincy is the Man! We all know of his musical genius and down to earth personality. He was the first African-American executive with a major record company when he became vice president of I believe it was, Mercury Records. I met Q back in those earlier days when I was a singer. I also know of his close connection with the inner-city schools. Quincy discovered and mentored one of the most successful young men to graduate from Locke High School. That young man's name is Tyrese Gipson, a singer/actor/model, who took the entertainment industry by storm in the late 90's, thanks largely to Quincy Jones.

Quincy is respected by so many people from so many walks of life. One such individual is Reggie Andrews, a music teacher at Locke High School, who was a most valuable supporter of our after-school program, Colors United at Locke. Mr. Andrews is respected and loved in the community by all who know him. Among the rare things that I find fascinating are things that Reggie and Q have in common. For instance, of all the people we have spoken with, not once have I heard a derogatory remark being made about either of these men. I appreciate the help and support we received from Mr. Andrews at Locke, and by writing about the inimitable Mr. Quincy Jones' involvement there. I can take this opportunity to also thank Reggie. I'm sure that Q will be glad to share space with this superb human being, Mr. Reggie Andrews, who is in my opinion, one of the finest high school teachers in the entire country.

Quincy has been, perhaps, the main reason that so many young black men who have attained success have learned to handle their business affairs well. I wish I could say that I know him better, even though we moved in some of the same circles during the earlier years. I do know about his greatness, and some of the challenges he's had to overcome. If that is not enough, then I boldly and unapologetically, commandeer the right to recognize and honor him as a great American, and a superior African-American.

Q, for all the joy you've given us through the wonderful music you make, for the truly rare example you set as a successful and caring human being, and for the sheer delight we feel when we see you in life or on TV, you are a special light that shines through some of the darkness that threatens to engulf our world. Our way of showing our appreciation for you, is with…**A Simple Thank You**

Chapter

R

Eleanor Roosevelt
American Icon

Eleanor Roosevelt gave a lecture at Huston-Tillotson College during my sophomore year. I remember well the day she flew into (what was named at that time) Robert Mueller Airport, in Austin, Texas. The basketball coach, Rip Collins, drove the college president, Dr. J.J. Seabrook, and his wife to meet the former First Lady and drive her to the campus. On an impulsive whim, I convinced my friend and fellow band member, Wilber "Bate" Stern, to drive his 1950 Pontiac, "The Stepper Mobile" (named after our extremely popular band, "The Steppers"), as an escort. The Stepper Mobile could have used a good washing, but that didn't cross our minds—to us it was a lark.

We followed a respectable distance behind Coach Collins; they never noticed us. Stern and I waited at the arrival gate. The former First Lady deplaned and coach Collins and Dr. and Mrs. Seabrook moved quickly toward the aircraft to greet her. They retrieved her luggage from the baggage claim area and proceeded to curbside where the rented limo, was waiting. Stern had parked the unwashed Stepper Mobile directly behind the limo. The coach placed Mrs. Roosevelt's bags in the limo, and Stern and I approached the former First Lady and introduced ourselves. Dr. and Mrs. Seabrook were not pleased with our antics, but preferred not to call undue attention to our surprise appearance.

 Mrs. Roosevelt shook our hands and began asking us questions about the college. She asked how many students attended the school, how many were there in the graduating class, did we have a football team, etc. We answered her questions, and pointing to the faded grey Stepper Mobile, I jokingly asked: "Mrs. Roosevelt, would you like to drive to the campus in our car?" Mrs. Seabrook's jaw dropped when the former First Lady answered in her high-pitched finishing school voice, "I'd love to." It caught us all by surprise. She was serious. I opened the door to the Pontiac and began to push aside music manuscripts, unused music paper, and trash. She stood ready to enter the Stepper Mobile when Coach Collins said: "Mrs. Roosevelt, I think it would be more proper for you to ride with Dr. Seabrook and Mrs. Seabrook instead." She looked slightly puzzled; the coach added: "Plus, it would cause a lot less confusion." She paused briefly and said, "Oh?" Coach said, "Yes, ma'am, it would." She got into the back seat of the limo.

Twenty minutes later Coach Collins, Dr. and Mrs. Seabrook, and Mrs. Roosevelt drove through the front gate and onto the campus of Huston-Tillotson College (presently Huston Tillotson University).

That night Eleanor Roosevelt gave her lecture to enthusiastic applause and when she concluded, the standing ovation she received was thunderous and prolonged. It was a fitting tribute to a great lady who had delivered a forward looking speech that encouraged us as black students (negroes back then) and promised that positive change was inevitable—just waiting for the proper catalyst. At the reception that followed her talk, I asked her: "Mrs. Roosevelt, what is the most important piece of advice you can give to a young man like me?" I wrote down her answer. Without hesitation she said, "Take seriously your education. Learn well and walk tall; America belongs to you as much as it belongs to me, but you must claim it." She also said: "Don't allow anyone to make you feel inferior. No one can make you feel inferior unless you allow them to do so." I had not been accustomed to that kind of straightforward encouragement from someone of her stature, but I received it wholeheartedly, and have never forgotten it. She stayed overnight with the Seabrooks. Stern and I washed the Stepper Mobile in anticipation of escorting her to the airport for her trip back to New York. Unfortunately we were not told what time she would be leaving and missed the opportunity. Besides, we thought we'd better not push it.

For days after her departure the campus was abuzz with a kind of lingering excitement, not only about the all empowering lecture she gave, but everyone was impressed mostly by the way she seemed to genuinely enjoy being on our campus. She was completely natural and relaxed at all times, and at one point made a comment that she wished she could spend a semester on our campus. Every student at the college felt that she cared about us, and wanted to see us make America a better place. I believe she really would have liked to have been a political science teacher at our college for a semester. I think she enjoyed hanging out with us.

IN HER OWN WORDS

"One of the best ways to enslave a people is to keep them from education… and the second way of enslaving a people is to suppress the source of information, not only by burning books but by controlling all the other ways in which ideas are transmitted."

"Will people ever be wise enough to refuse to follow bad leaders or not take away the freedom of other people?"

"No one can make you feel inferior without your consent."

Mrs. Eleanor Roosevelt made us feel special, and for that I am sending her posthumously... **A Simple and well deserved Thank You.**

(See Roosevelt photo pages)

Chapter

S

Tom Shadyac

Tom Shadyac's chapter is without a doubt the most difficult chapter for me to write. It was not because of anything this good, gifted and easy-going gentleman instigated, but rather a misunderstanding that was allowed to grow when an aggressive and ambitious individual in our organization saw an opportunity to create distance between Mr. Shadyac and me. There was envy-based discontentment that had been brewing even before this aggressive person came along. A lot of it had to do with the fact that I was quite guarded about to whom I would give Tom's phone number. He and his wife Jennifer had committed to supporting these children and I was not keen to have people trying to contact him for their own personal agendas.

I think he trusted me to be reasonable about the people I would allow to connect with him. I understood that he was a busy man. I suppose because he and his lovely wife Jennifer were so accessible and cooperative when they came to the Saturday sessions at Jordan High School that some of the students, and many of the adults (instructors), felt that it would be ok to call him up for whatever reason. This may not have been the only reason why some felt that I was in their way when it came to matters of running the program.

When I got involved, the name of the class was PAS, an acronym for "Professional Actors Society". I became the music teacher and we formed a twenty voice choir. I saw a great need for someone to take an interest in these under-privileged students the way some of the people I have written about in this book had taken an interest in me.

As a high school student I had many of the same issues as young people face today. The wonderful people who helped me, and the grace of God, made all the difference in the world as far as the success I have enjoyed, and the good life that I'm fortunate to live.

The time was right, and here was an opportunity for me to keep building on a promise I made to my godparents: Mrs. Maurine F. Bailey, whom I have mentioned throughout this book, and her beloved husband, Mr. Sterling Bailey, whom I have also mentioned. Soon I was captivated by the great hunger for opportunity that these children had, and their almost desperate desire to do well in life.

It was not difficult at all to convince them that a meaningful and successful life begins, in most cases, with an education. The students soaked up our teachings like 100 lb sponges, and they responded to the discipline we imposed when required. From the very beginning we did whatever was necessary to keep the class going. This meant that during the first week of school we walked the campus daily in order to recruit twenty students— the minimum requirement to sustain a class. We did a good job of getting kids into the class.

We counseled students when they had various problems, and our basic curriculum consisted of acting, music, dance, and writing, with emphasis on conflict resolution, youth crisis intervention, and self-management. Initially, I signed on for a one hour per week commitment, but after a few weeks it became, on average, 18 hours a day, six (and more often than not, seven) days a week.

There was no such thing as a day off. The word vacation was not in our vocabulary. The young people in our group, "Colors United" were the most wonderful, energetic, generous and grateful bunch of kids imaginable. I still think of them as special, and I'm always delighted when I happen to run into some of them, as I have done on occasion. The founder of the program, Phil Simms, was smart, creative, and committed, and as co-founder, I greatly admired him in spite of his eccentric and sometimes chaotic personality.

We worked for no pay-except the executive directors, and the instructors were paid. We worked six or seven days a week for nearly seven years straight and I loved every minute of it. The program grew each year, adding school sites and outreach to an increasing number of dedicated students and their grateful parents. As is the case in most organizations, some of us did not always see eye to eye and there were ulterior motives, and manipulation by one person in particular.

Due to a personal crisis endured by one of our most ardent financial supporters, funds ran out and we struggled to keep it together. The tension grew in the boardroom. Finally, we hired a woman named Shirley Quarman–may she rest in peace—as executive director. Her no-nonsense style was just what the organization needed. She looked into the situation, saw the problems, learned the truth, and within a year she had us on track.

The year before Mr. Shadyac got involved we had lost our offices in Westwood. Times were tough. We moved into a building in the backyard of a house that Lenny Kravitz and Lisa Bonet had purchased in Venice during their brief marriage. We had almost zero dollars in the bank, and after five solid years of working an average of eighteen hour days for absolutely no pay, and contributing our own money from time to time for the day-to-day operations, we were pretty much tapped out.

Our cadre of dedicated instructors were not being paid on-time and sometimes not at all. The program was about to fold. We had expanded this highly successful youth program into about eight schools, including an on-going relationship with CSSSA (California State Summer School for the Arts) at Cal Arts in Valencia, California. Thanks to two of its board members, Rob Jaffe, and, Marcy Davey, it was a successful venture. The students loved it, and worked extremely hard to win the yearly scholarships that Rob and Marcy made available.

We had also designed a program for elementary school children. The plan was to implement the program in order to reach kids at a younger age before they had been influenced by the gangs and peer pressure that could cause them to make choices that were not in their own best interest.

Shirley Quarman was strong and not intimidated. She saw the truth of the situation and immediately began to set things straight. She could not be bullied and she dealt with the nonsense head-on. The overt acts of sabotage ceased, and the perpetrators were pretty much put in check. Unfortunately, Shirley was suddenly stricken with cancer and within six months of her diagnosis she died. That was the beginning of the end of the organization.

While Shirley Quarman was executive director, she hired an office manager/assistant. When Shirley was diagnosed, she began to train the assistant. This new woman had previously been in charge of other 501 c 3 programs, and had knowledge and experience with non-profit organizations. When she took over, she ruled with an iron hand. My partner and I-as the heads of the organization, felt as though we were targets.

The new ED, saw the division that was growing between the two of us that was based on the fact that I would not accept the role into which he wanted to place me, after we had built the organization together. My partner wanted to replace me as co-founder with the person that had a hidden agenda.

I did not object when I was asked to step down as president of the organization to be replaced by a university professor who had a Ph.D. This made perfect sense to me, seeing as how we ran an education-based operation. As co-founder, I did not have the slightest problem with the new president, whom I believed would bring added prestige and credibility to the table. It was later suggested that I accept the title of "music instructor." This individual with the (by this time) not so hidden agenda, and no experience, would replace me (if not by title, certainly by leadership). This was totally ridiculous and unacceptable to me.

In my view, it was the same old story. A man of dedication and certain expertise helps to create and build something from the ground up. When that business or organization is well established, then, due to cronyism, he is relegated to a lesser position. If he refuses to acquiesce, he is somehow removed. Fortunately, I had the legal high ground.

As unbelievable as this is, one has to understand the mindset of the dictatorial person who was largely behind the scheme.

The students in the program knew the truth about him, but young people generally will not go against such a one. Although he was sometimes a bully, even the kids that did not fear him (and most of them did not) will stick to the code of not getting involved in another person's conflicts—and rightfully so.

The instructors also knew the truth, but because the founder of the organization, and a few board members, supported and encouraged him no matter how outlandish his actions, he was handled with kid gloves. Bottom line, this young man became completely out of control. He knew absolutely nothing about running a corporation, or any kind of business. Yes, he was smart, articulate and persuasive, and could boss some of the students, but there was little or no balance or compassion to his leadership. I occupied the position he wanted, and I was in his way.

My method of leadership was to treat every student the way I had been treated by the caring teachers who took an interest in me when I was in need of understanding and guidance. They treated me as a young adult with respect, kindness, and measured discipline when I got out of line. Because of their gentle but firm guidance, they "saved me from myself," so to speak. Their love and respect was the primary cause for my academic, professional, and personal successes. I patterned my approach to trying to help young people after their very effective teaching skills, and I refused to respect any one who wants to bully or disrespect others. Ninety percent of the students respected and trusted me for that. On one occasion, the spoiled kid threatened to "kick my ass"; he did not care that there were witnesses present. I think his intention was to show off in front of the students and, secondarily, to intimidate me. He accomplished neither: I think I dealt with each incident, measure for measure, but without bravado or inflammatory response. After all, I was the adult and it was my responsibility to conduct myself as such.

At the end of the school year, the students were given awards for various achievements, i.e. improvement with their grades, attitudes, community outreach (i.e. successfully encouraging kids to get out of gangs, and joining the after-school program, as well as for food distribution to elders and other needy residents etc). Because of their efforts, Jordan High School and Colors United were declared "neutral territory" by **all** the street gangs in Watts.

Every student received an award, and deservedly so. They were an outstanding group of former gang-bangers who worked tirelessly and successfully to stop the drive-by killings in the communities they served. The annual awards banquets were always fun-filled events for the kids and their parents, as well as our staff.

My passion was to help young people the way I had been helped as a teen-ager. I was fortunate, because by the age of fifteen I had encountered caring teachers that were able to reach me.

I was able to accept the discipline that Col. Carrington instilled in me as an ROTC cadet. When Ma Bailey corrected me at any given time, I received it, and acted on it. When Mama Chandler invited me into the teacher's lounge, kicked off her shoes, and spoke to me as an adult, I knew that it was time to tow the line. They never raised their voices. They simply showed me the consequences and the potential problems I would create for myself. They showed me how much I had to lose at school and later in life, if I chose to ignore their good counsel.

As teachers, they supported each other. This was not always the case in our program. Eventually, we lost our suite of offices at New World Pictures. That's when we moved into the house owned by Lisa Bonet and Lenny Kravitz. Miss Bonet also housed her non-profit organization in this facility and after three months at this new location, we were asked to pay a small stipend to her organization, which we did.

Having lost out primary source of funding, the board called a special meeting and asked Phil to start a for-profit division for which he would be paid a salary to run. I was asked to become a fundraiser for the organization. They offered me a straight commission on whatever funds I raised. I told the board that I would take a commission the first year, and suggested that it be on a decreasing scale thereafter. A contract was drawn and I began to send out proposals to raise funds for the program.

I have great respect for the students in our program, and for one particular young man's integrity, because he refused to join in with the lies that were being circulated. I was told by another student that this young man had been asked to join in but he refused. I saw this young man one day, and asked him about it. He told me that when an instigator approached him, he told him he would not say negative things about Kingston, because "That is not the Kingston I know." I thanked him for his honesty and courage. He told me that it did not take any courage for him to do what was right. I have dedicated a chapter in this book to him. He is a remarkable person not only for his refusal to support lies, but as you will see when you read chapter V, he is a winner in every thing he undertakes.

Some of the Board members believed, as did I, that the woman who became executive director after Shirley Quarman died might have had her own agenda. She started by convincing the board that Phil and I needed to stop teaching classes and stay away from the campuses, because the kids would only respond to his and my discipline, and new blood was needed. I understand that new people are needed in order for an organization to grow, and fresh ideas toward fulfilling the mission are necessary. When I was told to refrain from going on the campuses, I complied and began working in the office. Steve, the student that was responsible for our meeting Mr. Shadyac, and Ira, our main instructor, saw me in the office every day after I stopped going to the school sites. Yet it is my understanding that when asked, one of them said that I had not been there.

Let the Truth Be Known

Whenever a black person knowingly allows misinformation to circulate about a black man, it is most often automatically believed, especially when told to a person of another race.

One day I received a message from Tom Shadyac, and I immediately returned his call—was I ever shocked, and totally undone. He really "let me have it." I had seen him get upset once before, when he took a young actor that he had considered sponsoring and me to lunch one afternoon. After lunch, Tom said he wanted to go talk to his agent.

The agent was being a bit self-important for some reason, and Tom let the agent know that he expected the agents to do what he asked. He was not rude, he did not yell and scream, but he made it known in a quiet and forthright way that he meant business. After the meeting, I went back to the campus, and Tom went back to his offices at Universal.

The students were aware that I was meeting with Tom that day. When I returned to the campus for the after-school session, they were eager to know how the meeting had gone. I explained that the meeting went well and Tom had sent regards to the class. I remember saying to the students: "That is one man you would not want to cross." I gave them a brief over-view of the situation where Shadyac has been sort of unhappy with the way one of the agents was responding. I wanted the young people to know that just because Tom and his wife were down to earth and friendly, they must never take their kindness for granted. Of course they understood, and continued to always be respectful not only of Tom Shadyac, but to all of our supporters and guests. I was saying this for the kids benefit, because I had no intention or desire to cross anyone, and especially not someone who had been as gracious and concerned about these children as Tom Shadyac, and his wife Jennifer, had been. They are among the most genuine people I've met; they are unaffected, and care deeply for the plight of young people. I appreciate them for what they contributed to the program, but it is because of who the Shadyacs are as people that I grew to respect them the way I do.

When he got off the phone with me that day, I was devastated. He accused me of misleading him, being dishonest. I had no clue what was going on. My only hope was that he would do a thorough investigation of the bank records and discover that every single dollar was accounted for. The records would show that I had done exactly what was promised with the funds he and his wife donated, and that I had accurately reported every penny that we had received. Having been misled and believing that I had tried to "hustle" him, naturally he would not take my calls after that.

I was crushed. I called Ma Bailey (my godmother) in Dallas; I told her everything. I will never forget the words she told me: "If he's who you say he is he will come to know the truth about you." She was 97 years old at the time and still had a sharp mind. Before I hung up the phone, she said to me: "Don't you worry; Mr. Shadyac is a smart man. He will investigate this matter. If he looks into your past, from day one he can only find that (these are her words, not mine) your whole life has been that of an African-American hero." I never thought of myself in those terms and still don't, but her words were reassuring, and gave me some much needed relief. She said she would ask God to lead Mr. Shadyac to check me out thoroughly; then he would see the truth for himself.

She reminded me what she had told me since I was a kid: "Life is not a bed of roses." Ma asked me why he thought I was dishonest with him. Before I explain why, I want to say, I could have lied to him and probably been off the hook. But in spite of the turmoil I went through, I feel good that I never lied to him. If I had it to do all over again, I still would not lie to him. The one glimpse of light that shown through the despair I felt was that I knew and God knew, and I believe that Tom now knows that I encountered his displeasure because I feel that I was set up by certain peoples in my own organization.

My mind went back to the last time I had seen Tom before the misunderstanding occurred. It happened at Venice High School when he had come to watch a performance of the students. Mrs. Shadyac did not accompany him that particular evening. The students put on a great show, and Tom was quite pleased with what he saw. The two hour show was filled with songs, dance, skits, comedy and, relevant social commentary.

After the show, Tom hung out backstage with the students and staff for almost an hour. He seemed and looked, like one of them.

I walked him out as he was leaving and he told me how much he had enjoyed the show. He was especially pleased that he had seen a tap dance routine because he had purchased several pairs of tap dancing shoes for these students. That night he saw his money in action and was delighted. We briefly discussed what the projected budgetary needs were for the coming school year. Because the program had been expanded to include two additional middle schools and the East L.A. Skill Center, the budget would be more than the previous year. When I mentioned the approximate figure, he said he would discuss it with his wife and his CPA.

Was it a mistake not to tell him right then and there about the contract I had with the organization that paid me commission on the funds I raised? I do believe that if he had heard it from me, it would not have made one bit of difference to him. More importantly, it would not have given the person in our office -that "set me up" a chance to drive a wedge between Tom Shadyac and me. The irony of the matter is that I could have told him that night. We were talking about the kids and how they'd done. Suddenly he looked at his watch and said he had to run because his wife was waiting up for him. It was almost 11:00pm, and I did not want to delay him any longer.

When Tom Shadyac first agreed to support our program, I promised him that I would give him an annual report detailing the activities and the expenditures. I explained that the third year I would give a progress report, a financial statement, and complete breakdown of how the organization had functioned up until that point. This was the third year, and that report and breakdown would have been forthcoming.

I will never forget that unsettling conversation on the day of his admonishment. Tom asked me a question and he prefaced it by saying, "Kingston, tell me truthfully, the reason you didn't tell me that you were receiving a commission was because you thought I would not have given the money; is that right?" I could have easily said, "No, I just forgot," or some other made-up story. Instead I answered him truthfully. That was exactly the reason. I was going to wait until the third year after he had seen firsthand, year after year, with his own eyes, exactly where every cent of the funds he gave us had been spent, and how accurate the record keeping was and how punctual the reports had been. It was a conscious decision that I alone made.

When he became involved, the program was in such desperate financial need he was exactly right—I felt that I could not take the chance that he might not make the donation. I realize in hindsight that had I done so, it would not have caused our developing friendship to flounder.

My mistake was to not tell him my reason, because that too would have been the absolute truth with a reasonable explanation—if you only knew the many times I've wished I had done that. What I'm about to say won't be macho; it might make me look like a wimp, but it's the truth. I was so stunned, shook up, and surprised at Shadyac's discontentment that all I wanted was for the conversation to be over. When it finally was over, the anguish started to set in.

The new executive director and I had agreed that I would send that third year's reports to Tom and from that point on, she could make the reports. Contrary to that agreement, instead of waiting for me to send Tom my report, the ED wrote a report and sent it to Tom, while I was out of town.

I am not saying that she was blatantly dishonest, but as I stated earlier, some of us felt that she may have had an hidden agenda from the start.

I'm sure her report was accurate, because it was based on the records and bank statements, but I wanted to breakdown the commission structure.

When I asked the ED why she had done that, she replied that she did it because it was her job. I suspect it could have been for other reasons. It is never one's job; in fact it can be a dangerous and foolish proposition to interfere with the fiduciary relationship between a fundraiser and the donors with whom he/she has successfully established a relationship, unless a smooth transition is made.

Aside from losing Tom and Jennifer's trust, the most painful thing for me throughout this ordeal was discovering that so many people who knew the truth stood by and allowed the untruths to continue. Most notably, among them, were two people that I personally trusted.

Everyone knew without a doubt, that I worked on average eighteen hours nearly every day, either on campus, at one of the school sites, or in the office, and at night at home doing a myriad of preparatory things that only Phil and I were willing and/or able to do.

I had tried to reach Tom when I returned from Texas, because someone had told me that Tom liked Hockey. I acquired tickets for opening day at Staples Center for the Kings Hockey game. My plan was to treat him to a hockey game, and after the game maybe have a beer in the lounge, and hand him my beautifully bound three year report which would have explained everything in absolute detail. "The best laid plans of mice and men often go array".

I feel as though I lost a friend. I'm told that those who were jealous of that developing friendship were gloating. The thing that bothered me most was when Tom Shadyac said to me, "Kingston I trusted you. Now you have caused me to not want to trust." That went deep.

I will always admire Tom for his talent, and respect him for his ability to see the world the right way. I have been extremely blessed in my life, and I thank God, that in my entire adult life I've never needed anything and not been able to acquire it honestly. I put my music career on hold to devote full time to Colors United and I don't regret a day I spent with the students. Some might ask why I would do such a thing. I can say truthfully that it is because it became (as I stated before) my over-riding passion. When you impact young people's lives in a positive way and have the good fortune to see the results firsthand, it's a feeling that captivates and compels you to want to continue.

To know that you have prevented a kid from killing someone is a great feeling. To give young girls a sense of themselves that helps to keep them from teen pregnancy, and a lack of self-respect, is in itself a great reward. To help under-privileged students improve their grades, go to college, graduate and become productive citizens is a big deal for anyone fortunate enough to experience it. Those are reasons enough to cause one to continue. The most fetching thing of all, though, is to see the sheer unadulterated, unmasked gratitude in the teary eyes of grateful parents who thank you for saving their child from a certain life of drugs, crime, incarceration, and possibly an early and senseless death. That's why I put my career on hold, and in spite of the program's premature ending, it was well worth the eight years I invested. The program was one of the most successful of its kind in the nation. .

Tom and Jennifer Shadyac rescued the program, but the deception, backbiting and jealousy that destroyed the spirit of the organization had taken its toll. If things had continued that way, I have no doubt that the envy and resentment would have become completely malignant and even more destructive. Like my dear departed godmother said before she passed away at the age of ninety-nine in the year 2000: "They tried to harm you, and ended up harming themselves and worst of all, they deprived deserving young people help and hope."

Ma Bailey reminded me of a situation when I was a freshman in college. One of my music professors did not like me from the first day he saw me. He tried very hard to make trouble for me. His under-minding tactics, however, compelled me to stay on top of my studies.

My college piano teacher spoke up for me against the lies and attempted mistreatment. Years later, she explained why the music professor had a problem with me. According to her, he disliked me because I reminded him of a student who had graduated four years prior to my enrollment. She said, that student, like me, was from Dallas, and majored in music. He also had a band that played at night clubs, fraternity and sorority parties in and around Austin. It seemed that the professor had been cuckolded by the guy who had graduated four years before I enrolled. My piano teacher told me that the paramour was about my height, weight, and complexion. She told me that that teacher had once remarked that I reminded him of the guy that was fooling around with his wife. This is a foolish and dangerous game that I refuse to play.

Ma Bailey reminded me of other times when I had been lied on. She told me that people who have a lot to offer are often the victims of envy, jealousy, and resentment. I asked why this is so, she chuckled and said, "Honey, when you are a bright light, inferior people feel like they are in your shadow. Just remember that this is not the first time it's happened to you, and it probably won't be the last."

I do not think of myself as any kind of bright light, but I trust her wisdom. I asked what to do to prevent it. Ma told me, "You can't prevent it, not if somebody's got their mind set on trying to reduce you." It was like she was reading my thoughts. She continued, "No need to confront them, it will only give them reason to press on." She said, "The best way I've found to deal with it is to not let them know that you are aware of what they're trying to do. Protect yourself by watching the company you keep, and what you say and do around them, but don't let them know that you're on to them."

To my delight, I saw Tom Shadyac at the world premier of the movie "Seabiscuit." I was coming out of the theatre after the screening, and I heard someone call my name. I looked around and to my pleasant surprise it was Tom. He was upbeat, and told me he had enjoyed the movie and my work in it. We chatted briefly about the film and I told him I had seen him a couple of times on the Universal lot but did not approach him because it was too painful to risk experiencing that type of displeasure again. He looked at me and said: "Kingston, I want you to forget that whole thing." I said: "Thanks Tom, that means a lot to me." He saw that his ride was coming and started toward the car. I said: "Can I call you and take you to lunch sometime?" He said: "Yeah, call me." I went back into the theatre to get my lady-friend who had gone to the powder room. I was floating on air to hear him say that.

In life people come and people go and ordinarily you accept that fact and move on. However, for me it is not every day that I meet someone who is a high-quality human being such as any one of the people I write about in this book.

I realize that in this town (Hollywood) when you fall into disfavor with someone important it can be difficult at best to re-establish a connection. Sometimes it is because they might not want to reconnect, and sometimes because the people around them might block the communication. I don't know if either is true in this case. When I made my A to Z outline for this book, I knew that when I reached the letter "S" in the alphabet the person I wanted to write about would be Tom Shadyac. This is mainly because I want him to know the truth, which I suspect he knows, and perhaps because of the cathartic nature of this particular chapter, but mostly because Tom Shadyac and his wife Jennifer are people whose relationship is worth salvaging.

Tom is without a doubt an important player in this town. His success dictates that when he speaks people listen. If he had slandered me, my name would have been burnt toast in this town.

I am certain that his investigation proved that the derogatory things that may have been said or implied about me were untrue. However, as time goes on, I am still conflicted because, in my opinion, to lose the respect of someone who trusts you is to sow the seed of harsh, and not so easily dismissed, self-condemnation. On the other hand, had things been different, he might have continued to help the young people that we served, and that would have been a good thing. The unfortunate thing is that the backbiting seem to have gotten out of hand. It eventually destroyed a unique and successful program that was literally changing the inner-city communities of L.A. for the better.

My regret is that Tom and I did not complete the good works that I have no doubt that providence brought us together to do. It was a total misfortune that the program ended, not because it would become so successful that it would be no longer needed, but because of the attitude of certain adults. I deeply regret the misunderstanding and I take full responsibility for whatever part I played in it. I never set out to, nor did I cheat anyone.

The young people in the urban centers of Los Angeles-Watts, Compton, Venice and East L.A., lost the most. The City of Los Angeles lost the chance to export a proven successful youth intervention program that is so needed in every American city where racial conflict, gang and violence, and economic division seem to be on the rise, and increasing polarization is in motion. I lost the potential friendship of two people who I admire. That being said, I offer **A Sincere Thank You...** to **Tom Shadyac** for his desire to help make this world a better place, where all children have a chance to become living expressions of what is good, positive, caring, and lifelong ambassadors for peace. (See Shadyac photo page)

CHAPTER

U

Blair Underwood

I was introduced to Blair Underwood at a social gathering for a charitable cause. We spoke briefly and before the evening was over, I invited him to come to Jordan High School to see the great work these young people were doing in an after-school program. I explained that our "master" class was held on Saturdays at J.H.S., and that the Saturday classes were made up of students and kids from the various barrios and neighborhoods such as Watts, Venice, East L.A., Santa Monica, and Los Angeles.

Mr. Underwood agreed to visit the campus on the Saturday immediately following the evening we met. I gave him directions how to get to the campus, and where to park once he arrived. Our Saturday class started at 10:00 a.m. because this gave the students who traveled to Watts by bus, time to travel to the campus and arrive on time. As was our custom, my partner and I arrived early in order to unlock the doors to the auditorium where the class was conducted.

Blair was to have arrived at 9:45 a.m. Most celebrities when invited arrived on time. There were very few who showed up late, and fewer still that did not show at all. Still I was always a bit apprehensive until I actually saw them drive onto campus. That Saturday was no different. I waited for the guest in the security office near the parking area. I waited, talking to the security chief, Mr. Talmage Emerson, and at 9:30 a.m. Blair drove under the archway and onto the campus. I flagged him down and he followed me to a parking place just outside the auditorium entrance.

At 10:00 o'clock we assembled the kids onstage and introduced Blair Underwood. The students were very familiar with him, and as always they were polite, courteous, pleasant, but not intimidated by the guest. Blair had initially agreed to spend an hour observing and talking to the group. He saw how bright and talented these inner-city children were and he ended up staying through lunch—which he and the other guest helped to prepare. He, in particular, was pleasantly surprised when he discovered that the kids were familiar with just about all of his works, especially the one in which he played the role of a psychopathic killer. Blair had forgotten to mention this particular movie when giving his film and TV credits to the class. To his surprise and delight, the student had remembered that film as being his favorite Blair Underwood film. He was open, honest, unpretentious, and interested in the well-being of the kids, and we liked that.

He had a good time interacting with the students, answering their many questions, and his cogent answers were designed not only to inform these children, but also to help them gain confidence in their own ability to succeed. His was no Pollyannaish dissertation on the various questions and subject matter that the students presented to him. The young men in the class related to him because of his male prowess and natural "smooth." The female students, having been taught to not fawn over any of the guests, saw him as an absolute "heartthrob." Blair spoke lovingly of his family and pointed out the importance of having a good family life, and the support a family can offer, especially in times of stress brought on by the ups and downs of a sustained career. He stayed until the class was concluded, and promised the kids that he would come back.

When I left the organization 3 years later after about eight years, I started seeking work again as an actor and musician. I was booked on an episode of a new TV series," City of Angels," that was in its first season. It was a small role—in fact, I only had one scene, but it was important for me as an actor, to get back into the swing of things after about an eight year absence. When I received the script and discovered that Blair Underwood was the star of the show, I wondered how he would be to work with, and what his attitude on the set would be. As it turned out he was in the scene with me, but my character as a patient and his character as the head surgeon only exchanged glances in the shot. But even in that brief glance, he would be totally focused, and his glance was encompassing. When I arrived on the lot on the Culver Studios, I changed into my wardrobe, and finished with make-up. I went back to my dressing room to look over my lines and wait until I was called to the set. It was my first time on the set in eight years, and I was apprehensive.

On my way to my dressing room, I had to pass by Blair's room. His door was open, and I looked in and saw Blair Underwood sitting on his couch thumbing through a magazine. He had already shot his first scene and was obviously waiting to be called to the set to shoot the scene that we both would be in. Although the door to his dressing room was open, I peered in and knocked; he looked up from the magazine and said come in. I could tell by his expression that my face was familiar to him, but after all it had been some three years since he visited J.H.S. and spent the day with the students. I stepped inside and re-introduced myself. The minute I mentioned my name he recognized me from the after-school class at J.H.S.-Colors United. He asked how the kids were doing, and stated that he had not been contacted to make a return visit to the campus. I explained that I was no longer involved in the program. He seemed disappointed, and commented that it was a great program and too bad it closed down. I told him that I was hired to play one of the characters in the scene that he would be shooting just before the lunch break. Blair looked at his script and saw there were no lines spoken between our characters therefore, we had no need to rehearse. I stayed in his dressing room about ten more minutes before going back to my own dressing room.

About twenty minutes later, I was called to the set to shoot the scene. It took about 90 minutes to rehearse, block, and shoot. When the director said: "check the gate" (the camera gate) to make sure everything was clear, and the 1st AD replied after about 30 seconds, "The gate is clean," the director said, "print it." Six of the most important words on a TV or movie set is "the gate is clean" and "print it." The only other words that could be said to be of equal or greater importance are: "picture is up" and "that's a wrap." "Picture is up", means that all the lighting, the props, blocking, rehearsing, and any other technical or artistic preparations, and adjustments have been approved by the director. When "picture is up," is announced by the 1st AD, that means we are going for the main take and everybody knows that this is the take that requires your <u>very best</u> effort. In other words, this is the take that can get people fired.

"That's a wrap" means that the director, producers, executive directors and the "suits" (in television, the network bosses are referred to as "the suits") are pleased with the day's work, and the actors are free to go home for the day. My one scene, having been finished before lunch, I could stay for lunch and after I could either go home or stay and watch the other actors shoot their scenes. At lunch, Blair and I spoke again. I suppose maybe when he saw that my work on camera was professional (meaning that I showed up on time, knew my lines, took direction well, stayed focused, and did a good job of acting) he told me that he looked forward to our working together again. This is the best compliment an actor can receive from another actor whose work he, also, admires.

I am impressed by Mr. Underwood's talent as an actor, but more importantly, I am impressed and moved by his commitments of time and resources which he donates to humanitarian interests. I like him as an artist, and as a person, and I am grateful to him for the time, and the interest he has shown, and his willingness to continue to give to the at-risk youth in Los Angeles. **Blair Underwood**, please accept…**A Simple Thank you.**

Chapter

V

Alvin "Fro" Vasquez
Personal Hero

Alvin "Fro" Vasquez is a young man for whom I have the highest respect. Not only for his refusal to support those who were bent on spreading untruths, but for the total commitment that he and his younger sister, Ellia, showed from the very first day they joined Colors United. They were introduced to the program by their equally talented and bright cousin, Rosalee Velasco. Every instructor and most of the students noticed something special from the moment they took to the stage for our opening session. If memory serves me right, "Fro" as he prefers to be called was a sophomore, and Ellia was a freshman at Belmont High School, where they both attended, near downtown Los Angeles.

At six foot three, he was a strikingly handsome kid who held a black belt in Karate. As a senior at Belmont, he first competed on the U.S. Karate team. When he was a freshman at Cal State (where he attended college on a scholarship), he placed second for the U.S. national team in the international Karate tournament that was held in Korea that year. Fro was quiet soft-spoken and every bit a leader. He could do it all. He was a good actor who paid strict attention to what was being taught. It did not matter if the instructor was the wonderful Kathy Bates, well known screen writer, Bob Dolman, professional director, Michele O Hayon, or one of our regular instructors. Board Chair/dance instructor, Ann Marie Gillen, as well as, Nisha Folks, Ira McAlily, and Dave Dunard all agree that he was talented, focused and mature. He soaked up information and knowledge from the beginning of class till the closing circle at the end of the day.

Although I don't think he was that crazy about singing, he participated full out. Fro was an excellent rapper, a very talented actor, a dynamic dancer who always knew the dance routines. Never once did any instructor have to speak to him about horsing around or not paying attention. Sure, he would fool around with the rest of the students, but only between classes, or during a break.

Everybody had the utmost respect for Fro. He did not make a habit of trying to tell the other students what to do, or how to behave, even though he could have easily done so. If, however, someone was seriously wasting time on stage he would say in a fairly loud but not bossy voice, "People we are losing the light." This is a phrase that he picked up from various movie sets where he and a number of our other students appeared as extras. One of our students, Latoya "Lovely" Howlett, landed a leading role in the network TV series, "Dangerous Minds". I'm glad that "Lovely" handled her earnings wisely.

"Losing the light" means that the crew is taking too long setting up the shot, and the sunlight is changing too much to make the scene work, or perhaps, it's at the end of the day and starting to get dark.

Even in class, if some of us instructors would lose focus or get carried away trying to make a point, or taking too much time away from the issue at hand, Fro would say in a firm but respectful voice: "We're losing the light." The students would laugh, and if the unfocused instructor happened to be me, I'd get embarrassed, join in the laughter, and quickly get back to the point.

Being a Karate champion, his body was chiseled to perfection. I, on the other hand, was beginning to put on pounds from eating fast foods and the snacks that were always available for the young people after school. When my weight started to get out of hand, Fro started calling me "Belly Man". His relentless teasing finally caused me to start eating better and exercising more. When he noticed the change, and only then, did he cease calling me "Belly Man." He got me back on track at an important time of my life.

I understood why Fro and his sister Ellia were special the moment I met their parents. I had the honor of meeting their dear mother one afternoon when I dropped Fro off at home after class. Mrs. Vasquez is a lovely lady who has inspired her children to love and respect her the way that Ellia and Fro do, indeed. She's the kind of lady you want to have praying for you. To me it was like she exudes goodness. I am glad to have met her.

Ellia Vasquez

Take all those qualities and attributes that I assigned to Fro, duplicate them, add to that, what is called by young people today, a "hot chick," that's Ellia. She is about five feet eleven inches tall, educated, and a beautiful young woman. She, too, is an athlete and martial artist. Ellia is approximately a hundred 120 lbs, gorgeous brown eyes; she is sophisticated, but very friendly. That about rounds out her physical description

On stage, whether in rehearsal or performance, Ellia is an anchor. She is a good singer, good actress, fantastic dancer, and a leader who doesn't speak a lot. Her concentration is to the bone when the teaching starts. I can not think of a single moment since I've known them when I was not proud of both her brother and her.

When Ellia received her B.A. degree from Cal State I was just as proud as I was the day Fro walked across that stage and received his degree two years prior. I can imagine how elated their parents must have been. They both worked hard, stayed focused, and succeeded. I know each of them will have a good life and I wish them all the best. When Ellia graduated, I got the chance to meet their father. He is quite the proud father, and deservedly so. Their respect for him is apparent.

Following the graduation ceremony, I spent a couple of hours with them and I enjoyed it immensely. The senior Mr. Vasquez is a fun guy to be around, and he's got jokes. I can tell you first hand that these two young people are from good stock, and the way they have been raised has prepared them to go after what they want in life, and to face whatever challenges they might encounter with poise, confidence, and dignity. Since their high school days they have proven that they are loyal to family, and the people they choose to be close to are lucky to be considered friends. I salute Ellia, and I congratulate their parents for being so fortunate to have brought two magnificent people into the world. They have a lot to be proud of, and some wonderful years to look forward to.

And, finally, to **Alvin "Fro" Vasquez** for standing on your integrity when others around you were giving in to peer pressure and going along with things that they knew unequivocally to be untrue, please accept as a token of my respect and gratitude, A proud and delightful **Thank You,** from the "Un-Belly" Man.   (See Vasquez photo pages)

Chapter

W

T Bone Walker

It could be said that **Aaron "T Bone" Walker** was the first professional singer/ musician I ever met. He was also the first person to tell me that it was possible for me to become a singer. I have always loved to sing, and at the age of four I remember singing in public for the first time. I don't think that my mother had any thought of any of us being professionals; she loved to sing and it was an accessible and enjoyable pastime for our family. We sang as a group and appeared on programs in church during Easter, and at times when other opportunities arose. My brother, Billy, my sister Honey and me, were a pretty good singing trio; the congregations was very kind to us, and I believe that they genuinely enjoyed our singing.

All of my siblings were good singers and we loved to sing all kinds of songs, including blues, country/western, and, most of all, gospel. Mudear would take us to Gilmer, Texas (the place where my siblings and I were born) at least once a year to visit our grandmother and other relatives. We always looked forward to the visits, because besides getting to see our cousins who were mostly our own age, we knew we would get to sing at the church and loved doing that.

T Bone Walker was one of the most popular blues singers in the country at the time. It was rumored that he had even been to France to sing. He was without a doubt the most famous person in Dallas, except for maybe Bonnie and Clyde, who used to hide out in Dallas quite frequently. According to my Aunt Porter, with whom we lived when we first came to town, Bonnie and Clyde were respected by black folks and poor white people in Dallas because, like Robin Hood, they would give nice chunks of money to the folks who would hide them out and help them stock up on supplies. I'd have to say that T Bone Walker was more popular in Dallas among black folks, because they all knew him and his music. Only elderly black people knew and remembered Bonnie and Clyde. We kids did get a chance to see the car they were driving when they were killed. It was put on display near the viaduct adjacent to the Dallas Rebels (later named the Dallas Eagles) "Triple A" baseball team's stadium. It was a grey 1932 Ford. That car can be seen at "Whisky Pete's Casino, in Primm, NV, about thirty miles south of Las Vegas.

T Bone Walker was born in Louisiana, and raised in Dallas/ Ft Worth. He spent a lot of time in the neighborhood where I was raised,-"The Bottom," and even if he were not performing in Dallas he would come to town often because his driver/valet and best friend, Clarence Wakefield Sr., was also from Dallas. He lived in the Bottom with his wife and two kids when he was not traveling with T Bone. I saw Clarence Wakefield Jr.—Toogie, as he was known in The Bottom—one morning at the corner store, and he told me that T Bone Walker was at his house. I was excited because for the longest time we had heard that Mr. Clarence was T Bone's chauffeur.

It was a Saturday morning. My mother woke me up to tell me that she was leaving for work, and was taking my sister Tharsell (who was nine years old) with her. They would be home by one o'clock (Mudear only worked a half day on Saturdays). She told me to go to the store and get a box of Post Toasties, and have a bowl of cereal for breakfast. When Toogie and I left the store and got to his house, parked in front of his house, was a beige colored 1941 Cadillac Convertible with a khaki top. Toogie's mom, dad, and his sister, Clarice, were eating breakfast, and T Bone Walker was sleeping.

They lived in a row of "shotgun" houses on Colorado St. A shotgun house is a house where the living room was in the front and was usually also used as a bedroom, with the middle room as a bedroom. The third room was the kitchen, and out the backdoor at the rear of the yard was the outhouse. These houses were called shotgun houses because they were built straight, like a shotgun. In other words, you could stand at the front door and look straight out the back door, like looking through the barrel of a shotgun. Toogie and I went into the house. I said good morning to Mrs. Ethel and Mr. Clarence, and waved at Clarice. I asked what time will Mr. T Bone Walker wake up. Mr. Clarence took out his pocket watch, and said: "It's only bout eight thirty. T Bone will probably get up round about noon." I was taken aback. At seven years old I had never heard of anyone sleeping till noon. Mrs. Wakefield asked me if I wanted some breakfast; I said "No thanks."

The bacon smelled good, but we had been trained to not eat at other people's houses unless we had Mudear's permission. I took the cereal home, ate a bowl of Post Toasties, and went to my friend Gip's house on Comel Street, one block south of Colorado. I told Gip that I'd been to Toogie's house, and that T Bone Walker was there, but he never wakes up till noon. Gip was surprised, too. He asked his mom if anybody could sleep till noon like T bone Walker does. She told us that because T Bone Walker is a singer in a band, they probably don't get to sleep until four or five o'clock in the morning. Gip and I were amazed.

I could not wait to tell my mother and sister when they came home. I wanted to play with Gip until T Bone woke up, but his family was going to visit their Big Mama (the name that they, like many black people in the South, called their grandmothers), and would not be home. Gip was as excited about seeing his grandparents as he would have been to see T Bone Walker. Mrs. Lou Ada and Mr. Henry, Gip's mom and dad, were religious people, and were not at all interested in seeing a blues singer, even if it was T Bone Walker. Gip's real name is Henry Lee Gipson Jr. He was my first and closest boyhood friend. He had an older brother, George "Billy" Gipson, a younger brother, Alfred, and three drop-dead gorgeous sisters, Ada Lee, Helen Jean, and Evelyn.

Gip and I went outside and sat on his front porch. When I told him about T Bone's car, he couldn't resist seeing it. We ran to Toogie's house and stood outside looking at the most beautiful automobile we had ever seen. After about ten minutes or so, we went back to Gip's house and played until they left for their Big Mama's house.

It was now 11:00AM, I sat on my front step waiting for Toogie to come and tell me that T Bone Walker was up. I waited for what seemed like a lifetime, but still no Toogie. I decided to go back to his house; I started walking towards Colorado Street, when I saw the beige Cadillac turn the corner in the direction of my house. The Caddie stopped at the corner of Eads and Comel. There was a single story building that housed five businesses. On the corner was a grocery store, and next to it was the pool hall. The building next to the pool hall, was Brother Demus' Barber Shop, next to which was a beauty supply store, and at the far end of the building was the beauty shop. Mr. Clarence stopped the car. Toogie and Clarice were sharing the front passenger seat, and T Bone Walker was in the back seat with his guitar. This was the first time I ever saw the top of a convertible being lowered. When the top was completely down, T Bone Walker stood up, and sat on the retracted convertible top which rested neatly in place. I will never forget the beige gabardine suit, a matching rayon shirt with stitching on the collar. The suit and shirt were the exact same color as the beige Cadillac. It had an impact on me beyond anything

I had ever seen. T Bone made himself comfortable atop the back seat of the convertible. He took his guitar from its case, and crossed his leg, revealing the brown alligator cowboy boots that he wore. He asked the growing crowd that was forming: "Anybody round here like the Blues?" Everyone answered at the same time, saying things like: "Yeah, we love the blues."

He strummed a few notes on his guitar, turned the tuning pegs and said, "I'm gon play a little blues for ya, then I want everybody here to tell everybody you see that T Bone Walker is playing at the Rose Room tonight, starting at eight o'clock till 12:00 o'clock midnight." He asked: "You gon do that for T Bone?" The steadily growing crowd shouted "Yes!"

T Bone started singing, "They call it stormy Monday, but Tuesday's just as bad." When he finished the song, the people applauded, yelled, and asked for more. He sang another song titled "You Got to Bottle Up and Go." When the song was over, he asked: "Who come by Clarence's house trying to wake me up this morning?" Everybody started looking around to see who it was. I was scared he would be mad at me so I didn't say anything. Toogie pointed at me and laughing said: "He did, it was him." I was standing at the front of the car with no place to hide. T Bone must have sensed that I was afraid; he laughed and said to me: "Was it you?" I replied sheepishly: "Yes Sir, but I didn't wake you up." He laughed again, and said: "What's your name?" Feeling a little better, but still a bit embarrassed that I was being singled out, I told him my name. He asked me how old I was. I told him I was seven years old. He said: "You the same age as Toogie." I said "Yes, sir." He said: "Can you sing?" I nodded yes and said "I like to sing." Iona Bennett said: "He's always singing; he sings in church all the time." T bone: "Is that right?" Again I said: "Yes, sir." He chuckled and said: "You got good manners, too." Then he asked me: "You got common sense too?" Not knowing how to answer, I shrugged my shoulders. He asked the crowd: "Is he got any common sense?" I was glad when everybody answered in unison: "Yes!" T Bone said: "Wow! You must be something else. You can sing, got good manners and common sense, too." He continued, "Do you know any songs cept church songs. Do you know any blues songs?" I nodded uh huh. T Bone said, "Let me hear you sing a blues song." I was never shy about singing. I started singing part of a Tampa Red song: "One of these days, baby, your man gon make Tampa mad, Tampa gon git something from him darling, your man ain't knowed he had, cause when thangs go wrong, go wrong with you, girl it hurts me too."

I finished singing that one line and T Bone starting clapping his hands, and everybody else started to applaud. I felt great. T Bone Walker said to me:

"That's good. You wanna be a singer like T Bone?" I answered enthusiastically, "Yes, sir!" He said: "Well you gotta start singing T Bone Walker songs, not just Tampa Red's songs. Do you know any my songs?" I said: "I know the one you was just now singing." Although there were no blues radio stations in Dallas at the time. Mudear had some songs on 78 rpm records, and "Stormy Monday," being the biggest blues hit in Texas, was one of the records we listened to. T Bone said: "You know Stormy Monday?" I said: "Uh huh; you want me to sing it?" He said: "Just tell me the words." I recited the lyrics to "Stormy Monday," and T Bone said: "Now you cooking with gas." I asked: "Could I really be a singer like you?'

What T Bone Walker said to me in response to that question has remained with me, and is as responsible for my successes as any words ever spoken to me. He said to me: "Let me tell you something, and I want everybody standing out here to listen to what I'm saying. You got a talent that's good, but you gon need more than talent to be a singer or anything else worthwhile, but remember, good manners and common sense will help take you anywhere you want to go. Common sense means knowing how to stay away from trouble. It means you got to get your lessons in school, and stay way from anything that's gon land you in jail. That means no cuttin' and shootin' and draggin the gage." I asked, "What's draggin the gage?" T Bone said: "Ask you mama and daddy. They'll tell you exactly what it means, and tell you how come you got no business doin such thangs." Then he said: "T Bone's gotta go now. Clarence, Let's move on."

Mr. Clarence started the engine. Somebody in the crowd asked T Bone, "Where you fixin to go now?" T Bone said: "We going to the Hill, then to the Heights; we might even go up to service." A few people in the crowd laughed, and somebody said "Look out for Monday and Red;" The whole crowd laughed. The very idea that T Bone Walker was talking about going to "service" had to be a joke. Perhaps I should explain why that would have been such a big deal.

Doing those years, "colored folks" that lived in the Oak Cliff section of Dallas, lived in three segregated areas. Where we lived was called the "Bottom," because it was located near the banks of the Trinity River. The levy is the only separation, or protection from the overflow of the Trinity. The Bottom could be an exact comparison to the Lower Ninth Ward in New Orleans. Another section of Oak Cliff where "coloreds" live was called "The Hill," beginning at Eighth Street where the Bracken Village housing projects stand, and continuing south to Avenue A. This is a slightly better neighborhood than the Bottom. This is where Miss Billie's Kindergarten, and N.W Harllee Elementary Schools were located and where 99% of black kids attended K thru Eighth grade. This was also the main social center at the time.

The Star Theater (the only movie theatre in Oak Cliff for blacks) was located in a single story business structure, much like the one in the Bottom. Next door to the Star was the ice cream parlor, next to that was the barber and beauty shop, the record shop, and at the very end of the building was the pool hall. The third neighborhood was called The "Heights," beginning at Avenue A, and extending further south to Jefferson Blvd.

The Hill and the Heights were patrolled by two racist cops named Monday and Red. Every section where black people lived had its notoriously racist and mean cops. They were evil. If Monday and Red spotted you before you could hide, they would call you to the car. That meant trouble. They had this awful game they played that went like this. Monday would say, "What's your name boy?" The kid would answer: "My name is Ivory King,"

Monday: Do you go to school? Ivory: "Yes sir." Monday: "What school do you go to?" Ivory: "I go to school over there (pointing across the street) N.W. Harlee." Officer Monday: "You learnin anything at that school?"

Ivory: "Yes sir." Monday: "Do you know the days of the week?" Yes sir.

Officer Monday: "Tell me the days of the week." Ivory: (starts naming the days of the week) "Sunday, Monday, Tuesday, Wed... Officer Monday: (interrupts him). "Woa, woa, you missed one. Start over." Come closer and make sure I can hear you. Ivory: (moves closer to the open window of the patrol car and begins again to name the days of the week. This time very slowly and with more volume). Ivory: "Sunday, Monday... Tuesday...

Officer Monday slaps Ivory across the face "WHAM! Ivory was nine years old and probably weighed all of 40 lbs, at the most. I was eight. The blow knocked Ivory down and when he hit the ground, his head bumped and his nose started bleeding. Ivory was screaming with pain as officer Monday said to him, "Don't you know it ain't no Monday, It's MR. Monday." Ivory was on the ground holding his head, nose bleeding and in excruciating pain. I started to back away when Red called me and said: "I ain't said you can leave. Come here close to this car." I was terrified. I moved slowly toward the police car. Now, it was Red's turn to have his equally cruel "fun" on me.

Red: "You go to that same school too?" ME: "Yes sir." Officer Redd: "I bet you smart too, ain't you?" Pointing to a house three doors down that had a red roof, officer Redd asked: "What color is the roof on that house?" My knees were shaking, and I was flinching from anticipation of being slapped down.

Redd: "I said tell me the color of that roof boy." ME: --my mouth dry and voice cracking, I answered, "Mr. Red?" Officer Redd seemed disappointed that I had answered "correctly" but he was grinning when he said, "Now, see? We got us a smart little nigger boy here." Officer Monday chimed in: "Now that's a dumb little nigger boy laying there on that ground a crying; Git up from there." Ivory got to his feet and backed away from the police car. Officer Monday said to Ivory: Now tell me what day comes after Sunday? Ivory: (whimpering) "Mr. Monday." Without another word, Ivory took off running. Officers Monday and Redd doubled over with laughter. I ran down the hill and hid in Mrs. Yancy's back yard waiting to see if Monday and Red were coming after us. Ivory turned on Sabine Street and ran home. From that day on I hated Monday and Red as much as we hated the racist cop that patrolled my neighborhood, "The Bottom". His name was Officer Bill Burkola. His Modus Operandi was to get on his motorcycle and chase black kids while kicking them in the behind. Once he caught up with you it was almost impossible to avoid his big black shiny knee length motorcycle boot. His motorcycle could go just about anyplace a kid could run.

For a long time I was afraid to walk home from elementary school the regular way. Ivory, Gip and I would go through the woods and come out on Eads St. where Ivory and I lived.

Beyond the point where black people lived in Oak Cliff was called the service because it was an all white neighborhood. The only black folks that lived in this neighborhood were live-in domestic workers, who lived in servants quarters (usually a small detached house in the rear of the main house). For T Bone Walker to casually enter this area uninvited would have been a stretch, and probably not a pleasant one.

When Mr. Clarence started the car I asked T Bone if I could ride to the corner. He asked me where I lived and I pointed out my house which was three doors from the corner where the now idling Caddy was parked. It must have been without a doubt the most pitiful excuse for a house he'd ever seen. He looked at my house and looked at me and said (chuckling, to hide his embarrassment for me), "You sho can." I started to open the door and squeeze into the front passenger seat where Toogie and Clarice were seated. T Bone said to me: "Not up there, you ride back here with T Bone." He remained perched on top of the back seat, and I climbed in next to him; I could smell the freshly polished leather on his fancy boots. T Bone said "OK Clarence, drop this kid off at his house." When I got out of the Caddy I was literally dizzy with pride and joy. T Bone took a long look at our shanty and sort of shook his head.

This year, in August 2006, I just found out from my sister that, the house at 723 Eads St. had been a condemned undertaker parlor. My sister told me that when she found out by way of neighborhood gossip, she asked

Mudear and was told not to mention it to me because (since I was the baby in the family) she did not want me to be scared of living there. That was the only place my single mother raising four children could afford.

About five years later we had another celebration that consisted, as did almost all celebrations, of Mudear, my maternal grandfather who we called Papa. He lived in Plano, Texas, and came to visit us almost every Friday evening. My mother's two best friends, Miss Doretha, our Cousin Lorain, my two sisters, and my brother, were there. This was a big celebration that included a few more of my mother's close friends. It was big because we were celebrating being accepted to move into the new projects (Turner Courts) that had been built in the Bon-Ton section of South Dallas. Moving to the projects was, as the old folks say, stepping in high cotton.

I waved good by to T Bone Walker when Mr. Clarence drove away and turned east on Dodd Street. A group of kids ran along the side of the road until Mr. Clarence turned south on Cliff St. and headed to the Hill. One final note about the house we rented on Eads St. That house was such a shanty that the kids in the neighborhood would not make fun of it. That should tell you something about its condition.

It was about 12:45 PM when they drove away, and I ran straight up Comel, across Fleming, to the Car Barn, where the interurban transit ended its run. At one o'clock sharp, the interurban pulled to a stop and my mother and sister got off. Walking home, I was so excited when I told them about singing for T- Bone Walker, and riding in his Cadillac Convertible. As usual, my mother said (when checking to see if we were making up stories) "Boy, God hears you telling that fib." I continued to tell the story, so she knew I was telling the truth. By the time we got to the bottom of the hill and crossed Fleming everybody was talking about it. When we got home, I asked Mudear: "What does dragging the gage mean?" She looked almost startled and asked "Where you hear talk about dragging the gage?" I could tell by the look in her eyes, and the tone of voice that she wanted to know, and she wanted to know now! I told her that T Bone Walker told me that I could be a singer like him if I keep good manners, common sense, get my lessons at school, and don't be cuttin' and shootin' and dragging the gage. Mudear: "Well he told you right." I asked again what it means; my sister was all ears. Mudear: "It means somebody smoking reefer." I asked: "What is reefer?" She said, "None of your business, you just better not ever do it, cause if you do you'll get a whipping like you ain't never had." I had heard enough. I told her that T Bone Walker wanted us to tell everybody that he was singing at the Rose Room tonight at eight o'clock. I asked: "Can we go?"

She looked at me with that, "boy, are you crazy?" look and said: "No, we ain't going to no Rose Room. I got T Bone Walker records you can listen to, but I ain't thinking bout no Rose Room. I don't care who's playing there. Besides, we got Sunday school in the morning." My sister "Honey" asked if she could go to Iona's house. Mudear said she could go "but don't wear out your welcome" (meaning don't stay too long). I asked if I could go to the park; she said yes, but come back in an hour cause she was going to fix me a sandwich and a glass of milk. Mudear said she and "Honey" ate lunch at Miss Dees' house. "Come back and eat lunch, then you can go back and play till before dark." I walked to the park singing "They call it stormy Monday but Tuesday's just as bad, Wednesday's worse, and Thursday's also sad. The Eagle flies on Friday, and Saturday I go out to play, Sunday I go to Church and kneel down and pray." For the next two weeks, I was in a T Bone Walker frame of mind.

T-Bone's in the Bottom

Two years later, on a Friday afternoon I was walking home from school with a group of friends when we crossed the street on Eight and Denley Drive, a man driving a pickup truck yelled out of the window: "T Bone's in the Bottom." A woman waiting for the bus asked: "T Bone Walker's in town?" The man in the truck said: "Yeah, he's down in the Bottom." I took off running. I cut through the woods and took a short cut. When I got to the Bottom I asked somebody, "Is Mr. T Bone here?" I was told that he just drove down Dodd Street on his way to the Heights. I was crestfallen, because had I stayed with the kids I was walking with, I could have seen him cruising up Denley Drive.

Still, I'll never forget the time when I was seven years old, and I sang for T Bone Walker, and rode in his convertible Caddy. But more importantly, I remember what he told me about having good manners and common sense. I have kept both as fundamental and necessary tools in my survival kit, and like T Bone said they would, those tools have served me in every aspect of my life. Although it has been a long time coming, there's no better time than now to recognize the late great **T Bone Walker** with… a **Long Overdue Thank You.**

Jeff Washiashi

Personal Hero

In the mid 1980's my acting career was not going too well. I supported my family with my thirteen piece band which had pretty solid bookings during the summer months. The rest of the year I broke the band down to a seven piece party band. My days were free, and partly out of curiosity I applied for a sales position at a Japanese owned company. I was hired, but never dreamed I would eventually be placed in the position of Executive Director. This gave me the distinction of being the first and probably the only African-American to hold such a position with a major Japanese corporation. When I interviewed for the job, not believing that I would even be hired as a salesman, I told them that I would have to take off every Thursday at 3:00 PM, because I had to coach my son's baseball team.

Mr. Yasue, Vice President and the head of the American office, said that would not be possible. I stood up, thanked him for taking the time to have me in to interview, and I left. It was raining cats and dogs outside, and when I reached the door I turned, bowed and thanked him in Japanese. The only Japanese words I knew were "thank you" and "you are welcome,"-words that I had learned from a friend who had served in the Army and had been stationed in Japan. Mr. Yasue returned the courtesy also in Japanese. As I reached for the door he said—in his broken English, "Thank you very much." Then, in Japanese he said *"ammio toko."* I asked him what *ammio toko* meant. He said "Rain man;" *ammio toko* means rain man. You came here in the rain;" then he laughed like a little boy would laugh, and said, "you are *ammio toko*". He stopped laughing and said in a very serious tone, *"Sayonara."* Playing along, I bowed again and left, thinking that that was the end of that. A couple of days later he called and asked me to please come to the office.

When I walked in, he said in playful voice, "*Ammio toko.*" I bowed, and he asked me to please sit down. He said he liked me, and would like to give me the salesman's job that I had applied for. I said thank you. Then he said, "There is only one problem; you will not be able to take off at 3:00 o'clock on Thursdays. I stood up and said thank you very much, but I have to volunteer my time to my son's Little League baseball team. Although acting jobs were not as plentiful as I would have liked, I was serious about time spent with my kids. Plus, I had a dance band that was "the" social band in Pasadena, and the surrounding areas. Music has always been there for me and I was never desperate.

Mr. Yasue asked me to please sit down again, I did so. He said, "OK, I like you. You want to help your kid; you have the job." I couldn't believe it. The pay was quite a bit more than an American company would pay a salesman. It was straight salary, no commission, and my Christmas bonus for the first year would be two thousand dollars. I could have fallen off my chair. This was an exciting time. I had my detractors but there were also good people that I respected who would be hired.

Each year that I remained with the company the bonus would increase. He ended up hiring six more Americans. I worked my butt off and was "Top Salesman." The money was fabulous by American standards. I loved it and I told Mr. Yasue that I wanted to learn to speak Japanese. A week later, he hired a Japanese lady named Yukiko as office manager, and one of her duties was to teach an hour long Japanese class every day after work. It was not mandatory and most of the American salespeople did not attend, but I did. The Japanese language class was suspended after one week because of a lack of interest on the part of the American sales team. It was an opportunity for me to learn another language and I hated to see it end. I have a solid work ethic—thanks to Miss Billie, I always have, and I believe I always will. If I agree to do a job, I will give a full day's work for a full day's pay. I was Top Salesman because I made more sales than the other sales people in the company. It's as simple as that. The backbiting started, but I did not let it phase me. I was having fun.

One day Mr. Yasue gave me the title of Executive Director. He said, "Mr. Takarabe wants you to come to Japan. You need more training. Will you go?" I had never been to Japan, so I went for two weeks. I spent Christmas, 1987, in Japan. I returned to the states and three Americans had quit the company. Six months later one of them came back and apologized for what they had tried to do, but we did not hire her back.

When I was given the title of Executive Director of the company, the JEG family tried to take over the office: the J-E-G (jealous, envy, and greed) triplets. Not everyone was pleased that I had gotten the position. There were three disgruntled employees out of a staff of twelve. The ring leader was a female who I will call Sherry. She was without a doubt the main instigator. She actually purchased a ticket, got on a plane, went to Japan, met with Mr. Takarabe, the Founder and president of the company, and Motohashi, the co-founder and Executive VP. She was outraged that they would hire a "black" man in that position. Saying: "It's just not done in America." Rafi was an Iranian guy who had a tremendous crush on himself, and JB, another American, was the somewhat paranoid co-instigator with Sherri, the globe-trekker, who went to Japan to try to get me fired. I was informed about her trip to Japan, and was told that her complaint against me did not carry the weight with Japanese businessmen the way it might have with an American employer. Other personnel in the American office at that time were Colonel Fred Delisle, US Army Retired. The Head instructor of this Japanese management training school was an American gentleman named Galetz. He was a good guy, but left after about six months, to become head of a large security company. Like Col. Delisle, Galitz was also a gentleman for whom I have great respect and admiration. Col. Delisle, and his dear wife Fuji will always be special to me. Other personal were Yukiko, Hideko, Kurita, Joe, Mark, and Angi Kobyashi another guy that I highly respect because he told the truth when pressured to lie to Mr. Takarabe in order to cover for a mistake that one of the Japanese managers had made. Mr. Yasue, Senior VP, who I hold in very high esteem, was the head of the American office. He hired me, and later gave me the ED position.

Yasue was an honest and fair taskmaster who was aware of everything and everybody in that office. He could not be influenced by the JEGs or anyone else. He knew exactly what was going on, and was completely loyal to Mr. Takarabe. And of course there was Jeff Washiashi, a Japanese-American who was born and raised in Hawaii. Every morning before starting work, the entire staff would form a circle and do a fifteen minute exercise routine; after which we would sing the company song. It was a daily ritual that I enjoyed from beginning to end. I suppose that beginning the day with music took me back to Miss Billie's kindergarten, and I loved it. Perhaps that is why I was top salesman. After the exercises and the songs, I was ready to sell, sell, sell, and sell I did. I never let it be known that I was a professional singer and musician.

The irony of it was that I had never before had success trying to sell anything. As a teenager, I once tried to sell encyclopedias, and another time I tried to sell Fuller brushes. I never made one sale, and I hated it. The only reason I applied for the job at KYG was because Diane Sawyer did a segment on "60 Minutes" about Khanrisha Yosei Gakko's training methods—known as "Hell Camp," which was mandatory for many companies in Japan. This was the 1980s, during the time when the Japanese were "buying up America". A week or so after the Diane Sawyer,

"60 Minutes" piece, a gentleman named Larry Richardson, and his wonderful wife, Demaris, and their two kids, Tracy and Jai, were attending a gathering at our Altadena home. I mentioned that I would like to take a Japanese training course I'd seen on TV. Larry said that he had seen the "60 Minutes" segment, and had recently read that Kanrisha Yosei Gakko (KYG) was opening an American company in California. I became very interested.

Diane Sawyer had reported -in affect, that KYG was the main reason that the Japanese were buying American companies large and small with breakneck speed. I wanted to take the thirteen week training course and discover their secret. As it turned out it was no secret at all. The Japanese just took the business principles that an American named W. Edward Deming had taught them after World War II, as part of the reconstruction of Japan, and put them to good use.

Americans knew little or nothing about those management techniques and skills although they were created, developed and largely ignored in the US. As a result, America fell behind in commerce while the Japanese applied the principles vigorously, and the resulting business acumen made them top heavy with economic efficiency and manufacturing superiority i.e. Sony, Toyota, Honda, etc. I studied the techniques diligently, learned them well, and applied them successfully at every opportunity.

One morning after the exercise and song, Mr. Yasue told me that a Japanese-American fellow was coming in for a job interview. I told him that I had three morning appointments and would be out of the office until after lunch. Yasue said he would handle the interview.

When I returned to the office later that day, he told that he liked the Japanese-American fellow and had hired him. His name is Jeff and he will start work tomorrow.

The first day Jeff Washiashi started work at KYG there was something that everyone in the office liked about him. He was soft-spoken, focused, and extremely bright. He did not believe in cutting corners, and he treated everybody with respect.

Jeff had been at KYG about three months. One afternoon following lunch, some of the sales people were in the conference room before returning to work. I had an appointment and I announced my leaving. Like the morning exercises, and songs, it is also the custom in many Japanese companies, and it was absolutely mandatory in KYG Inc., that when any of the office personnel exits the office, he/she must say, in a strong voice: "Shitsurei Shimasu." Translated to English it means, "I'm going to leave." When entering the office, he/she must say, in a strong voice: "Hairi Masu?" which means in English: "May I enter?" When I got to my car, I realized I had forgotten the written directions to my meeting. I returned to the office, and when I entered I overheard the JEGs talking about me. It was not a flattering conversation. I did not announce my return, instead I listened. No one knew I was there. I heard two males and the female voices saying that I did not deserve to be Executive Director, blah, blah, blah. Then an amazing thing happened. I heard Jeff Washiashi say something like: "I don't see why you guys are always putting him down. All I've ever seen him do is try to help us." With that I quietly stepped outside of the office, and a few seconds later I entered and announced my return. I went to my desk, picked up the directions I'd forgotten and announced my departure. As I drove to my meeting, I was moved by what I had heard. I never let Jeff know I had overheard his remarks, but from that moment on, I respected him and wanted to be his friend. A year or so later, Kanrisha Yosei Gakko closed the American office. After work on the final day, I invited Jeff to join me for a beer. I told him that I was going to start another business distributing air and water filtering systems. I asked him if he would be interested in being partners with me. He said he would think about it and talk it over with his wife Susan. A few days passed, and I got a call from Jeff. He agreed to come in with me. We rented a small office in West Covina and formed "Rainbow Enterprises." We worked hard, but not much happened, so we dissolved the company. Jeff got another job and I went back to music full time and acting when a decent role came up. I am thankful to be able to say that I have done well, and so has Jeff. Until recently, I never told him why I made an effort to be friends with him. It was for the same reason that I have such respect for Alvin "Fro" Vasquez. Despite Jeff's soft spoken, non-confrontational personality, he, too, stood on his integrity and refused to join in with a disgruntled group which had been captured by the JEG triplets. The fact that he would defend anyone would have impressed me, but because he spoke up for me in my absence, his actions placed him in the winner's circle in my mind. I shall always remember that there seemed to be almost a smile in his voice when he told the instigator and her disgruntled crew that I had only tried to help them. People with that kind of integrity seem to have at least one thing in common; they have been raised right. Such is the case with Fro and Ellia Vasquez, Jeff Washiashi, and others.

Like most people, I decry disloyalty, because it encompasses the worst of human traits. Unwarranted disloyalty is the mother of deceit, and the father of gross pusillanimity. In my view, it is driven by weakness, envy, jealously, feigned superiority, dishonesty, arrogance and fear. At best, it animates pity, and begs the question, how do you sleep at night?

My purpose for writing about the "JEG triplets", and other adversaries, is not to whine or complain. It is to remind young people, and others of Ma Bailey's statement: "Life is no bed of roses." Whatever we do in life, no matter how noble, or well-intentioned it might be, there will be detractors, naysayer and dream killers along the way. <u>DO NOT ALLOW THEM TO DETER, OR DEFEAT YOU</u>.

I am fortunate to have a few friends to whom loyalty is one of the corner-stones of their character. They know who they are, and do not have to be named, because some of them have already been mentioned in this book, and like the Washiashi family, they too, occupy a place of gratitude and respect in my heart and mind.

Blessed by Heaven

For a long time Jeff and his lovely wife Susan had tried to get pregnant and they were now beginning to wonder if it was going to happen. They are people of faith as well as character, and I was thrilled when Jeff told me one day that Susan had conceived. Because Jeff and Susan are truly decent people, and their hearts are right, he and Susan received the ultimate blessing for any couple who was beginning to question whether they would ever have a family. They were blessed with beautiful twins Lindsey and Brandon —a girl and a boy. How happy I am for them.

Today they have the beautiful family that they so richly deserve. I have no doubt that Brandon and Lindsey will be raised by two wonderful parents who will instill in them the values and give them the unconditional love that is in Susan and Jeff's hearts. They have purchased a home and are raising their family in Orange County, California.

At Christmas time Susan takes the time to write a really nice update in the "Washiashi News Letter." In it she brings their family and friends up to date on the highlights of the whole year. Often they are gracious enough to include the latest photos of the twins. I want them to know that I look forward to receiving the "Washiashi News" and I will continue to wish them well. Jeff and Susan are very special people.

To Mr. Jeff Washiashi, for your integrity, courage, honesty and friendship, I send you and yours… **a Simple and Sincere Thank you.**

(See Washiashi photo pages)

Alfre Woodard
Actor, Activist, Wife & Mother

In addition to her enormous talent, great looks, and natural charm, Alfre Woodard's involvement with humanitarian causes is also well known. Actors for South Africa, an organization to which she belongs, had been active in the liberation of South Africa long before Apartheid ended. She and the organization are no less active in the development of a free South Africa.

I had the pleasure of meeting Miss Woodard at a fundraising function at Universal Studios in Hollywood. The affair was sponsored and facilitated by Oxfam America –an international organization with a mission to create lasting solutions to global poverty, hunger, and social injustice. I discovered Alfre's interest in helping youth, and made a mental note to ask Patricia Duff, (the person who had invited her) to speak to Alfre about perhaps getting involved with out youth program.

I did not speak at length with Miss Woodard that evening, but I ran into her and her husband, screen writer, Roderick Spencer on several occasions. The chance meetings with Alfre and Roderick were usually at some affair that supports humanitarian concerns, to which Alfre had contributed her time, talents, and/or other resources.

In 1996, Colors United sponsored a county-wide youth conference for high school age students. The weekend long gathering was held on the campus at the University of Southern California (USC). In attendance were, Ed Begley Jr., Edward James Olmos, popular Disc Jockey, Theo, and the legendary math teacher that Edward James Olmos portrayed so masterfully, in the highly acclaimed 1988 film, "Stand and Deliver," Mr. Jamie Escalantes.

Alfre Woodard graciously accepted the young people's request to speak to the gathering. Her talk was engaging and inspiring. Many of the students commented that her words had encouraged them to stay in school, get a good education, and pursue their dreams. One young lady who was having self-esteem issues stated that Alfre had made her feel differently about herself. This young lady said she was now convinced that she can achieve any goal, and was highly motivated and eager to start. Alfre added something special to the conference. Her willingness and ability to speak plainly to young people (especially teen-aged girls that are faced with peer pressure, and various other dilemmas,) helped them believe in themselves. In many ways her contribution to the success of the event was priceless.

Many, if not most of us, are familiar with Miss Woodard's work as a successful and highly sought-after performer. Her resume and accolades include four Emmy awards, several Academy Award nominations, and scores of TV and movie performances. Alfre, Roderick, and their two adopted children, Mavis, and Duncan, live in Santa Monica, CA.. This suggest, that a superb talent, an adored wife and mother, a beautiful woman, who finds time to help improve the lives of disenfranchised, and suffering people, can indeed have it all.

I invite you to join me, in sending Miss Alfre Woodard, **a warm and wonderful Thank you.** (See Alfre Woodard photo pages).

Dennis Weaver
Actor-Musician-Humanitarian-Ecologist-Philanthropist

Dennis Weaver was a one of a kind actor, and a one of a kind human being. Born in Joplin, Missouri, he has had one of the longest careers in the business, beginning on Broadway in 1948. Dennis also starred in nine television series, including "Gunsmoke," for which he won an Emmy in 1959 for his portrayal of "Chester." He earned two Emmy nominations for "Gentle Ben" and "McCloud" and played leading roles in 40 motion pictures. He has a star on the Walk of Fame in Hollywood, and on the Trail of Fame in Dodge City, KS. Other entertainment and civic honors include awards from the Screen Actors Guild, the Publicist's Guild, Hollywood Women's Press Club, Women of Los Angeles, and Brandeis University's National Women's Committee. He has been honored by the Festival of the West and received the 2002 Cowboy Spirit Award and several Western Heritage Awards when he was inducted into the Cowboy Hall of Fame.

Dennis served as a Naval Air Corp Pilot before graduating in Fine Arts in Theater at the University of Oklahoma. In high school, he had been a star in football and basketball. As a track and field athlete in 1948 he was a finalist in the Decathlon in the United States Olympic Trials. In his twenties, as a member of the famed Actors Studio, he made his Broadway acting debut in "Come Back Little Sheba" and was subsequently signed by Universal International, and brought to Hollywood. He has also released several country music albums, and in his one-man Shakespearean performances he plays 19 different characters.

I met Dennis in 1974 when I was elected to the National Board of Directors of Screen Actors Guild (SAG). Dennis Weaver was President of SAG at the time. It was an exciting time to be involved with a Union that was making progress in a number of areas. I became Chairman of what was known as the Minorities Committee. I also became the Chairman of the Feature Films to Television Sub-Committee, and was a founding member of the SAG Film Society Committee. I am proud of the progress and the gains that were made during that period. As a member of the National Board of Directors under Dennis Weaver's leadership, we worked hard to create a Film Society whereby actors would be able to view pre-released films for a yearly fee of fifty dollars. We see some twenty-five films per year. That averaged out to be about two dollars per screening.

Getting the Film Society off the ground was no small task. We worked closely with the Writers Guild of America which was headed by the very capable and knowledgeable Allan Rifkin, without whom the undertaking would not have seen the light of day. The major studios that supplied the films to us were quite fickle; one day we were in, the next day they had changed their minds. As a matter of fact, on the day that our very first screening was to be held, one hour before the doors were to open, we did not know whether or not we would have a film for screening. The name of that first film was "The Day of the Locust," the John Schlesinger film, starring Donald Sutherland, Karen Black, Burgess Meredith, William Atherton and Geraldine Page. The much anticipated film was about the ins and outs and broken dreams of Hollywood in the 1930s. We were on pins and needles until the studio decided to allow the screening about thirty minutes before the first of six hundred people were to be let in.

In the beginning, screenings were shown at the old Writers Guild Theatre on Melrose near Doheny, in West Hollywood . Once the film arrived from the studio, we all breathed a sigh of relief, and the show went on as scheduled. After the first year of providing the films, the studios decided to disallow the screening of pre-released film, and movies were given to us for showing after they had been released and in theatres for two weeks in order to not interfere with the opening weekend box office receipts (a wise move for the studios). Screen Actors Guild Film Society Today is a highly successful tool for actors to view and study the work of fellow actors, and filmmakers in front of, as well as, behind the camera. The SAG Film Society has been duplicated by any number of film societies and festivals.

The Ethnic Minorities Committee also made great strides during our tenure, and the Features to TV negotiations in 1976 yielded the greatest measure for measure gains for actors to date. That was also the year that cable TV was introduced to the industry as a "potential" financial force. The Guild agreed to leave cable off the table because no one knew if it would fly. Under the direction of Guild President Dennis Weaver, and National Executive Secretary, Chester Midgen, our diversified, coherent, and effective National Board made great gains in a number of areas. Dennis Weaver was the driving force behind those accomplishments. Most actors today have no idea how indebted they are to Dennis' contribution to their well-being. In these years that have followed Dennis' tenure, SAG still has not come close to gaining parity with network TV's pay scale and residuals, as far as cable is concerned.

His work as an actor speaks for itself. He is one of the few actors like the late Jack Lemmon, Michael Landon, the talented Jack Nicholson, Sidney, Denzel, Tom Hanks, and a few others whose work has always been pretty much about quality. Dennis was a consummate professional who understood the business, and would not compromise his integrity. He was also cool under fire. The SAG Boardroom was no place for the faint-hearted. I have seen Dennis defuse a tense and even a heated situation with his enormous intelligence (which is usually wrapped in his genuine

Missouri drawl) and his penetrating insight into human nature. A living testament to his coolness is the love of his life, Gerry who told me, and a group of close friends, that in sixty-three years of marriage Dennis never once raised his voice to her. That is what I consider to be coolness that is almost beyond some people's ability to comprehend.

In negotiations with the stout-hearted television executives or the fiercely determined negotiators of the MPTP (Motion Picture and Television Producers), his skill and power were not to be underrated. None the less, his acute sense of fairness—which I believe is based on his concern for a struggling humanity—*never* weakened his resolve to do what is right for everyone, but what was <u>best</u> for actors.

One of the things that I admired most about Mr. Weaver was that his was no proselytizing, fire and brimstone, judgment and condemnation type personality. He was a quiet and deeply spiritual individual. His humanity is legendary: his committed efforts to feed the hungry of Los Angeles, led him to create the food bank that he called "L.I.F.E." an acronym for: "Love Is Feeding Everyone." Dennis and his co-founders, Valerie Harper and Tony Cacciotti along with wife Gerry, and a group of dedicated volunteers fed **180,000 people** in Los Angeles **each week** for nearly ten years. In 1986 for his efforts, he received the "Presidential End Hunger Award" from President Ronald Reagan.

Dennis was not just a celebrity figurehead that sat behind the desk and let everyone else do the grunt work. He and Gerry were on the front lines with other Celebs that he recruited, along with some "everyday" people. Together they were loading and unloading, storing and distributing much needed food to those who were in serious need, and who otherwise might not have had food, nor hope. Countless people have benefited from his desire to help. His quick wit and down-home humor was an ever-present part of his demeanor.

In addition to working together on SAG matters, my wife and I got to know Dennis and Gerry on a personal basis as well. For more than thirty years, I have been fortunate to think of them as friends. Aside from being an actor and entertainer, Dennis is an excellent singer and musician, who has recorded and released several country music albums. His family-oriented comedy variety stage-show featured wife Gerry and singer-composer son Rusty.

While getting to know them, I discovered that we shared a spiritual connection, and another thing that we had in common was that Dennis and Gerry have three fine sons, Rick, Rob, and Rusty. We have three terrific sons as well. Dennis Weaver, the highly celebrated actor, was at ease and accommodating with people. His talent was so finely honed that what you see on screen is so natural that it is impossible to see the work that goes into his performances. As for his being a giving actor who was willing to take a chance on someone as yet unproven, some folks might not be aware that he gave a young Steven Spielberg his first major shot as a director on the 1971 TV movie, "Duel." He also took a chance on me, and helped me understand something about acting when I first made my transition from singing to acting. I appeared on his long running TV series "McCloud." He was so generous as an actor and so encouraging as a major star that I will be forever grateful.

Dennis and Gerry's passion has always been for the preservation and care of what he called his Mother Earth. Everything they did was with that in mind. Thirty years ago we interviewed them at their beautiful beach-front home in Malibu. What he said then about our nation's foolish disregard for the earth is timelier today than when he spoke to us back then. Today's calamities such as Katrina, Rita, and the destruction caused by earthquakes, tornados, hurricanes etc., prove that his insight surpassed mere sagacity and reveals him as a true visionary. I'll let you be the judge. The following is one small portion of that two hour interview that was given thirty years ago, transcribed from Dennis and Gerry's own words.

Note: ME= Kingston speaking, S= Sande, my ex-wife, GW= Gerry Weaver, and DW= Dennis Weaver. This interview was done in 1976 and is timelier today than it was then. It confirms Dennis Weaver's visionary insights without question. .

S: "Dennis and Gerry, You have been so generous with your time. Thank you so much for allowing us to speak with you. Your insight and openness has been far beyond expectations. With that we will conclude unless of course you feel that there is something that you'd like to add".

GW: There are two things that I wish Dennis would touch on. They are things that I feel could be so helpful to people who read this book. We have a tremendous urge to go around and talk to everybody as much as we can, and Dennis is so articulate. He speaks so beautifully about the preservation of the environment and what we can do to help heal our mother Earth.

I have such respect for his love for God and his unending service to and love for mankind. I just thought you might like to hear what he has to say about those two things.

S: Absolutely; we'd love it.

DW: Well Sande, since she mentioned Mother Earth, I'll start with that because Mother Earth is a living organism and has very strong feelings and we are abusing them terribly. Poisoning water, cutting down her rain forest, poisoning her soil, allowing it to erode, and we're making all kinds of deserts, and the ozone layer is being depleted, radiation is coming through and altering all kinds of forms of life on this planet, and mother earth is reacting to that just as you or I would react. What would you do if some somebody put poison in your arteries in your blood stream? What would you do if somebody poured acid rain on your hair? What would you do if somebody tore the skin off of your body? You would react to it; you would do something about it and that's what's happening. The tragedy is that people in their ignorance do not realize that we are creating all of these great natural—I call them unnatural catastrophes that we are facing now. And, we will face more of them, including earthquakes, droughts, and all kinds of volcano activity which will increase the kinds of unusual weather patterns which destroyed 15 million trees last year in England (This interview was done in the late seventies) with a hurricane that they have never had before.

All these things are happening because of our actions, because of what we are doing, and people look at it and say, "Boy this earth is really acting crazy, isn't she"? Well, of course, she's acting crazy and so we've got to change the way we live, the way we relate to the earth. We've got to change the way we think; we've got to change our priorities otherwise we are going to suffer the consequences. So anyway... you know... I always like to use the analogy of the human body and Mother Earth, because the human body is made up of billions and billions of cells and they all have to work together for the body to work.

We think of the body as one, although it's made up of billions and billions of pieces and parts... and if any part, if any group of cells in the body become diseased, the whole body is affected. The body becomes debilitated no matter whether it's a heart condition or lung condition, or cancerous, or whatever it is, or just a cold. It affects every part of the body. Mother Earth is made up of billions and billions of cells and the cells of the earth are you and me and everybody else in the world. When any part of those cells is diseased everybody else is affected by that disease. And to me... environmental abuse is a disease, poverty is a disease, hunger is a disease, war is a disease. Wherever those things exist on this earth, we all experience them in some way, shape or form either directly or indirectly. We all suffer from it, so it behooves us all to eliminate the diseases of the earth... you see...and that's what we should be about.

ME: "What are some of the ways ordinary people can go about doing that?

DW: The best way to do that... the most final way to do that is... This is the answer to everything, is to feel the consciousness of God within, and once you feel that consciousness within, you want to give it to everybody else. It's a spiritual law. You can't feel it without wanting to give it to somebody. If everybody felt it, there would be tremendous change in the behavior of human beings on this earth. We wouldn't have to have the police forces, or the armies that we have. We could spend our time, our energy and our money doing that which improves the quality of life rather than destroying it. We wouldn't be making useless armaments that only become obsolete and do not create a healthy economy and do not create good jobs. Instead we would be making things which at one time create good economy and good jobs and at the same time benefit mankind.

So that's why it's so important to have that as the foundation of your life, communion with that which you eternally own, which is the peace and bliss of God's presence.

ME: Wow, that's powerful stuff, and it makes a lot of sense to me as it no doubt will make to a lot of people who read this. Thanks again.

DW: You're welcome. ME: "And thank you, Gerry, for suggesting that we ask Dennis to share that with us".

GW: It was fun.

Passionate environmentalists, Dennis and Gerry moved to Colorado in 1989 to construct his "Earthship." This "new world", solar-powered home is unimaginably beautiful, completely self sufficient. It requires no generators, electricity, no conventional water source, and is virtually indestructible. This magnificent 10,000 sq foot home was primarily built from recycled materials, and is recognized as an inspirational model for sustainable living. The documentary "Dennis Weaver's Earthship" aired on public television for years and is still available at www.dennisweaver.com.

His semi-autobiography, "All the World's a Stage," is beautifully written and is a must read. It is a totally engrossing book filled with Dennis Weaver's wit, charm, passion, humor, and never before revealed information about the life and work of this great artist/ humanitarian/philanthropist. The book concludes thus: "Tomorrow's children await our answer. Tomorrow's world awaits our creation. Join me today, for the sake of tomorrow. Thank you for caring.

Love,

Dennis."

On February 7, 2006 at the age of eighty-one, Dennis lost his battle with cancer, and I lost a dear friend. The legacy he left, and the tremendous good that he did will live on as a shining example of what the human spirit can achieve, when the heart is willing and the commitment is real.

The following poem by Emerson must have been written for people like Dennis and Gerry Weaver, and all those who follow a path of service, inner-peace and agape.

SUCCESS

To laugh often and much; to win the respect

of intelligent people and the affection of children;

to earn the appreciation of honest critics,

and endure the betrayal of false friends,

to appreciate beauty, to find the best in others,

to leave the world a bit better whether by a healthy child,

a garden patch or a redeemed social condition;

to know even one life has breathed easier because you have lived.

This is to have succeeded.

Ralph Waldo Emerson

Dennis Weaver's life was a living portrait that embodied, and reflected, each and every line of Emerson's vision of success. He used his celebrity to support his unwavering commitment to saving the environment, ending hunger, and eliminating poverty in America. In 1989, he founded The Institute of Ecolonomics, a non-profit organization that promotes sustainable development principles and practices. IOE, is dedicated to sustainable living through education programs, affordable housing, and environmental businesses. Dennis was quiet, fun-loving, and low key. Sort of an undercover saint he was. To learn more about the institute, please visit: Ecolonomics.org, or contact, Robert Wood, @ (970) 626-3820.

Dennis Weaver, I realize that you have fans and admirers throughout the world, an adoring family, and a life that is to be envied. It was our misfortune that you left us before this book was completed, but you knew how much your friendship of thirty plus years meant to me, and others like me, who knew you well. My spirit overflows with gratitude in knowing that you were a gentle giant, a magnanimous soul, a fun and loving gentleman, who more than earned the many honors that have been bestowed on you, and like the other great ones in this book, you too deserve much, much more than, **A Spirit-filled Thank You.**

(See Weaver's photo pages)

Above: Mrs. Maurine F. Bailey, directing the Harry T. Burleigh Choir at
Lincoln High School's tenth anniversary, 1945.
Below: In the front yard of the Bailey home. L to R, Carl AKA Kingston,
Mrs. Bailey, her devoted husband, Mr. Sterling Bailey, Carl's former wife
Sande, Kingston's son, Carl Anthony. 1976.
Photo taken by my middle son, Kevin age 6 yrs. Courtesy Kingston's photo archives

Above: Top right, Mrs. Myrtle Salone presenting flowers to Mrs. Bailey, honoring her @ St. Paul AM Church. 1997.
Bottom right: Five great Educators, being honored for fifty years of
service. L to R, Mable Chandler, Thomas Tolbert, Josie Washington,
Mrs. Bailey, And L. C. McGaughey.   Photos courtesy of Myrtle Salone.

It's official ! Street named for Mrs. Bailey is now , Maurine F. Bailey Way.
Below: MFBCF Board members @ ribbon cutting ceremony. L to R,
Judge Joseph E. Ashmore Jr. Legal Advisor, Lurline Jackson, VP Bessie
Slider Moody, President Rev. Dr. Gerald Lee Britt Jr. Founder and
Chairman of the Board Kingston DuCoeur AKA Carl Mathis Craig cut-
ting ribbon with Dallas City Councilman, Leo V. Chaney Jr. Student,
Philmore Peterson V, and Dr. Hazel Partee. LHS Maurine F. Bailey Con-
cert Choir sings in the background. April 2003.
Photo courtesy of Maurine F. Bailey Cultural Foundation Inc.

Mrs. Billeia Montgomery (miss Billie) at her piano, in her kindergarten classroom of three, four, and five-years old children. Kingston: Top row, center, John Hopps Jr. , front row, third chair from the right, David Lee Perry, third row from the top, third chair from the right. Photo courtesy of L.G. Slider.

 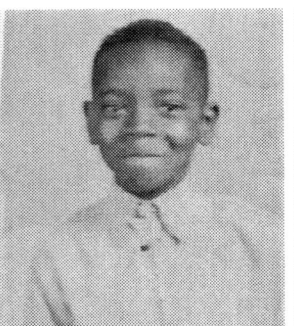 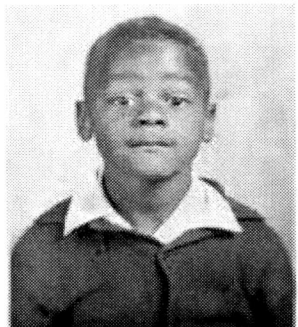

Above: Three classmates at Miss Billie's Kindergarten School. L to R, John Hopps Jr., Carl Mathis AKA Kingston DuCoeur, David Lee Perry.

Below Left. Dr. John Hopps Jr.. (Physicist) Dr. Hopps was one of the distinguished scientist that discovered and developed Fiber Optics, and brought Nano-Thecnology to prominence. As Deputy Under Secretary of Defense, he was also one of the leading scientist assigned to develop an Anthrax vaccine.

Below right. David Lee Perry, is one of the most beloved, and respected City Council members in the city of Plano Texas.

Kingston DuCoeur and Muffin , the horse that played Seabiscuit in
Gary Ross' great film, "Seabiscuit" On location in Lexington, KY 2003.
Photo by Francois Duhamel, Courtesy of The Kennedy/Marshall co.

Left: L to R Chris Cooper, Kingston DuCoeur, Jeff Bridges, Toby Maguire
(top). Photo by Francois Duhamel.

Above: Toby Maguire, mounted and Kingston holding the reins, 2003 @ Santa Anita (Oak Tree) Race Track.
Photo: from Kingston's photo archives

Above left: Hall of Fame Jockey, Gary Stevens standing by a ststute of the great Jockey George Wolff, @ Santa Anita Race track, 2003. Photo
 Above right: Hall of Fame Jockey, Chris Maccarron & Kingston, at Saratoga Raceway, Saratoga, NY.
Photos: courtesy of Kingston's photo archives.

Above: L to R Toby Maguire, Elizabeth Banks, & Kingston. On the set, Santa Barba, CA
Photos: Kingston's archives.

Gary Ross, directing Chris Mccarron and Gary Stevens @ Keenland Race Track, Lexington, KY.
Photo: Kingston archives.

Below: L to R Front: Producer, Kathleen Kennedy, Kingston Du-Coeur, Jeff Bridges.
2nd row L to R, Executive Producer Robin Bissell, Director of Photography, John Schwartzman.   Photo: Kingston's photo archives.

Last day of principal photography, five months later. In the make up trailer,
taking off the Seabiscuit make-up for the final time. L to R, Jeff Bridges, Elizabeth Banks, Kingston, Chris Cooper. John, a production assistant looks on.
Photo: from Kingston's photo archives.

Kentucky wrap party. L to R. Jockey, Joe Stein, Chris Mccarron, Gary Ross, Gary Stevens and, Kingston DuCoeur. Photo: from Kingston's photo ar-

Top: Kingston DuCoeur chatting with Jeff Bridges at the Los Angeles wrap party

Below: L to R, Lovely Elizabeth Murphy, KingstonDuCoeur , Robin Bissell & his beautiful wife, Kristen, back stage at the Screen Actors Guild (SAG) Awards.
Photo: Kingston's photo archives

ENJOYING AN EVENING OF FUN AND DANCING are top ranking off
of Lincoln High School ROTC, when the ROTC held its first Dinner-Dance. They
(left to right), Annie Ruth Davis, Major Carl Mathis, Lt Col Leon King, Claudia H
ar. Col Andrew McLeod, Billie Jean Roberson and Melba Moore, Lt Col Hudson Grif

Above: Lincoln High School ROTC Ball. Far left, Annie Ruth Davis and
Major Carl Mathis AKA Kingston DuCoeur.

Below: My senior autograph book, page signed by my personal
heroes, Mrs. Maurine F, Bailey, Mrs. Mable M. Chandler, and
Lt. Reginald W. Carrington. Photos courtesy Kingston's personal archives.

- 244 -

Above: Kingston visiting with Mrs. Chandler at her home In Dallas, TX 1996.

Below: Kingston and Mrs. Chandler strolling in her font yard, 1996.
Photos: Courtesy of Mable M. chandler's Estate.

Photo by Errinn Cosby, courtesy of the Cosby family

Dr. William H. Cosby Jr. 2006

*The glory of friendship
Is not the outstretched
hand, nor the kindly smile
nor the joy of companionship;
it is the spirited inspiration
that comes to one when he
discovers that someone else
believes in him and is willing
to trust him.*

Ralph Waldo Emerson

DULUTH HERALD, WEDNESDAY, JANUARY 10, 196

Cosby's Humor Strikes at Will

BY DOLORES ORMAN
Of the Herald Staff

Chatting with Bill Cosby by telephone Tuesday gave this reporter the feeling that she was playing straight man in an unrehearsed, impromptu comedy act. You never knew when the humor was going to strike.

Cosby in informal conversation is much like Cosby in concert. There is the unexpected and the ad lib. The actor-comedian's performance hinges not only on the unpredictable wanderings of his mind, but on the mood and rapport of his audience.

Persons who attend his concert at the Duluth Arena at 8:30 p.m. Friday will be just where Cosby likes his audiences—at home in a familiar environment rather than in the strange and somewhat newness of a nightclub.

The musical portion of the Cosby show will be handled by the Pair Extraordinaire, a duo that has received raves for their fresh improvisational approach to old and new songs. The pair are Carl Craig, a folk and pop singer, and Marcus Hemphill, a jazz bassist.

"They are very, very groovy," Cosby said. "They've been more than well received by audiences throughout the tour. They kind of go along with the sense of feeling and relaxation of the show."

Cosby wrote the liner notes for one of the Pair's record albums. In his comments, he said, "I first met Carl Craig and Marcus Hemphill when we appeared on the same bill at the hungry i in San Francisco. I'll admit that the first time they got on the stage, I thought the rest of the band must have missed the plane. But when Marcus played that first note on his bass and Carl began to sing, I knew that I had made a marvelous discovery.

"I am no musician, but it is clear that Carl and Marcus have a sound that is uniquely their own. It takes a special quality of musician to create that kind of sound out of one voice and one bass fiddle."

Cosby's concert tour started Jan. 5 in San Diego, Calif. The group will have performed in 25 cities when they end their tour Jan. 26 in Philharmonic Hall in New York City.

Then after nightclub engagements in Las Vegas and Lake Tahoe, it's off on another 12-day tour.

Above: Bill Cosby and The Pair Extraordinaire having fun and thourougly entertaining audiences on the Las Vegas Strip.

Below: A somber press conference shortly after the Assassination of Dr. Martin Luther King Jr.
L to R, Marcus Hemphill, Bill Cosby, Carl Craig AKA Kingston DuCoeur. 1968.

Photographer unknown. Courtesy of the Cosby Family archives.

- 249 -

Above: John Denver points out his next ski run to event photographer at The John Denver Ski Classic at Heavenly Valley Ski Resort in Lake Tahoe, North Shore as other skiers look on.

Below left: John Denver poses with Kingston's former wife, Sande.

.

Below right: Kingston at John Denver Ski Classic Heavenly Valley, Lake Tahoe
Photos takes February, 1986. courtesy of Kingston's photo archives

John Denver and Kingston DuCoeur, at ABC Television Studios in Hollywood, on The John Denver TV special, Cir. 1980. Floor Mgr. Lower right corner   Photographer unknown. Courtesy Kingston's photo archives

Above left: Polly Draper, Actor, Director, Writer, devoted wife and mother.

Above right: Gregory Hines & Polly Draper Starring in "The Tic Code", a film written by Polly Draper, Film score and original music by Michael Wolff.

Below left: L to R, Michael Wolff, Russell Hines, Polly Draper, Aldo, and Alfredo Pineda.

Below right: Jazz Musician, Michael Wolff (Polly's husband).

Photos courtesy of Michael Wolff and Polly Draper.

Left: Belenda Sadberry & Domingo Maldinado, lead actors, on the set filming Michael Wolff's music video " No Happy Ending". 1992..

A real wedding: Beautiful Bride, and Happy Groom, Nancy and David Keith make their way down the isle. It's official. Oh Happy Day.

Photo courtesy of Kingston's photo archives

Above: Nancy and David Keith toast each other before cutting the cake.
Below: L to R Groom David Keith, Kingston, Beautiful Bride Nancy Keith, Django Craig, Polly Draper & hubby Michael Wolff. Knoxville, TN, April, 2000. Photos: Courtesy of Kingston's photo archives.

Above: Patricia Duff with Colors United students in Washington D.C. for President Bill Clinton's inauguration, January, 1993.

Below: President Bill Clinton, and Kingston DuCoeur, @ inauguration, 1993.
Photos courtesy of Kingston's photo archives.

THE WHITE HOUSE
WASHINGTON

February 10, 1999

Mr. Kingston DuCoeur
Living Literature Colors United
Suite 1495
9911 W. Pico Boulevard
Los Angeles, California 90035

Dear Mr. DuCoeur:

Thank you for your assistance with the White House Millennium Council's "Save America's Treasures" visit to the Los Angeles Theater. The Living Literature Colors United performance brought excitement and meaning to this occasion.

At the theater, you helped us to see that if we are to honor our past and imagine our future, then we must preserve not only the sites that exemplify our nation's history, but also the sites that are historically cherished by our nation's people. Thank you for helping to make the "Save America's Treasures" visit to the Los Angeles Theater an enormous success.

Sincerely yours,

Hillary Rodham Clinton

Above: L to R, CU supporter, Mrs. Parez, First Lady Mrs. Hillery Rodem Clinton, and Kingston DuCoeur in Los Angeles, Summer, 1999.
Below: CU students in front of Jordan High School auditorium 1999.
Photos courtesy of Kingston's photo archives

LIVING LITERATURE
COLORS UNITED

Top left: Kingston and Patricia Duff, at the American Spirit Awards in Hollywood, CA, 1994.

Top right: Candice Block and Susan Jameson @ President Bill Clinton's inauguration, Washington DC, January, 1993.

Below: Patricia Duff holding her American Spirit award, and surrounded by Board members of "Show Coalition" 1994.

Photos courtesy Kingston's photo archives.

Above: Thanks to an incredible effort by Patricia Duff, and Gail Simms, CU students are photographed in new winter cloths for their trip to Washington DC for President Clinton's inauguration where they participated in the "Bells Of Hope" ceremonies. Kneeling, front row: L to R., CU Founder/ CEO Phil Simms, Jordan High School Principal, Grace Strauther, CU Co-Founder and President, Kingston DuCoeur.

Below: R to L, Colors United Founder & CEO, Phil Simms. Kingston DuCoeur, Co-Founder & President @ Venice High School 1994.
Photo courtesy of Kingston's photo archives.

Above Damon Wyans with Colors United students @ Columbia pictures Studio

Below left: Actor, Clarence Gillary, Nancy Stafford (2nd from the right) on the Set of their TV Series Matlock with the Colors United students. 1995.
Photos courtesy of Kingston's photo archives.

Top: Patricia & her precious daughter, Caleigh.
Photo by Steven Wolosker.

Below left: (Triumvirate), Kingston DuCoeur,
Ann Marie Gillen, Phil Simms. Bottom right:
Carl, Woody Harrelson, and Kingston @
President Bill Clinton's inaugurtion.1993.

Photo by John Thomas. Courtesy of Kingston's photo archives.

Farrah's Smile

Above: L to R Farrah Fawcett, Kingston, Patricia Duff. Top right Brownie Pineda, top left, Rosalee Valasco.
Below: L to R, Ann Marie Gillen, CU student Tyrone Barrow, Farrah Fawcett and Kingston DuCoeur, Hollywood ,1996.
Photos: courtesy of Kingston's photo archives.

Left:: Colors Straight Up
Director, Michele Ohayon
And Morgan Freeman at the
Beverly Hills Screening of
Michele's Documentary film
"Cowboy Del Amour" 2006.

Below: Kingston DuCoeur
and Morgan freeman, 2006.

Above left: Gertrude Gipson elegant beauty. Above right: Muhammad Ali & G.G.

Below left: Florance LaRue (singer with The Fifth Dimension) with G.G.

Below right: Gertrude Gipson (G.G.) interviewing Keenan Ivory Wyans.
Photographer unknown. Courtesy of the Gertrude Gipson Penland family via Shonte P. Abraham.

KURT HURTTE SIGNS EXCITING NEW SINGER

SANTA MONICA—The Kurt Hurtee Productions office announced this week the signing of new-comer to Los Angeles, terrific Kal Craig, vocalist and M.C. and have hooked him into the popular Zanaibar night club in Santa Monica, opening this week-end.

This twenty-three year old singer, recently returned from the Armed Services, where his many appearances as a singer created quite a sensation in the European sector.

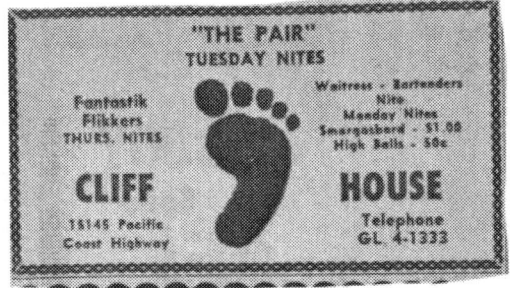

Top left: Zanzabar clipping
Top right: News ad announcing
The first appearance as Duo
"The Pair Extraordinaire."
Righr: Photo of "Cliff House
booking. Photos from Kinston's
Photo archives.

Below left: The Pair Extraordinaire's first college concert was at Los Angeles Trade Tech.
Below right: First major TV show was "Hollywood A-Go-Go. It was the first TV variety show to use Go-Go dancers in a caged setting. 19665.

Photos and news clippings from Kingston's archives.

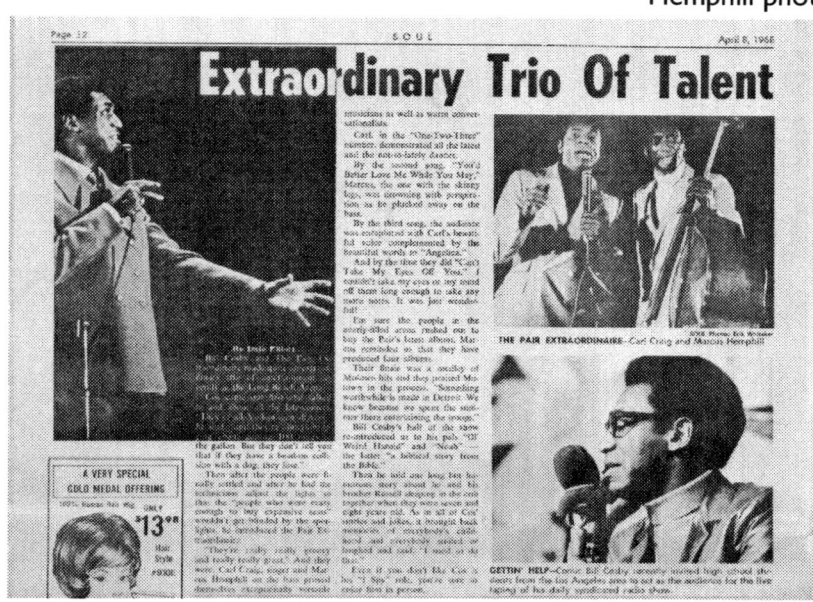

Above: Soul magazine article on The Pair Extraordinaire appearing with Bill Cosby. Below: L to R, Carl Craig AKA Kingston DuCoeur, Bill Cosby, Marcus Hemphill on stage, at the Frontier Hotel in Las Vegas.

Photographers unknown. From Kingston's photo archives.

Left: On The Mike Douglas Show. R to L. Mike Douglas, Bob Cummings, and The Pair.
Below left: Promo shot
Photo by Jay Thompson.
Below right The Pair on The Dean Martin Summer Show.
Bottom: Kingston with girl friend, Bonnie.
Photo from Kingston's archives.

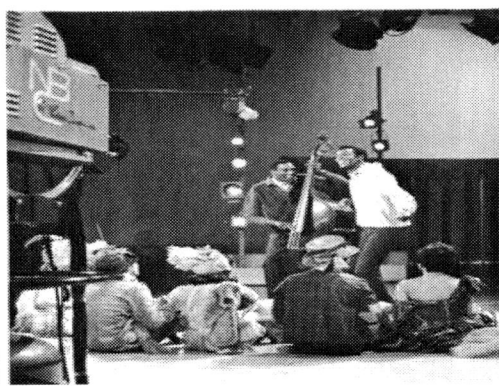

Top left: President JFK, television address, June 11, 1963.
Top right: JFK and Soviet Premier, Nikita Khrushchev, 1961.
Above: President Kennedy, signs the nuclear Test Ban Treaty in Bonn, West Germany,1963. Photographer unknown. Courtesy of Kingston's photo archives

Bottom right: My dear sister, Mrs. Frankie Roland and me. She was the pharmacist at Parkland hospital, and witnessed President John F. Kennedy's arrival at the Emergency room. Frankie said, contrary to news reports at the time, he was DOA. She described the chaos and panic that surrounded Mrs. Kennedy, and Mrs. Connally. Photo courtesy of Kingston's photo archives.

Jack Ruby, Strip Club owner, in his office with two of his employees, Cir, 1960.

Below: Jack Ruby murders Lee Harvey Oswald on National TV. In Dallas, Police Station, Nov.24, 1963.

Bottom: Jack Ruby Mug shot.
Photos courtesy of Robert J. Groden from JFK The Case for Conspiracy.

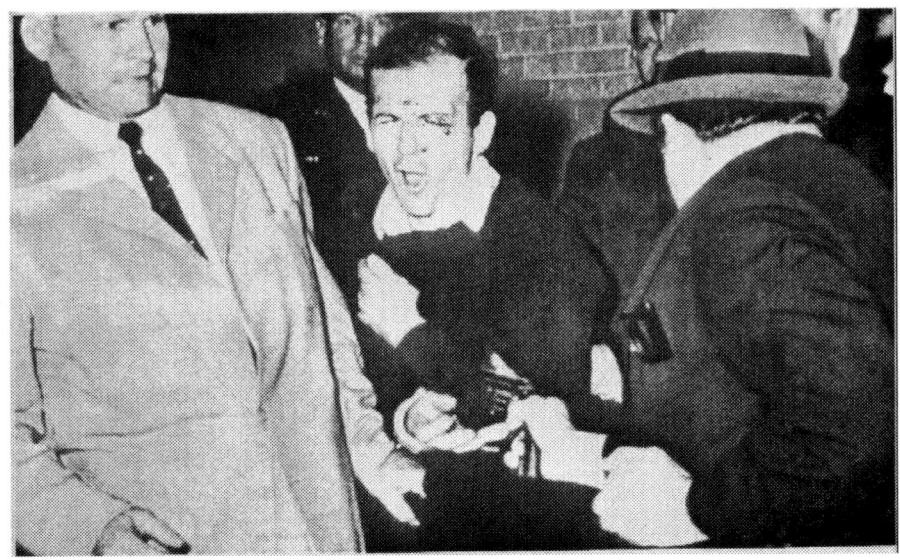

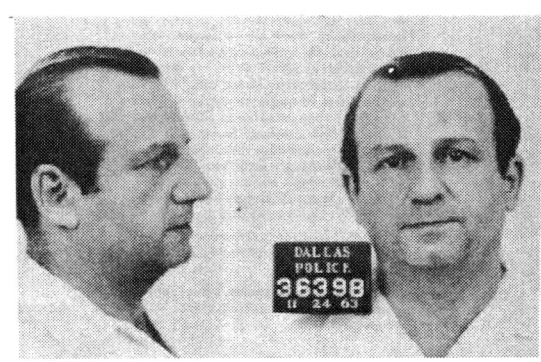

Above: Wilmer Maurice Lacy , The most gifted, well-read, intelligent, honest, and soulful friend I ever had. Photo taken in Los Angeles, 1960. "To The Bird."

Below: The inscription Maurice Lacy wrote on the back of the photo. This is the only photo I ever saw of him. I'm honored that he took this photo for me. He signed it : The Cloud.
Courtesy Kingston's photo archives.

It's not a very good picture man, but I haven't seen one of me yet that was. Be cool,(as if you could be anything but).

The Cloud

Wilmer Maurice Lacy, Los Angeles 1960

Top Left: President Nelson Mandela, Freedom, February 1990 .
Top Right: Mandela & Walter Sisulu give the Afrika Salute in Capetown, 1990.

Below: Nelson Mandela meets with students at his home in Orlando.
Top photos by: Gideon Mendel Magnum. Lower photo by: Peter Magubane.

Above left: My favorite South African family, The Mahlanza Family. Front center to top: Timothy, Mosa, Sembe, Mrs. Mahlanza, Mr. Mahlanza, Kingston ,at the top center.
Above Right: Jane and Joe Ashmore.

Below : Kingston with the Ashmore Family.
Photos courtesy of Kingston.

My beloved mother, Mrs. Nathalie Mathis
1910 - 1976

Above: Kingston and his mom two years before she passed
away.
Below: L to R, Me age eleven, my sister Tharsell age 13,
Mom, & her dad, Jesse Gipson, at his home in Plano, TX.
Photos courtesy of Kingston's photo archives.

Left: My late sister, Mrs. Norma Bell.

Below Left: My late brother, Billy Joe Mathis.

Below Right: My dear sister, Tharsell. "Honey" Watson.

Above: Edward James Olmos with students and supporters at Sony Pictures Studios..

Below: Edward James Olmos, Damon Wyans, with youth supporters at Columbia Studios. 1995. Photos courtesy of Kingston's photo archives.

Above left: Sidney Poitier, recipient of the 2005 Gertrude Gipson Penland Humanitarian award at the Hollywood Renaissance Hotel, presented by the Regalettes Philanthropic and Social Club, founded by Gertrude Gipson.
Above right: Kingston DuCoeur, Actor, Musician, Writer, working the runway at the event's All Male Fashion Extravaganza.
Below left: Kingston removing his jacket.
Below right: Grammy Award winning Guitarist,, Kenny Burell

Photos by Earl L. Dotson. Courtesy of Regalettes.

Above: G.G.''s youngest daughter, Shonte Pendland Abraham, with her Godfather, Sidney Poitier.

Below: At the podium, G.G.'s first born, Reve Gipson, M.C. for the evening.
Photos by Earl L. Dotson, courtesy of the Regalettes.

Above left: Actor, David McKnight, Star of "The Five Heartbeats, strutting his stuff on the runway. Right: Musician/Producer, Panther.
Below left: Actor, Harry Lennix, Chief of Staff on ABC hit TV Series "Commander In Chief."
Below right: Vocalist, Charlie Wilson (Gap Band), Sings and modeled.
Photos by Earl L. Dotson. Courtesy of The Regalettes.

Top: Eleanor Roosevelt arrives at Robert Mueller Airport, Austin TX L to R, Mrs. Opal Seabrook, Mrs. Roosevelt, Coach Collins (white Pants),
H.T. President, Dr. John J. Seabrook (dark suit).
Below right: Mrs. Roosevelt attends a Reception following her talk.
Bottom right: Eleanor Roosevelt at the home of College President, Dr. and Mrs. Seabrook, where she spent the night. 1960.
Photos courtesy of Huston-Tillotson University.

Mrs. Roosevelt

Above: Eleanor Roosevelt delivers her speech.

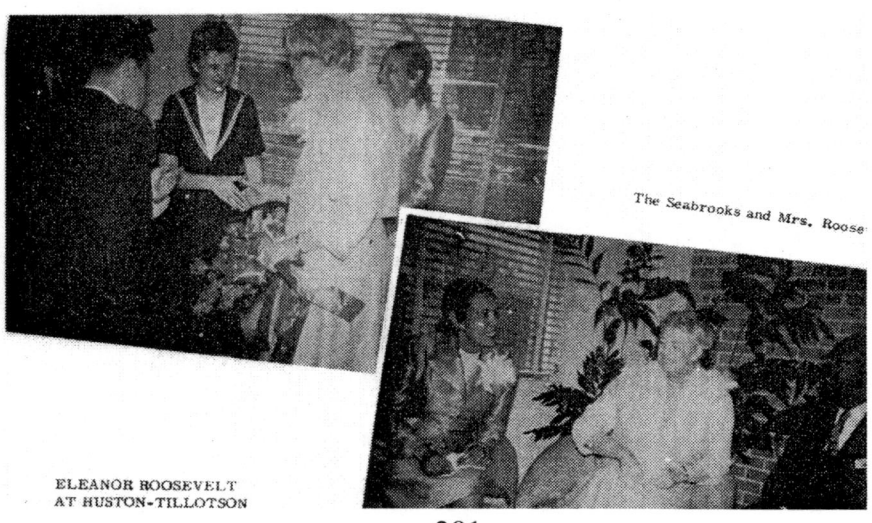

The Seabrooks and Mrs. Roose-

ELEANOR ROOSEVELT
AT HUSTON-TILLOTSON

Top left: Tom Shadyac.
Top right: Kingston DuCoeur,
and Tom Shadyac.
Left: Tom, Shadyac, Bob Dolman,
and Laura @Venice High show.

Below: Former Colors United student Clatvon Thomas, with LA Lakers,
Koby Bryant, back stage at the Forum before the Lakers vs. the Houston
Rockets, 1997. Photos courtesy of Kingston's photo archives.

Alvin "Fro" Vasquez

Above left: Fro rapping on stage. Above right: Fro & Patti Zamora.

Below: L to R Fro, Django, Kingston, Ira, and Stanley performing on stage.
Courtesy of Kingston's photo archives.

Above: L to R Rosalee, Velasco, Ellia Vasquez, Myra (in white).
Below: L to R, Patti, Stanley Elam, Ellia Vasquez, Leslie Hernandez, Fro
Vasquez.

Above: Flag raising ceremony at Kanrisha Yoesi Gakko (KYG) Japanese Executive Training school, USA @ Calamigos Ranch in Malibu, Calif.

Below: Jeff Washiashi, KYG graduation ceremony, Malibu, Calif. 1988. Photos courtesy of Kingston's photo archives.

Kingston, in Japan quizzing Japanese students at graduation
ceremony, December 1989
Photo courtesy of Kingston's photo archives.

Kingston with Japanese office staff at the KYG Shinjuku office
1989.
Photo courtesy of Kingston's photo archives

Top left: Colonel Fred Delisle, head Instructor, (USA School) with two students. Top Right: L to R, Mr. Yasue VP, USA School (my favorite KYG Executive) and Mr. Motohashi, Exec. VP of Kanrisha Yosei Gakko, at the Thousand Oaks Mall, Thousand Oaks, Calif, 1987. Below left: Senior Instructor, Angi Kobyashi and his lovely family, at their home in Tokyo, Japan, December 1989. Bottom Left: Susan & Jeff Washiashi holding their best Christmas gifts ever, beautiful twins, Brandon and Lindsey, Christmas 2000. Bottom Right: The Washiashi Family, 2004.

Left: Dennis at home in Colorado.

Right: Dennis & Gerry Weaver, at their 40th wedding anniversary at SRF Lake Shrine Temple in Pacific Palisades, October 20, 1985.

Below: Dennis and Gerry, Country & Line dancing in Colorado, 1993.
Photos by Alice Billings.
Courtesy of the Weaver family.

Above: Kingston and Dennis and Gerry Weaver's sons, Rusty and Rick. Dennis & Gerry's son, Rob, was unavailable for the photo

Below: Mrs. Gerry Weaver, Dennis' faithful and beloved wife of sixty-one years, and Kingston at Dennis Weaver's memorial at SRF Lake Shrine Temple , March 2006. Photos courtesy of the Weaver family.

Above Alfre Woodard. Photographer unknown.
Below: L. to R, Kingston, Ed Begley Jr. , Oscar, and Alfre Woodard.

Photo courtesy of Kingston's photo archives

Chapter

X

Malcolm X
American Icon

Malcolm X, along with the likes of JFK, Mrs. Rosa Parks, Dr. M.L.K., Jr., Nelson Mandela, Bill Cosby, and Muhammad Ali, are among the greatest contributors to the uplifting of the human condition in general, and to African-Americans in particular, during my lifetime.

I realize that there are countless men and women who deserve to have their rightful place in history. My wish is to focus on, and thereby contribute to the preservation of the legacy of those whose lives have made a monumental difference in my lifetime.

There are many titans of humanity such as Harriett Tubman, Sojourner Truth, John Brown, Abraham Lincoln, Nat Turner, Cinque and others that I could write about in keeping with the overall context of this book. In my heart and mind I shall continue to revere, honor and express my gratitude to these and other great souls who fought, and continue to fight, for human freedom. The struggle for equality will be etched in human history until the sands of time run out. It is evident that controversy is the inevitable shadow that is cast by greatness.

Some will argue that John Brown's attempt to destabilize the institution of slavery in America was misguided, due to ignoble reasoning. They argue that his belief that black folks were helpless and infantile was in itself degrading. I counter that argument by saying: "Who cares?" Had his motives been to help demolish slavery in order to lead them into the fires of hell, or to feed the whole slave population poisoned Kool aid a la Jim Jones? (-although it is clear that John Brown's motives were certainly not to do such a thing) I say "so what?" The need was for freedom for an entire race of the most creative, loving and forgiving people on the face of the Earth. The point being: help me to become free. Because being free, I have a chance to prevent the dastardly or diabolical schemes, against which I can not defend in leg irons and chains. I believe, as did Patrick Henry, that death is preferable to slavery.

When Malcolm X came on the national scene in 1954, as Minister of the Nation of Islam's New York Temple, he was the most feared and hated man in America. He was telling the truth about the underbelly of American society. His bold stance and fiery rhetoric inflamed, informed and ultimately enlightened a nation. He forced America to take a reluctant look at its flawed character. Rev. Al Sharpton is certainly no Malcolm, but he is today's most fiery exponent of the spirit of truth that was defined by Malcolm. The unfortunate episode that was the Tawana Brawley affair, gave the American media the tool that it needed to trivialize his message, thus stripping him of his slowly increasing influence among non-whites.

Other ethnicities were beginning to resonate to the elements of truth that were being validated by the day to day realities. Will his persistence one day render him a statesman? It is a question that is not often asked, and has little or no source, nor capacity from which an answer to the question can be gleaned. Some believe that his style and his approach to the truth that he attempts to tell, overshadows whatever substance that might upon closer examination breed some form of credence. His energetic and revelatory witticisms are fertile and gravid with opportunity for those who rely on the controversy that his name invites, to discredit him.

Those pundits and other opposing forces, black and white alike, often receive him as though he were a stand up comedian auditioning for a spot on the next available television show. Any present or future truths that he might manage to reveal have already been relegated to the annals of suspicious innuendo. This is partly due to the fact that Tawana Brawley unfairly duped him into being labeled not Rev. Sharpton, but rather Rev. Al Charlatan.

Politics defeat the truth by discrediting the bearer thereof. Those who honestly seek the truth are often swayed by perceptions that are largely false. Smoke and mirror tactics are often the hallmark of political enterprise. To the ideologues, the truth is never the issue unless their side is telling it. Many of us who consider ourselves to be morality-first exponents, are usually the most gullible when it comes to those smoke and mirror tactics, and the ever present spin doctors. It is quite possible, though extremely improbable by today's standards and practices, that a Rev. Al Sharpton, however sincere, will become a respected "public figure." Some of the choices he has made have been perceived as being self-serving and with conflicting purposes. Yet he can speak, he can entertain when he speaks, and he can hold his own with the best of the debaters. There is hope that someday when he ceases to get in his "own self's" way he might emerge as a legitimate spokesman for a people that seem to be losing their way. We vilify those who can see, and are capable of gaining and holding our attention. Who among us can—who among us will—successfully advance the cause of freedom that is being so blatantly eroded with every tick of the clock?

We need a Malcolm X today—not so much to point out the ever-increasing injustice that marches steadily and stealthily towards neo fascism, to the goose-stepping cadence of what we blindly think of as "days gone by." We need a Malcolm, again, not to point out the injustices, because the injustice is the same as it was before the Voting Rights Act, and the Civil Rights Act were passed into law. We need a Malcolm to effectively wake up little Susie and mobilize Uncle John. It seems to me that in spite of the average African American's slim possibility to "win the lottery" whether by purchasing a ticket or making a hit record, once that slim possibility comes to fruition what seems to follow is a "where do we go from here" outlook. It appears that we compete with ourselves to see who can best expedite the constant flow of self-loathing. Self-hatred is being borne from the womb of the denial of the fact that "I am my brother's keeper" and is nurtured by the ignorance that frames that denial.

The runaway slaves of the 19th century, thanks to that powerful goddess known as Harriett Tubman, survived because they believed in each other and cultivated survival tools that were fashioned by the notion that "I **am** my brother's keeper." It was a bond so strong that it inspired white people who had good hearts, minds, and unparalleled courage to risk their lives and the safety of their families to create and distribute additional tools for survival. They held out long enough for President Lincoln to deliver the legal blow to the same evil that threatens to raise its ugly head again, this time under the guise of classism.

We need Malcolm today in order to convince young black men that their acts of cruel indifference towards one another is a poison that we ourselves mix and serve to each other as individuals, and drink the damage collectively as a race. We need Malcolm X to show us that we can grow and change like he did when he made his pilgrimage to Mecca in 1964. He realized that the truth that he loved so much was beyond the limits of his prior knowledge, and outside the scope of his narrow, albeit moving, rhetoric that marked phase-one of his quest. We need Malcolm to convince us that we are in the midst of phase two. And we needed Dr. Cosby to warn us, and show us that phase two can only be mounted successfully by making the necessary changes the way that Malcolm did. We must heed the only effective call to arms, which is our intellect. The only acceptable weapon is our awareness.

The only effective way to win the emerging battle is not on the football field. It is not on the basketball court, at the Grammys or the Academy Awards. **I do not criticize our athletes, entertainers, or our notable public figures.** Without the likes of Oprah Winfrey, Barry Bonds, Maya Angelu, Denzel Washington, Halle Berry, Shaquille O'Neal, Mary J.

Blige, Kanye West, Venus and Serena Williams, Kobe Bryant, Morgan Freeman, Condoleezza Rice, Tiger Woods, Bill Cosby, and others, our image in the world would be far less sparkling. Our call to arms is to mount a successful challenge to win the **academic** decathlon. It is a call that must be answered across the width and breadth of America. When we begin to win **that** race, then we will be able to steady our focus, and dedicate our resolve to win the victory. Victory must be won in order to participate and compete in every phase of wealth, and wealth distribution in this new millennium.

We must begin to learn anew how to survive the silent distraction that is already too far along the path that is leading us to complete, and open, disenfranchisement. If we don't heed the "Cosby call," we ourselves will be complicit in turning our own beautifully created race into a nation of pirates, preying on each other's weaknesses, and trying to survive on the bile of our discontent. The enemy within is too well stacked and the enemy at the door is too well armed.

We need Malcolm X to awaken us from Dr. M.L.K., Jr's beautiful dream, and make it a reality before it becomes our self destructive nightmare. Malcolm lived and died to fulfill his mission to see African-Americans become beacons of hope and assurance of freedom for our people. Malcolm's spirit designed a matrix that his life made manifest. Is there hope that another will rise and come forth to show us, inspire us, and force us to begin to save ourselves? Guns, knives, and the "dumbing down" of our children will not help us to claim our rightful place in this nation, a nation that was literally and figuratively built by the salty sweat of our brow.

We are no longer unique under the sun. Today, the whole world has access to our soul, economic control of our bodies, and increasing disrespect for our minds. To **Malcolm X**, who was the antithesis to self-loathing: as you ply your trade on the other side of this reality, I send you a **Simple and a Courageous Thank You.**

CHAPTER

Z

ZACK
(My dog)

Whoever said you can't buy happiness forgot about little puppies.

Unknown

Cats are love on four legs.

Dogs are our link to Paradise. They don't know evil or jealousy, or discontent.
To sit with a dog on a hillside on a glorious afternoon is to be back in Eden.

Milan Kundera

Even the tiniest Poodle or Chihuahua is still a wolf at heart.

Unknown

They never talk about themselves, but listen to you talk about yourself, and keep up an appearance that they are interested.

Jerome K. Jerome

I allow my cats to express themselves. Never interfere with their romances, and raise them with dogs to broaden their outlook.

Murray Robinson

If dogs could talk, it would take a lot of the fun out of owning one.

Unknown

Cats don't have to be put on a pedestal, they put themselves there.

Anonymous

If your dog doesn't like someone, you probably shouldn't either.

Unknown

A simple thank you goes to our dog "Zack" for always being there, alert, loyal, and protective.

A simple thank you also goes to "Mama Cat" –our kitty, for her perfect poise, and graceful presence.

EPILOGUE

I truly hope that you had an entertaining, and informative experience as you explored the various chapters of ICONS, IDOLS, & PERSONAL HEROES. It is my desire that you will reflect on those things that you found agreeable, and discuss with friends and family, anything that might be contrary to your own beliefs.

If I may, I'd like to encourage our readers to focus on, and instill in our youth (especially young African-American men and women), the ever-increasing importance of education. For the average American, it is the primary source of achievement, and one of the most accessible pathways to true and lasting equality. Our children deserve to understand that a good education is, without doubt, the main escape rout from the "New Slavery" that Pope John Paul II alluded to on page 106 of this text. Look on page 165, and review Nelson Mandela's words on education. They reinforce the statements that former first lady, Eleanor Roosevelt, made on page 191. Those three pages are well worth reviewing, and will take less than a minute to highlight the consequences that await the uneducated in the new America. (Please check pages, 106, 165, & 191, now).

As adults, we must become more vigilant about our schools, and what is being taught –and more importantly, what subjects are being systematically omitted. Each of us must begin to demand that subjects of the humanities be reinstated in schools where they have been removed. Insist vehemently that Civics, and Government are required subjects, so that American students, as citizens of democracy will be able to recognize and resist the doctrines of hate mongers and extremists who are the well entrenched and recurring enemies of freedom.

And finally, the most important aspect of ICONS, IDOLS, & PERSONAL HEROES, is not the wonderful Icons that we know and love, nor the Idols that entertain and uplift us, but those most deserving of our respect and adoration are the Personal Heroes that influence, and inspire us to dream, and encourage us to believe in our dreams, and, most important of all, are those Heroes like Miss Billie, Ma Bailey, Mama Chandler, Colonel Carrington, and others that this book salutes and honors. The real Heroes are those who find a way to convince us that we can be more than our environment, or our circumstances so often dictate.

I want young men and women everywhere to look around, take stock, and appreciate the "everyday" people in their lives who believe in them, as the beautiful souls I've mentioned, believed in me.
In closing, I extend to you -the reader, **A Simple and most Sincere, Thank you.**

To Order

ICONS, IDOLS, & PERSONAL HEROES

Please send check or money order to:

Pacific Blue Publishing
501 W. Glenoaks Blvd. suite 746
Glendale, CA 91202

To order by phone: (818) 241-4797
Or
E Mail : kducoeur@sbcglobal.net

Or visit: www.kingstonducoeur.com

$19.95 Purchase price
Please include, $1.65 tax
Plus $2.95 S & H
$24.55   Total

Make check or money order payable to Pacific Blue Publishing

Thank you